WORTH SAVING

A Memoir

Judith Stih

To my parents, Mollie and Rudy

whose strength in adversity helped me become who I am today

and to my Lord and Savior Jesus Christ

For I never felt alone, not one single day

Contents

And So it Begins...... 1

Mollie 3

Rudy 10

The Lady in Black 14

War 19

The Crew 21

The Garage 28

Music in the Air 32

Peace in the Sun 36

Some Things Never Changed 38

Amazing Mom! 39

Windward 42

The Drama of it All! 48

Oh, the Special Times! 51

Give Credit Where Credit is Due 55

A Promise Broken 60

Left Speechless 64

A Cold Beer on a Hot Summer Day 67

Oh Happy Days! 72

The Real Test of Sobriety 76

Those Wonderful Visits 82

Dad Gave Us Back Our Family 84

Post AA Changes 89

Forever Changes 92

Two Lost People 96

Mom & Dad Move On 98

Regrets 106

December 22, 1997 109

The Viewing 112

New Year's Eve 115

Just Hang On! 118

God Bless Moms 126

East McDowell, #5 Mesa, AZ 129

In the Blink of an Eye 136

The Decisions We Make 141

Arizona Long Term Care Program 147

If at First You Don't Succeed... 152

Seven Years of Journaling 157

The Fall That Changed Mom's Life Forever 158

The Real Goal 170

Nightmare! 172

The Alzheimer/Dementia Clinic 177

Mollie's Journal 181

Carol Hoffart Silvernail 189

Another Christmas with Mom 195

A Brand New Year! 197

Ahh, the Orange Grove! 199

Some Days Were Diamonds....Some Days Were Stones 213

Caring for Your Loved One 216

Mom Is Beautiful 221

Flapjack Arrives 224

Father's Day 230

Oh, You Are My Kenny! 237

Oh to God We Give Thee Glory 242

The Long and Winding Road 244

Those Halloween Handouts 250

You Are My Sunshine...257

I Walk With Jesus Every Day 264

You Can Not Over Dream God..266

Through the Years 270

Because We Believe 278

We Made it Through the Rain..291

I Never Saw it Coming 294

Love Has No Number...302

Respect and Love...308

The Tea Reading Experience 309

Love Me, That's All I Ask of You 310

The Medium 316

Acknowledgements

I would like to thank the following individuals, without whom this book would never have been possible. I am especially grateful to my most special partner and husband, John. He has been my rock and supporter armed with love and patience through this journey that has taken seven decades. I could not have survived this without him!

Thank you to my editor and special friend, Jan Larson; my sister Carol for her every day 9pm calls; my brothers Louis and Kenny; Cheryl Moritz, who for over 30 years of friendship I was privileged to have with me on this journey; my friend Mary Hentz, when I needed to get away a key was always waiting; my cousins Linda Hoffart and Susan Kovatch who flew to Arizona from Ohio for 1 day for mom's 100th birthday; Mom's caregivers, Lois Susic, Randa Williams, Brenda Thacker, Kathy Goulet and Wardine Taylor from Comfort Keepers; Shonna, the author who helped me during the "Author in Residence Program"; Hospice, all the staff I knew I could call 24/7; Apple, my iPhone always was there for that video and pictures; and my neighbors, so much love for Mollie.

Chapter 1

And So it Begins......

I am standing by the front window and I can hear my Dad start the car. It then whizzes past the dining room window down this very narrow drive. At the bottom is a street light. I stand there thinking "Hit the light," "Hit the light." Then, I was thinking, the light would crash onto the car and hopefully this would all be over! What did I think would happen? He would be killed, of course. One of them had to die to end this horrible existence this family was living through.

Minutes before my Mother was kneeling on the carpet in the dining room. Dad was beating her. I was hitting him over the head with the broom. She was screaming and I was screaming. When he pulled his hands off her she felt the top of her hair and screamed "My hair, my hair!" At that point he stopped and ran out the back door. I knelt down to comfort her, to help her up, to tell her I thought her hair was just fine. She barely made it to the dining room chair. That is when I heard the start of the car and immediately went to the window. Yes, I wanted one of them to end this cycle of fights and drinking. This was the first time he hit her. Would this happen again? One of them had to die.

It was 1957 and I was a few months short of 17 years of age. I have 3 other siblings but I cannot remember where they were that night, especially my younger sister who would have been 9 years old. When Mom and Dad argued I don't remember just where my other siblings were. They may have just been out of the house with friends or at work. Most of the big fights would occur later after supper since that is when Dad would come home from work. That is when the two of them would communicate most often by shouting at each other.

When Dad did miss the lamp post, and drove hurriedly down the street, I went again to Mom. She had stopped crying. I had never seen my Mother cry. But that night I did. She quickly pulled herself together and went up to her room. I still remember the house had an eerie silence. I sat there in the living room just staring out the window wondering what would happen next. I thought they would eventually kill each other and Mom did not have a chance against Dad. But she did know how to use words that would set him off. Whether she was right or wrong made no difference to me at the time. The problem was they fought and fought hard.

I started to think back to how this all began, or at least when I first noticed it. I recalled coming in from the playground at St. Paul's Catholic School, kneeling in the front pew and praying the same prayer every day, "Please God, make my Dad like other Dads." Now I wondered, what did I mean, what did I think was 'other Dads'? But it was evident that as far back as 8 years old I knew things around this house were not like on television. *I Remember Mama* was a program we loved to watch on Friday night. It was the only one of 4 available when we got our first TV. What a wonderful family! No, ours was not like *I Remember Mama*.

I sat there contemplating my next move. Do I report him? Do I call my Uncles and tell them? Do I tell the school? For sure I did not want my friends to know so telling school was out of the question. Where do I go for help? I seemed to be the only person keeping these two from killing each other. I was actually afraid to leave the house and go roller skating, to a friend's or even an after school program. I felt like I was their "security guard," always on guard. I went to bed thinking there was no hope this family will ever be any different. I needed to remember it was up to me to keep a careful watch over Mom.

I have no idea how Mom and I went to bed or remember when Dad came home. All I remember is the next day everything seemed quiet. This argument would keep them from even talking to each other for a week if I was lucky. I had one week of peace and one week to focus on school. My grades had gone from a's in 6th grade to c's in 7th grade. For sure they were not going to help me get a job. I was already thinking of how to earn some money. Mom had gotten me a job cleaning the lady's house across the street so I could just have a few pennies of my own. And I did some babysitting for some relatives. But I wanted some real money.

I now think back and see how little I was capable of. How sad to even recall my simple thoughts and inability to see that I was unable to fix the situation. Silly as it may seem, I thought I had the recipe. Now years later when people ask "What was your dream growing up?" I actually cannot think of one dream I had for myself.

Chapter 2

Mollie

Amalia Elizabeth Skolaris was born August 28, 1915. Mollie, as she was called, was preceded in birth by Mary, Edith, Esther and Frank Jr. She had another brother, also named Frank, who was born after the death of Frank Jr. Mary was 12 years older than Mom and would play a large part in Mom's life, as you will later read.

My Grandfather came over from Austria to work on the railroad. Four years later my Grandmother joined with the four children. The boats back then were a very rough ride, especially with four children in tow. My Grandmother was a woman of strength and managed the journey.

They lived in the city for a short time when a horrible accident occurred with little Frankie being struck by a streetcar and killed. After my Mother was born they moved to the country where they had a small farm in Geneva, Ohio. One year later, little Esther was raking leaves when her skirt caught fire and she died of her burns. Mom said she always felt that her Father was disappointed she was not a boy since he had lost his only son. But, shortly after, they had another son who they again named Frank.

For some reason my Mother also said she went through most of her childhood very intimidated by her older sisters and feeling somewhat insecure. She was always very insecure. I knew there was something about her when I saw her around other members of the family. It wasn't until I was older and knew what the word "insecure" meant.

Grandma would take Grandpa to the railroad station on a horse where he caught a train to Cleveland to work on the railroad. He was gone all week. The family was left alone to tend the garden and to try to help Grandma through her nightmares of losing her two little children. My understanding was life was very stressful yet it prepared my Mom for her life and tough times.

The workload on the farm was divided up with Mary and Edith working outside in the garden while Mom and Frankie were taking care of the inside cleaning and cooking. My Mother was by far the best cook. As for keeping the house clean she knew how to organize! She also knew how to never sit down! If she didn't sit, no one sat. I never learned how to just sit and relax as I always felt there was something else to do. If Mom caught us sitting she would say "Well, if you have time to sit I have something you can do." If we wanted to rest or sit we had to hide!!!! I am sure that is the way she was brought up since they had a farm and everyone had their chores. However, she never stopped that manner of living, always multitasking and doing it right the first time! She would always remind me "Judy, if you do have time, just do it right the first time!"

Grandma passed at age 65 from colon cancer. It was on my Mother's 30th birthday, August 28, 1945. Mom said two weeks before Grandma passed she went out to take care of her. Grandma was in bed and Mom said when she brought Grandma breakfast or lunch on a tray she would put it on a pretty lace cloth. She was so proud of the way her Mother smiled when she would come in the room with this tray. I find it amazing the things we remember forever. Mom had brought my brother Louis and I with her. We were 5 and 4 respectively. There was a swing on the front porch and we would sit there and swing and hit the wall over and over and over! Kids! But this was the wall that backed up to Grandma's bedroom and she was basically dying. So Mom came out and yelled at us. When Grandma heard Mom yell she said, "Mollie, let the children play." When you hear of these stories you can feel in your heart the sadness she felt when her Mom passed, and then of all things, on Mom's birthday. I have little to no remembrance of my Grandmother but when Mom told that story I felt I always knew her. I wish I could remember more of my Grandmother.

The story I love was the one Mom tells about Grandpa and the record player. As she had said, she felt insecure since following the death of Frank Jr. Then she, a girl, was born rather than another boy. But on one particular night after dinner they put on the record player. She said Mary, Edith and her Mom were sitting and listening when her Father came over and asked HER to dance! Can you imagine? My Mom was about 8 and she still remembered her Dad asked HER to dance! It always seems to be the little things we remember. We should never hesitate to create small but important memories in someone else's life.

Mom was a star on the basketball team and the basketball team would not let anyone forget it! The picture hung in her room until the day she died. She moved to Cleveland where she got a job as a nanny. I wish I had asked her many questions about that position, but all I remember was her saying "I loved taking care of the children, cleaning the silver and keeping house." She also said the lady of the house taught her to cook. She taught her well because Mom was an excellent cook. I would go so far as to say she was a gourmet cook since she could not only cook, but she made unusual and delicious dishes. My sister-in-law says my Mother was a housekeeper and cleaned homes, but if so my Mother never described her positions in those words. She did describe the children and told me all she wanted to do was to be a Mother and have children of her own.

Mom was a beautiful girl and my Dad loved taking pictures of her with his small camera. (see pictures) You can see why Dad fell in love with her. I am not sure if she realized then how pretty she was.

Chapter 3

Rudy

Rudolph William Hoffart was born on July 14, 1911. Rudy was preceded in birth by Edward, William and Frank. Joseph, John and Alvin followed Dad. Grandma and Grandpa Hoffart also came over from Austria. All the boys were born in Ohio.

When my Dad was eleven he was hit by a car which left him with a plate in his head. This resulted in a classification of 3A from the Selective Service. From the beginning my Father loved going to the movie show. Word is that Uncle Ed, the oldest, would get his allowance and save it while Dad would take the money and ride the streetcar or go to the movies. Ed obviously was a saver and in later years would own a restaurant with apartments above where his brother John and my Aunt Betty lived after John returned from the war. Sadly, little Alvin died around 8 years of age from diphtheria. Grandma cried just about every day for years until Uncle Frank and Uncle John went to war. Dad said that event changed her whole attitude. Dad said while they were gone to war, Grandma never mentioned Alvin.

My Grandfather owned a wallpaper and paint store. Two of the boys, Uncle Joe and Uncle Frank, could wallpaper a wall. You could look up close and not see the seams. They were also unbelievably talented at painting houses inside and out. It seemed there was paint in their blood. Uncle John learned to cook in the Army and was the cook at Uncle Ed's restaurant when he returned. My Grandmother Hannah was a great cook. I remember on Saturdays she came to our house for Mom to do her hair. I would sit and eat French toast with sugar rather than syrup and she would say "Judy, you're going to get very sick from all that sugar." I think it's amazing I remember her saying that. She was very kind.

We come from a long line of Catholics. Father Kirby was considered a part of the family and we children called him "Uncle" for the longest time. When Dad was 18 he traveled with Father Kirby to

Canada. His brother Ed wrote to him explaining how much the family missed him.

My Grandfather had to have been what some would call "well-to-do" because he owned a car, a brand new car at that. I am not sure what the make was but I was told they didn't have a garage so they chained it to a pole and locked it. Then one morning they came out and it was gone! Auto thieves way back in the 1920's!!! Dad said they then built a garage!

They were also a drinking family. They enjoyed a shot and a beer! We must consider that there was no TV. Some families had a radio, but most evenings were spent sitting around this very large round table in Grandma's dining room, talking and enjoying a "shot and a beer!" As mentioned, my Dad loved to go to the movies. There was a movie theater near their home and he would go as soon as he got his allowance. Then Grandpa moved because he felt the older two sons were hanging out with the wrong crowd. Dad was devastated, but where they moved was a new movie theater being built. It was called The La Salle. Dad watched every brick being put into that building. Even now I love to watch *TCM* because I always wonder what movies Dad watched and why he loved these movies so much. Mom said he loved Ruby Keeler. I think the next dog we get we will name Ruby Keeler for Dad.

Grandpa ruled with a strict hand. I think most parents did back in the early 20's and the belt was used a lot! We seem to learn how to parent from our parents although sometimes we learn what not to do in parenting from our parents. Amazing now remembering what now seems so trivial. Due to the depression, Dad had to quit school and go to work. He only had an 8th grade education and Mom said Dad was heartbroken when he had to quit school because he loved school, with his favorite class being history. He would have loved to have been able to travel and told me he always wanted to travel to London. He had two great big pictures on the wall of the cathedrals in London.

Rudy grew up with a large family, a painting family, a strict Father, experienced the depression first hand, and a family of 5 brothers who loved to enjoy a "shot and a beer." All of this would dictate his demeanor in years to come.

Chapter 4

The Lady in Black

Father Kirby got Dad a job at the church during the depression as a janitor. It was there that he noticed this pretty girl coming to church every Sunday where they would exchange smiles. He began to watch for her and open the door as she would arrive. Mom thought this nice young man opening the door was so handsome. Dad says he started going to the mass where he originally saw Mom in hopes she would be there. How cute! Smiles led to dating and dating led to marriage. Their dating during 1937 and 1938 was made more enjoyable because Dad had a car! Yes, the church had lent him a car so he could fulfill his janitor duties. He also then fulfilled his fun duties with his girlfriend Mollie! I have enclosed a picture of Mom by the car, taken by Dad and published in a small newspaper that my brother Louis owned. The wording is lovely and it will make you smile!

Dad was an amateur photographer, at best. We have lovely pictures of Mom taken downtown, in the parks, everywhere. Those were the days! Mom became pregnant before their wedding date so she and Dad pushed up their wedding in 1939. Mom's sister Mary decided Mom should wear black. They settled on dark navy (see picture)! Mom hated that wedding picture and would never show it to anyone, but I found it in her albums one day. I said "Mom, why did you wear black?" She would correct me and say "dark navy," and then respond very quietly "Because Mary said so." So you're thinking the same thing I am...what??? Mary??? "Mom, you were 24. I am sure you could decide for yourself." When I would question things Mary had told her to do Mom would say as she always did. "Well, Mary said I had to because I was pregnant with Louis." Where was Dad in all this? I have no idea except he was dressed so nice with a big black hat. Maybe he had no idea she would come that day wearing a navy dress. The most important part of the picture is they were both smiling!!

Yes, times were tough therefore these two lovebirds moved into Dad's parents' home while some of the brothers were still living at home. Even though the home had 4 bedrooms and a big front porch it was crowded for a couple newly married and expecting their first child. My brother told me "Mom had a tough time and so Dad went to the pries. He allowed them to move into the church cottage." I was heartbroken thinking of her so young, being told to wear a dark dress and now moving in with my Grandparents. Obviously no privacy, and of course being pregnant in those days before marriage was, well, you didn't get a gold star...let's put it that way!

So there I am feeling sorry for a young woman with her first child, living with her husband. But Mom said "Judy, it wasn't so bad. I was so happy to be married. I could not believe I had married your Dad. I was giddy with love." Her exact words. Whew...I felt better! It was really wonderful to hear about all those wonderful days they had as newlyweds, their first child together, and moving to a little cottage. This was especially nice to hear considering all the trauma in my life with them many years later. I always knew, in my heart, they loved each other. At times my Dad had a very sweet demeanor. Mom was very sharing and caring and always took the best care of us when we were sick.

So, what went wrong?

Chapter 5

War

Before the war broke out my brother Louis was born October 17, 1939. I was born December 30, 1940. Dad's brother Frank had taught him the skill of repairing radios and automobiles and they both worked at the same automobile shop. However, if you ever decided to fix cars on the side, you would need a compressor for painting and Dad had one. The factories were not making appliances and new cars but rather war products. You had to fix your old car which created a lucrative business for auto body shops. If you had a compressor and knew how to do repairs, you could make some really good money. With a wife and two small children to feed Dad sold his compressor. This was a hard decision, but times were tough. That decision to sell his compressor was an extremely sad one for Dad and created even harder times. This change in the economy had to be heart breaking for Dad and Mom. I think of these hard issues with them whenever I experience a tough situation. Yes, this very day, when things just don't seem to go right and I find myself losing something, having to make a change I really don't want to and other issues, I think of my parents and the strength they left behind for me.

Dad then found a job in the factory for $.50 an hour. Later his brother found him one for $.60 but the rules at that time were you were not allowed to change jobs. The family first lived in the church cottage and Dad used his salary to purchase a stove for Mom so she could now bake and to help heat the cottage. Later they moved to 1518 Clairmont Ave. where I was born and Mom was near her sister Mary. Now Mom had two children under two years of age. She was also very sick when I was born. So much so that she did not attend my christening.

The story is my Aunt Edna was my Godmother. Upon arriving they all discussed what my name was to be. Mom had wanted the name Karen. The day of the christening the group decided this was a Jewish name. Mom and Dad wanted a German name due to both their parents' heritage. Since I was in no position to remember exactly how it happened, I was named Judith. What a joke. Karen was very German and Judith was very Jewish. In those days that was the thinking. I think Dad loved it because his name was Rudy and now his only daughter was called Judy!

I am sure everyone has heard of all the restrictions and sacrifices families had to make during those times. Each has a story of their own but Dad says everyone worked as a family. He did not hear of one story where someone broke the rules or cheated on what they could purchase. Mom says they were allowed one egg a week and she and Dad decided my brother and I should have it!

When the war ended, the government started building large density buildings called projects. They were one and two story homes attached in groups of 6 or 8, a playground for the kids and a large parking lot. Doesn't sound like much but, WOW! You felt you won the lottery if you were chosen to rent one. My parents were the 3rd couple to move into the Euclid Projects. My Mother says it was their first real home and it was brand new!! They were so excited as it was such a wonderful place. She could not wait to fix up the house and cook in her own little kitchen. By this time my brother Kenny was born. Mom and Dad had a two bedroom, one bath unit on a corner at 770 E. 203rd Place, Euclid, Ohio. Everyone made friends and there were many children for us kids to play with. I met my best friend Kathy there. Much later these projects were torn down and replaced with a senior apartment center and other buildings.

Chapter 6

The Crew

Louis Frank Hoffart was born on October 17, 1939. Judith Hoffart entered on December 30, 1940. Kenneth Rudolph Hoffart made up the family, or so they thought, in 1943. Carol Hoffart was our "Christmas Carol," arriving on December 21, 1948.

We each took our place in the "Q" putting Mom through the wringer. Oh, no, that's what Louis did. He actually put his arm through the wringer of the wringer washer, which is all we had in the early 40's. He has the scar to this day. Can you imagine, you hear a scream as you are washing in the tub, the wringer is turning and you look to find Louis's arm up to his elbow!!! It's amazing and so were the medical programs they had "way back when." He did not lose his arm.

When my Mom became pregnant with my sister, Carol, they qualified for a 3 bedroom home in the projects and we moved to 20216 Chickasaw, just across the parking lot from where we currently lived. So now rather than 3 children in one bedroom, the boys had their own room and my sister and I had ours. After my sister was born Mom explained to the doctor that she had to be home for Christmas with 3 little kids. In those days you stayed in the hospital a minimum of 5 days. However, Mom was not going to miss Christmas with 3 little children.

My sister was about 3 months old when I was diagnosed with rheumatic fever. At that time, they kept you in bed for up to 3 months. So, here was Mom, running up the stairs when the baby would cry, running up the stairs to give me meds, and probably running up the stairs just because I would cry "Mom, where are you?"!!!! Soon I started asking Mom to let me feed the baby. With Carol's bed in the same room as mine she would come up with a bottle, put Carol on my lap in bed and I would change her diaper and feed her! I am not sure who was happier, Mom, me or the baby who was getting her bottle!!! Meanwhile, Kenny was not the youngest, but he was at one time the smallest for his age. Cute little blond boy, sweet, and did everything his older sister told him to do! Probably why she thinks he was so sweet! The picture shown was taken of the 3 of us. Ken was 4 and the photographer told him "Don't move." He claims that is all he remembers about that day. As you look at the picture you understand how cooperative he was. This picture is just so much "Kenny."

Kenny was cute but he was always sick. He had pneumonia four times as a child and was small, but he wasn't sickly to speak of in that he ran, played and did everything a child his age would do. When he was 15, he went to the hospital to have a hernia taken care of. While filling out the admittance form, my Mother was asked why this child looked so pale and small for his age. She responded that he had pneumonia four times as a child and just was always small. What my Mother did not know was that at the University Hospital the first open heart surgery had been performed. Actually it was my understanding this was the second in the United States. (If anyone has information different than that I would appreciate the information.) So there they were, surgeons looking for their next patient. Celebrating this new field of surgery and checking records to see if there was someone that would benefit from this new life saving procedure. And there was Kenny. In the hospital for a hernia, four times pneumonia, pale skin and small for his age. My Mother was approached by one of the surgeons and asked if they could do some testing on Kenny. She said she was so happy since she always worried about the "little guy." And believe it or not, little Kenny had a hole in his heart. As they explained, he could have just dropped over in gym class with no advance notice of a problem. Kenny came and went from that hospital for almost 5 months!! It all began with the testing and then the actual surgery. Everything was explained to my parents yet my Mother says when she went to see him after the surgery he was in a machine bigger and longer than an iron lung! She fainted. The good news is Kenny lived! Kenny came and went from the hospital those five months, being able to come home for Christmas and his birthday in March. He also contracted rheumatic fever during his hospital stay.

In the months and years to follow after the surgery Kenny grew and grew and grew. The pictures taken at Easter the year before showed him two inches shorter than me and the following Easter while home from the hospital almost my height. In the following years he was getting even taller and healthier. When he would come home for visits, my Mom would carry him up and down the stairs. As you have read, my Mom spent a lot of time going up and down stairs!! The expenses were totally paid for by the Heart Foundation at that time and my parents were spared any stress with bills, etc.

We have come a long way in the last 60 years. At this writing Kenny is 73, playing volleyball and tearing down the kitchen, including the ceiling. On the 50th anniversary of his surgery Kenny sent Mom a card! (see card) It was an emotional Moment for everyone! It brought back many memories. Thank you Kenny! Mom was so happy to receive that card! It was a far cry from what open heart surgery is today but is just an example of how far we have come. There were those that took the chance, some not making it, but gave many a chance to others for a new life.

I Love You

Thanks, Mom, for Everything

I Love You

Mom, there are times
when I need someone
to lift my spirits,
encourage my dreams,
give me a gentle push
in the right direction,
and you're there
for me...

OPEN

A BIRTHDAY KEEPSAKE

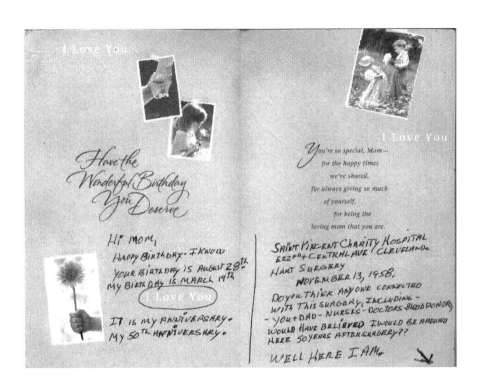

I Love You

Have the Wonderful Birthday You Deserve

You're so special, Mom —
for the happy times
we've shared,
for always giving so much
of yourself,
for being the
loving mom that you are.

I Love You

Hi mom,
Happy Birthday. I know
your birthday is August 28th
My birthday is March 14th

I Love You

It is my anniversary.
My 50th anniversary.

Saint Vincent Charity Hospital
E22nd + Central Ave Cleveland.
Hart Surgery
November 13, 1958.

Do you think anyone connected
with this surgery, including -
- you + Dad - nurses - doctors - blood donors
would have believed I would be around
here 50 years after surgery??

Well here I am.

26

TODAY   NOVEMBER 13, 2008
YESTERDAY NOVEMBER-13, 1958
                      50 YEARS

THANK YOU MOM

KENNY

LOVE YOU MOM!

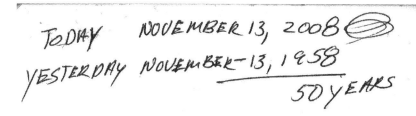

AMERICAN GREETINGS

TAKE GOOD CARE OF YOUR SELF
+ ALL THE PEOPLE AROUND YOU.
LIKE YOU TOOK CARE OF ME!

Keepsake bookmark is detachable.

HAPPY THANKSGIVING

Kenny / Carolyn

00001

27

Chapter 7

The Garage

In 1945 my Grandmother passed of colon cancer and in 1946 my Grandfather fell down an elevator shaft to his death. In all this sadness there arose a new life for Mom and Dad in the form of East 140th Auto Body. With the monies left to Mom from her Dad's passing, she and Dad decided to put Dad's skills at painting and repairing cars to work. They purchased some property on 140th St. in Cleveland and so began the beginning of a dream they both had to start out this new business together. The site was a lot with overgrown weeds, a small building in the front and an old 2 car garage in the back. When I say old, I mean very old. Since it was a garage, we referred to Dad's shop as "the garage!" "Where is Dad?" we would ask. Mom would say "Down at the garage." Mom says she would go down and sand the cars. Dad did the fixing, painting and striping. In the 40's cars would have a stripe around the middle and it was said Dad could match the paint perfectly and was the most skilled striper!!! The site they chose was not at random. It was just down the street from Fisher Body, the maker of Chevrolet. Many of the executives would go to Rudy for the striping of their cars.

I asked my Mom once "Who took care of us kids?" which she replied "A lovely Romanian woman." I wish I could remember her but I have absolutely no recollection. Mom also said this set up did not last too long because what she contributed to at the garage was not really enough to pay this lovely woman. And then, softly she would say "But I really didn't like the idea anyway"! Mom claims Dad would leave to go and have a beer with his brother leaving her to sand the cars. This is only one side of the story, another question I would have liked to have asked Dad but now, too late. When Mom was no longer working with Dad, she began to mistrust Dad when he would come home late from work. He might tell her he just had a lot of work but she said she could smell the alcohol. She really wondered if he again had spent the afternoon at the neighborhood bar. Mom began to mistrust him to the point Dad could never again gain her trust even though I am sure he worked his heart out and many times was working late. However, this was the beginning of their arguments and the end of a beautiful dream of working together.

Working together as a team on the dream of a business they had built began to spiral out of control. Never in the almost 20 years Dad owned the shop did it return. What happened? What happened was they were two people who loved each other but I firmly believe they never learned to share their feelings and discuss how they felt. Screaming was probably what they always heard during arguments at home and screaming is what they did. I do not picture either of them saying "Let's sit down and discuss this"! But the body shop itself was a total success. Unless you count the times people would pick up their car and not have enough money to pay for the work! Dad didn't have helpers until my brothers were older and would go down on weekends and help him. I stayed home. Mom would make me clean my brothers' room!! I hated it. She would say "Your brothers are down at the garage with Dad, sanding and polishing" and therefore we cleaned the house!! Later my brother Kenny, who was very talented in repairing cars after learning from Dad, worked for years with the same company as an auto body repair man. He was considered the best auto body repairman in the state. I was not told that, I knew that!

My Father had found his love, painting, fixing cars, and now a place of his own. He had worked at one of the top car dealers for a while and had learned much of the art of painting cars. These cars were not made of fiber glass as they currently are, and required a lot of pounding out dents. It was very hard work. But, when those cars went off the lot, they were beautiful!!!! Everyone who knew Dad knew he was a true artist. Mom meanwhile was caring for 3 children under three.

Later as we children grew, Mom still distrusting Dad, they chose this plan where Dad was to at least call Mom when he was on his way home so she could warm up his dinner. She would get very upset if he just popped in the door and she was not ready. She got really upset if it got later and later and he was not home. There was one specific situation I remember clearly, even to where the phone hung in the kitchen.

Remember, there were no special phone programs where if someone was on the phone and you were trying to reach them, the person talking would get a beep or signal that someone was trying to reach you. No, in those days all you got was a busy signal. So on this particular night, I think many times Dad tried to call Mom letting her know he was coming, but I was on the phone. So Mom waited and waited and her mistrust and anger just built up. Of course, she did not know he was on his way home. Meanwhile, I am sure Dad knew there was going to be an argument and so he was already building up his anger as he drove the 30 minutes home. He knew he didn't have a chance! I think her anger built as well as his and then it all exploded. He came through that door like a cyclone, came into the kitchen and pulled the phone off the wall right in front of me! Boy, I knew I was in trouble and probably why I have remembered it all these years. But it was both their faults that these episodes of anger existed.

In later years my brothers and I would come down to the garage and simonize cars to make some money. I would always walk around to see what was interesting. There was one door in the back that was always locked. Dad told me that was where he kept his inventory of paint. I believed him, no reason not to. He also had a huge calendar that some supplier had given him which showed an almost nude beautiful lady on it. I found this in very bad taste and for sure it should not be hanging in a place owned by a good Catholic family. Well, of course I took it down, rolled it up and hid it behind some cupboard. Sometime later I heard my Mom and Dad talking in the kitchen. Dad told Mom that the supplier noticed the big calendar was missing. Mom said, "Was Judy down there lately?" Dad affirmed that I was so Mom then called to me in the living room with "Judy, did you take down Dad's calendar at the garage?" I remember this so clearly, where I replied very calmly "Yes." That was it! Just a calm "Yes." I think I remember this because I was so proud of myself. Today I see how that might have bothered my Dad and the supplier. I think of it as a funny memory. There were not too many, but I loved this one.

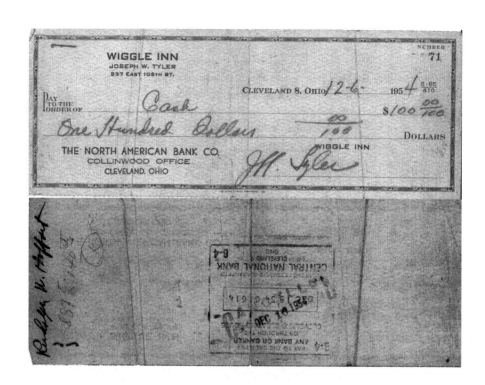

WIGGLE INN
JOSEPH W. TYLER
537 EAST 105TH ST.

NUMBER
71

CLEVELAND 8, OHIO 12-6- 1954

$100 00/100

PAY TO THE ORDER OF Cash

One Hundred Dollars 00/100 DOLLARS

THE NORTH AMERICAN BANK CO.
COLLINWOOD OFFICE
CLEVELAND, OHIO

WIGGLE INN
JW Tyler

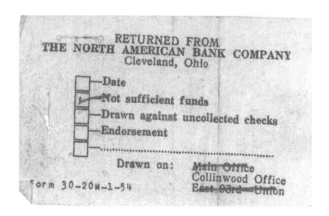

RETURNED FROM
THE NORTH AMERICAN BANK COMPANY
Cleveland, Ohio

☐ —Date
☑ —Not sufficient funds
☐ —Drawn against uncollected checks
☐ —Endorsement
☐ ....

Drawn on: Main Office
Collinwood Office
Form 30-20M-1-54 East 93rd—Union

31

Chapter 8

Music in the Air

There is sadness within this family for everyone, not excluding our parents who created the platform for such theater almost every day. Underneath the issues were two talented people. My Father was so talented when it came to music. The harmonica was the only instrument he played and he played it well!! But he also knew the sound of good music. Long before there was stereo Dad had 2 speakers hooked up to his Orthophonic which is what he called his elegant record player encased in this gorgeous large wooden cabinet. I wish I had a picture because you cannot possibly picture what a piece of art it was. He loved organ music and had quite a collection of records. What I did not know is he was speaking at the public library downtown on his collection. What is sad about this is not only did I not know, but me the reader who loved the library, would have loved to have been there with him.

For some reason I also love old music. Today I turn on SiriusXM 40's Junction every single morning to listen to the music Mom and Dad woke up to. I just love it and know every song. To me, having an art and sharing it alone, outside the family wall, there has to be something missing for the artist. I can picture Dad getting so excited about being asked to speak, actually doing the lecture and then coming home with no one to say "How did it go Dad?" I have an idea of why he did not share this special event with us but it's just one more way we could have had something to do together. Possibly creating some kind of Father-daughter bond. You see, Dad's love of music did not bother Mom but his huge collection of records was a sore spot in Mom's everyday life. For one thing, there was no place to store them! Dad had built shelves in their closet and it was full, from top to bottom. Where did Mom keep her clothes? I have no idea, should have asked her, wish I had. If you pulled open the drapes to the closet it was lined with specially built shelves, the width across being the exact width of a record. It was very organized.

Meanwhile we lived in the projects, watching every penny. There was Dad out scouting for more organ music records and other antiques. I am sure some of their arguments were due to the buying and collecting. But one argument sounded like all the rest. Shouting, screaming and sometimes hitting. We never listened for the words. We never cared what it was all about, we just knew it was another horrible example of them not being able to talk to each other and settle their differences. I accidentally found all these records (I know you're wondering how I knew the closet was full of records).

It was just before Christmas and my brothers and I were anxious to know what Santa was bringing so we did what little kids would do, we went looking. Small house, not many places to look, but Whalla!!! We pushed open the curtain to their closet in their bedroom (a place for sure we did not belong), and there was a pair of gloves, scarves, a "cotton candy" game (YIPPEE!!) and a small airplane kit for my brother. We were so excited. We were giggling and dancing until it hit us there would be no surprises at Christmas! I remember going to my bedroom and sitting on the bed realizing how horrible this Christmas was going to be. I promised myself I would never again try to find a present of any kind! But my thoughts then turned to my younger brother who was only four. What Louis and I had done totally might have ruined his "Santa" experience. Another question I should ask him someday!

My little brother has always been my little brother. I care for him, love him and worry about him every day. He has the best wife, Carolyn, and he told me when he first met her "I am going to marry Carolyn someday." He doesn't remember saying that, but I do. I am happy he has found such a loving marriage. Don't we each deserve it? You would think after what we witnessed growing up we might be very strict or have a lot of anger. I guess we all decided we never wanted to live our life under those circumstances and have made every effort to always be a nice, caring and loving person. But wait. Dad and Mom were nice, caring and loving also. In fact, I think they were very nice, caring and loving. Sometimes life happens, we get off track and finding our way back can be long and hard. It's like a run-away train where they just could not find the brakes. But there was hope.

As of this writing, my brother Kenny celebrated his 50th wedding anniversary with his wife Carolyn. My brother Louis also just celebrated his 51st wedding anniversary with his wife. John and I celebrated our 54th anniversary. Long marriages. Much love. Maybe we did learn something. If so, I am sure my parents are proud of us.

Chapter 9

Peace in the Sun

"Inside the book between the lines was a place to rest and absorb the magic!" I am not sure who said that, but it sure describes my love of reading. The Euclid Projects were just down the street from Roosevelt Elementary. I found this on my first day of kindergarten. Wow, I saw all these books and we got to take them home! Along with my friends Kathy and Carolyn we would walk almost every day skipping and laughing, so excited, we were going to get a book! As soon as we would get home we would put out the blanket and read. I still remember walking into the library and thinking "Wow, this is going to be such an exciting afternoon." I was as young as 6 and loved the freedom of leaving the house. I remember staying in my room and reading and enjoying the peace and quiet. I also think it was my outlet for blocking out all the loud conversations down stairs. This was by far my favorite pastime. There were no televisions yet, at least in our home. When I was reading I forgot everything in my life. Sort of like if you're a golfer. When you are out there on the course all you are thinking is "Hit that ball. How far? Which club?"

When my Dad would go to see his brother, my Uncle Bill, I would go with him because my cousin Marlene loved to read and lay in the sun on a blanket. I was always looking for some quiet place and there was such peace there. I know for sure, now, that I am not an introvert. As you can imagine as a young girl in this environment, I valued every little bit of peace and quiet I could find. To this day I am an avid reader, especially non-fiction. I cannot possibly learn everything there is about life, art, spiritualism and other facts of the universe we live in, but I can find it all in books! There is something for everyone in a book. The library is your best friend. The computers now have it all, but no E-book for me! There is such a feeling of peace and relaxation sitting with a book on your lap!

As soon as my children were old enough to walk, I would take them to the library inside the elementary school one block from our home. After a few times all I had to do was say the word "library" and I could get them to do whatever, i.e., eat their lunch, put their toys away, etc.! What I never realized was what it took to write a book! I can now appreciate all the time and concentration a writer experiences. Finding time was my biggest obstacle, plus writing about your life requires remembering some specifics; some you enjoyed remembering and some you wanted to bypass. As I learned from one of the artist I worked with during the three months of an "author in residence program," you need to write the details!

Details, details, details!

Chapter 10

Some Things Never Changed

It seemed none of the wives worked until Mom took a job in the cafeteria at the junior high school about 1/2 mile from our home in the projects. Dad was furious and began a long struggle with this issue between them. Mom said, "When I shut the door and went to work that first morning it was the worst day of my life." She loved being a Mother. Four children, no automatic washer, no second car to get her to work. She walked to and from and still came home to fix supper. I don't know the discussions between them and don't believe Dad ever accepted Mom going to work. I think there were still some issues with this but "it was not a factory" so somehow she did it anyway. Dad worked in a factory during the depression and I guess he had some bad memories of what it was like for the women.

Meantime we attended St. Paul's Catholic School which was about half way to where Mom had to walk. It was a pretty good walk for us, going under the bridge and then the walkway that had a slight uphill section. This had to be extremely hard for Mom. Now I realize just how hard. Guess I was caught up with friends, etc. and never realized it. Mom stood on her feet all day then walked home to do exactly what she did when she was home all day washing, cooking, etc. I remember it was also a change for me. I was used to coming home to see Mom ironing and listening to the Cleveland Indians baseball game. Now I was coming home to chores. Mom was determine to keep up with everything so we each had some chores now.

One thing that never changed was Mom's feelings of her duty to her family. Dad still got his pork chop dinner, the towels were hung in the morning to dry, but taken down before he came home, and the house was wound up tighter than a baseball! So Mom now was bringing in an income, small as it was. I guess it made a difference.

Chapter 11

Amazing Mom!

Mom always dressed simple, but nice. Every picture I have of her you can see her outfits always matched. She never had a lot of money for clothes but she knew how to dress. She was also a wonderful seamstress. She made almost all my clothes until I was about 12 years old. She made my first communion dress and told me it cost $2.00 a yard which was very expensive back in 1948. I still have the dress. Beautiful rows of ruffles, puffed sleeves and satin collar.

Mom sewed for both my sister Carol and I, always making the same dresses for each of us as if we were twins. Then, one Easter when I was twelve years old, Mom made the most beautiful pink and gold metallic striped dresses. The dresses buttoned all down the front. I later sewed and I would always think of how Mom made all those button holes, smack down the front of the dress and they were perfect! I remember everyone stopping to look at my sister Carol, who was four years old, and remarking on how cute she looked. That night I told my Mother I did not want to have the same dress as Carol. I explained that yes, I thought I looked nice, but I didn't want to wear the same clothes as a four year old. My Mom was so sweet and told me she would never do that again, and she didn't!

When Mom went to work at the school there were no more new clothes from Mom's sewing machine. It certainly changed Mom's life, but she tried very hard to ensure it did not change ours. I remember once Mom washed the clothes early in the morning, very early! Then she hung them all over the house from lines she had set up, to the bars in the bathroom, everywhere! On this particular day my friends decided to take our lunches to someone's house. Seemed like it was my turn. I then remembered helping Mom hang towels, etc. all over the house, so I ran ahead, grabbed all the towels and underwear and threw them in the bathroom. So the girls came, we laughed, ate and then one of them said they needed to use the bathroom to which I explained "Oh, it's not working, Dad is going to fix it tonight!" Four children, gone all day, of course there was much to do. I am sure Mom was overwhelmed at times and now I understand. All I can tell myself about these issues is "Judy, you stayed and helped." Maybe it's this part of the story that makes me remember the difficult times for Mom. I probably was very unhappy with coming home from school and not riding my bike but now I am glad I stayed and helped even though I was probably a little grumpy at the time!!!

Mom was a good Mother. She was a good cook, she kept the house clean, she sewed and she made the best potica this side of the Mississippi! The potica was a Slovenian pastry but not at all created using a pastry base. She would make this over the holidays for people. One time, I was about 28 years old, I left my house at 2pm to go help her and returned at 6am the next morning. We stayed up all night baking and playing cards. The recipe required you to create the dough and then pull it very thin with no holes. My Mom used the dining room table to spread the dough. It was so thin that when you ate it you could hardly see any dough at all. All you saw was the nut mix inside that consisted of ground walnuts and egg whites. It was my job to slowly stir this mixture on the stove, mix and lick the spoon. And lick the spoon again and again! Once in a while I would hear my Mom murmur "This seems harder to spread tonight," which was probably due to a few teaspoons less of mixture. Once the dough was prepared it had to rise so Mom and I played cards. After rolling and filling the dough, it had to rise again, so we played more cards. A recipe made 3 loaves and she had over 100 orders. So now you know why I did not return home for hours...yum!!! One year I got out the video camera as my friend Dottie and I wanted to try to make potica. We had Mom sitting there as we followed the recipe, but even with Mom trying to tell us exactly how long to mix the dough, pull the dough and mix the nuts and egg whites, actually doing it was almost impossible. There were plenty of holes even as Mom would say "Now be gentle girls." We just never got the hang of it.

In the summer of 1955 we purchased our first home. We had lived in the projects, moving from a 2 bedroom to a 3 bedroom. Mom transferred to Roosevelt Elementary at that time. The walk was longer but we finally moved out of the projects. You would have thought this would have for sure made Mom and Dad so happy that some of their issues they would put behind them.

You think?

Chapter 12

Windward

18108 Windward was the first home my parents owned. It cost them $12,000 and had three bedrooms, one bath, a small kitchen, a beautiful dining room with two walls of windows, a large living room with a fireplace and a basement. It also had a three car garage that sat way back on the property and was ready to be torn down! Of course, with everything in our lives, this home had a story to tell that we could not ignore.

My Dad operated the 140th Street Auto Body, as described, while we still lived in the Euclid projects. I think Mom and Dad tried to qualify to purchase a home but for some reason nothing happened. Then one day Dad got into a discussion with Harold the mailman. Harold offered to carry the mortgage if Dad found a home that was not too expensive. This old house was in a great neighborhood but probably the worst one in all three blocks. But, it had character, a large front porch, and a beautiful large back yard where hundreds of daffodils were planted, an old three car garage in the back and most importantly it was just walking distance to the lake. This neighborhood, which we referred to as "down near the lake," was about three streets of beautiful old homes and close to all shopping on E. 185th Street.

At one corner was shopping including a drugstore, bakery, fish market, clothing stores, and a dime store where I would later work. Further down was a movie theater. At the other end was Lakeshore Blvd. with access to a bus line, a hospital a mile away and a Catholic boys' school, St. Joseph's. At the end of E. 185th Street was a large clothing store. The whole neighborhood always purchased clothing there and it was where we purchased our Easter outfits.

As to the story of the new home of ours, it seems that an old lady died in the house and she cared for over 50 cats. You knew the story of the cats was true because the kitchen stunk! I think they found actual food dishes on the shelves and, of course, there were no litter boxes to be found. The smell was so bad Dad knew he would have to take down the cupboards. Then they realized the smell was into the walls so these old plaster walls had to be taken down! They sanded all the floors and Mom put down carpet. I could lay on the floor and read the newspaper and still smell cats! Dad's brothers, great painters, all helped in painting the outside and inside and Mom and I spent the summer cleaning the rest of the house. Every day Dad dropped Mom and me off. I would listen to Eddie Fisher songs and we would wipe down every piece of woodwork and clean the bathrooms. It took us all summer.

Mom would walk to the corner deli to get us lunch. I was 15 and fell in love with the deli guy who I am guessing was about 24! How funny! Mom would say, "Do you want to walk up to the deli with me?" "You bet!" During that summer, Mom had an opportunity to be interviewed for a job at Bailey Meter where Aunt Mary worked. This job would be so much better for Mom, as she would be sitting rather than standing all day at the school cafeteria. One day after Dad dropped us off at the house to clean, we walked to the bus stop to catch the bus to Bailey Meter. I waited in the waiting room while Mom was in the interview but she had forgotten something. She asked me to run home to get it. I caught the bus and when it stopped at our street, knowing time was of the essence, I ran as fast as I could to retrieve this paper all the while knowing I needed to catch the bus as it made the swing back down the street towards Bailey Meter. I fell. Boy did I fall. I remember this so well because I still have the scar on my arm. Yes, 60 years later. I had no time to bandage the open sore. I just keep wiping the blood with a rag I had retrieved from the house. I was so excited for Mom. Imagine, no more standing on her feet! Well, that was short lived. When Dad heard he put a stop to it. No wife of his would work in a factory, not peacefully said, and it ended all conversation. This might be due to memories of when he worked in the factory during the war and saw something, who knows what, of the ladies who worked the assembly lines. Didn't matter, Mom was devastated and knew when the summer was over, she would again be walking to work and standing in the kitchen at the school.

Mom had to walk down Windward to E. 185th and then walk down to Roosevelt Elementary. She had gotten a transfer from Euclid Central Jr. High since it was closer to our new home. She would walk

43

down Windward, cross E. 185th, and continue down the following long street to E. 200th every single day; rain, snow, whatever. I know this to be true because for a while I walked with her. Many times I thought "Mom should be sitting at a job at Bailey Meter," but I never mentioned that possibility to my Mom. In the 10th grade, starting a new school and also having to walk, I walked with Mom every morning. It was quite a walk but the other option was to attend the high school in Cleveland. My parents decided I would instead attend school in Euclid. The school my brother was attending at the time was an all-boys school named St. Josephs. My choice was either an all-girls or regular school. My parents could not afford two private schools and did not want me to attend the Cleveland school in my neighborhood. I have no idea why. I never asked. So they signed me up for a school in Euclid. They used my Uncle's address since I belonged to the Cleveland School District. So, we both walked. She went as far as E. 200th and I went further to 222nd. It was good we walked together because there were some mornings it was dark. Dad was very worried about that so most mornings in the winter he would drive both of us. But there were many long, cold, walks. It was OK with me, I was excited to go to high school and Euclid was brand new. I think it was harder for Mom walking home after a long hard day than it was for me.

Regardless of all this, we all sat down every night to a good dinner!! This sounds unbelievable, but somehow Mom always felt she was supposed to fulfill her duties to her family. It was like it was ingrained in her. I am sure it was her upbringing watching her Mom work in the fields, in the garden and taking Grandpa to work on the horse. These women were strong women!!

Meanwhile, the house had a double entry staircase into the kitchen. You came down the steps from the upstairs and could go right into the kitchen or left into the living room. One day my brother and I were cooking something in the kitchen and it started a small fire. I screamed "Fire fire!" My Dad came running down the steps, turned into the kitchen and in such a hurry missed the two steps into the kitchen and bounced all the way to the floor. I still remember that fall and his face. He was in such a fright over us calling "Fire fire!" to only find this little grease fire in a pan. But we had to go into the dining room so my brother and I could hide our laughter at the look of Dad slipping on the steps. Of course he did not get hurt and we actually felt bad about him slipping. I remember this only because here we were with what we thought was a huge problem and who did we call but Dad. To us Dad could fix or take care of anything! And he could. I don't care what it was Dad could fix it. My Father was a jack-of-all-trades, meaning he could fix anything! We had an opportunity to purchase an old freezer. Dad looked it over and said it would take an $8.00 part and encouraged us to purchase it. We did. He fixed it! That freezer worked for years even after we later gave it to my cousin.

Dad eventually put a toilet in the basement and we painted some of the walls, put in some old furniture and a record player so my brothers and I could have a place, as teenagers, to bring friends. My brother Louis also had a short wave radio in the basement. Between the little furniture and the radio, we teenagers had a place to go and play music and be teenagers. This was a blessing for us, or rather maybe an escape. We were teenagers and needed a place to go. You would think my parents would have thought they died and went to heaven finally having their own home and things would settle down. Maybe the stress due to a higher mortgage than the rent in the projects just added to their already short tempers with each other. I know it was a lovely house and should have been a happy relief from the projects in Euclid, where we had lived for about 12 years, but.... *it was in __this__ house, in front of __that__ living room window, where this story started!*

So, no, things did not change with our first home of our own.

Chapter 13

The Drama of it All!

Of course Dad was the "person in charge" as us kids thought of him. So, what happened that night was a shock. If we could be shocked at anything. This long dream of both of them to own a home and for us children to leave the projects should have brought the whole family together. But if it could get worse, it did.

I remember it was the night this salesman was coming to the house to show me some silverware. In those days we tried to put together a trousseau! He no sooner entered the house when Mom and Dad started a spat in the kitchen. I guess they knew someone was in the living room so they retreated to the bedroom upstairs. You could hear them upstairs but to the salesman's credit he just kept talking, bringing out one different pattern of silver and then another. I was so embarrassed but did not know what to do. So I kept talking. They got louder and he just kept talking! Not just talking but actually trying to sell me this silverware. I mean, here I am going to be 18. I guess you could tell from the fighting upstairs I was in no position to agree to a sale of anything. I am sure this salesman is not alive to read this book, but if he were I am sure he would remember this night. I bet he talked about this pitch for a long time. The man left but not after being there for at least 90 minutes. It could have been longer, I mean he just did not give up! Either that or he was trying to help me keep my mind off the shouting upstairs. I have often thought of that. He was helping me! It seemed he had just left when I noticed it was quiet upstairs. Then, I heard my Dad crying. I held my breath. I remember right where I was standing in the living room as I listened to him cry. It was horrible. Yes, Mom had cried, but Dad?

I was afraid to go upstairs but then Mom was coming down anyway. She went to the phone and called a doctor. The doctor came to the house in those days. I moved to the end of the living room so she would not see me and sat there scared to death. As I write this I am wondering, where was Carol? It sounds amazing but I remember these arguments so vividly but do not remember where my younger sister was. I wish I had talked to her about that on our nightly calls later in life.

The house was so quiet you could not help but hear the soft sobs of my Dad. The doctor came with this black bag and went upstairs. Soon, I did not hear my Dad crying. Mom came down with the doctor and he spoke very quietly. He left and Mom turned off the lights in the kitchen, saw me in the living room and told me it was time to go to bed. And that was that! Imagine, she tells me it's time to go to bed and turns off the lights. What?! Well, Dad had experienced a nervous breakdown. I remember the next morning he did not come out. The next time I saw him he was sitting at the dining room table eating. He was home from work! Dad was never, ever home from work! This already scared me! Dad actually was home for at least a week. That was not good because he was the only worker at the shop. Now, as I understand breakdowns, this man obviously felt things were just too big to handle. Did someone give him another bad check? Did he not have enough money for the mortgage? What could bring a strong man, my Dad, the person who always could handle everything, fall apart?

I remember thinking I could not wait to get out of school and get a job so I could help pay some bills and maybe that might help everyone. That thought actually stayed with me the whole time I lived in that house. I was somewhat jealous watching the girls at school talk about the college they picked out. Still, I knew I had to just get a job and make some money.

To this day I wish my relationship would have been better with my Dad. Maybe it wasn't our relationship, maybe it was we just didn't hug. I think my Dad could have used a hug, just one hug. I would have given anything now, as I write this, to have given him a hug. I actually felt he would be embarrassed if I had since he always showed us he was the head of the household! What caused the argument I have no idea. Since the salesman was with me I actually do not remember the words. Whatever the issue, it involved both of them and I am sure Mom was under stress. They both were having trouble carrying these burdens. I do remember Mom said we were not going to be eating as many breaded pork chops because Dad needed to lose some weight and we were all going to get healthy. Now, looking back, I had so many chances to ask Mom exactly what happened. Sometimes you just don't want to talk about those times. I will forever remember the salesman sitting there talking and talking, hardly taking a breath, trying to out talk the shouting upstairs. Also I guess I didn't ask Mom because it just didn't matter anymore.

Chapter 14

Oh, the Special Times!

Special times with Dad were few but wonderful. I remember each one and cherished them then, and now. Like I said, under all the anger and problems there was a man who was very sweet and gentle and caring. I did get to see it on some events with just the two of us. Skating. Dad loved organ music so he would ask me if I wanted to go skating at the roller rink at Euclid Beach Park about three miles away. I loved it! I would go around and around and see Dad outside just humming and listening to the music. Now when I think of it, I can somewhat feel what Mom felt like when she said how happy she was that her Father asked her to dance rather than her sisters. For my Dad to ask me to go with him, anyplace, without my other siblings was special. Movies. My Father was a movie buff and loved old movies. I was never invited to go with him except for one time to see *Limelight*. It is a memory I have cherished the rest of my life. Limelight is still played once in a while on *TCM, Turner Classic Movies*. It would be Charlie Chaplin's last movie. It is the story of a ballerina where Charlie Chaplin befriends her. Even 70 years later it is still a beautiful story. As a girl of 10 watching a ballerina on the stage was special. I loved the story. I think Dad loved watching Charlie!

Later in life I found a music box with the song and sent it to Dad. After my Dad died, I was sitting in bed writing in my journal. I always turned on *TCM* because I like to see the movies my Dad enjoyed. Those movies from the 20's and 30's were, well, you have to actually like old movies to understand. I liked thinking about how they didn't have special cameras for special scenes and wondered how they created some scenes. "Where do you think the camera is?" I would ask myself. One particular evening 16 years after Dad passed I was feeling very low, both reminiscing and missing him. It felt like something told me to "turn on *TCM*" (I am sure you have had those moments). I stopped writing and changed the station and guess what? There was Charlie Chaplin, the ballerina and *Limelight*! The last time I had seen the movie was with Dad. I kept thinking of that day and how I just couldn't take my eyes off the screen. As much as I loved watching it with him 65 years ago, this evening, in bed, I felt like he was there and we were watching it together again!

Another example of how thoughtful my Dad was, was how involved he got when I joined the orchestra at school. I had wanted to meet kids at my new high school so I joined the orchestra. The band leader said "We have three instruments you can play, base fiddle, drums or cello." I chose the base fiddle. A year later I was asked to be in this band some boys in the orchestra were putting together to play at weddings. Since I did not have a base fiddle I was told I could use the school's, but could only take it out on Friday and return on Monday. With us playing mostly on Saturdays I had little time to practice with the band. We called ourselves "The Satellites," twelve guys and me! My favorite song, when it was my time to play a solo, was *Little Brown Jug*. One night, my Father surprised me and came to hear us play. I was so surprised to see him in the audience. Dad did not do much in the evenings because he was so tired from work and I thought he really did not pay much attention to the fact I had joined this school band. I mean, really, I did not think my Dad paid that much attention! About two weeks later I came home from school and in the corner of the dining room was a beautiful, blond Kay Bass. If you know instruments you know that is a special instrument. I have no idea where he found it but I am sure he just kept checking the newspaper ads. Shock. Happy. One of those "I cannot believe it" moments. My Dad was not affectionate and we did not discuss what I liked or didn't like or what I wanted. We did not have conversations like that. All I can think of was he was very happy and surprised at this band we put together and proud of me up there "pickin" away!!! But Dad was a lover of music. Maybe he was happy to see that I had really made an effort to get involved, even to playing an instrument. If I could have one more minute with my Dad, I would love to hug him and tell him what that meant. To this day I have no idea where he found the money to purchase such an item just for me to play in a band. It was way out of character for our family. So today I say to Dad "Dad, that was so special and I love you!! "

Another example of Dad's love that he and I had a hard time expressing was around skating. Skating at Euclid Beach while Dad listened

52

to the organ music created for me a love of skating. Dad also loved listening to Joe Vero who played the organ at our local Rollerdrome. As luck would have it, I had met two girls at school who went very Friday night and they invited me to go. I wanted to go because this boy I saw at school did not notice me, and I found out he skated there. I later found out his skating partner was my cousin Nancy! Small world. So I started going skating. I then decided I wanted to do more than skate around the rink so I told my Mom I wanted to take lessons. Well there certainly would be no monies from my parents so I had to start cleaning the neighbor house and babysitting some of my cousins' children. But I saved enough to purchase a nice pair of skates. I mean really nice!!

Now I was going out there every week end with my Dad taking me and listening again, to the organ player, Joe Vero. Dad would actually go up in his booth behind the glass partition and sit and listen and talk to Joe. I was not satisfied with just lessons to turn backwards and "flee-hop" as they called it then. (I have no idea what they call it now.) So I started to learn spins and jumps and just started spending every minute I could at the rink. I remember a test I had to have to get a medal and Mom and Dad came. They sat in the front row. At the end of my four minute dance, my teacher and I had choreographed, I ended in a spin and came down directly in front of the front row. It worked, and there I was, and there was Dad, sound asleep! I actually was not upset. This was a week night and I knew he had to be exhausted. The fact he came meant a lot. Yes, I still see him sleeping there.   I was then, and am today, proud of him for taking the time and coming to see me! Today I see girls with their Fathers. Hugging. Giving a kiss goodbye when they are leaving to go someplace. Especially when I was a substitute teacher and watched cars pull up to drop children off. Kisses, hugs, all these moments and signs of affection I missed. I know I was an affectionate person, but you just didn't do that around our house. Why? I ask myself that every day. Yes every day that I hugged my children I would wonder "Why didn't we do this with my Dad and Mom?"   I cannot see any reason except maybe they didn't do this with their parents? They probably did it with us when we were little so when and why did it stop?

I can now think of many opportunities I had to hug my Dad, kiss my Mom, write little notes and leave them around the house, send a card and just make a call. I was 22 years old before I remember doing this. If your family is not of the affectionate nature you need to remember that you are allowed to hug, kiss, call, or write cute notes. If they rebuke you, don't take offense. Do it again and again and again. I am betting they will get the idea. Little by little, shy as they might be with these ways of saying I love you, they will someday, when you leave or say goodbye, acknowledge your hug and hug you. Don't give up no matter how long it's been that way. Remember, someone has to be first.

Might as well be you!

Chapter 15

Give Credit Where Credit is Due

As far back as I can remember of holidays, Valentine's Day, Easter, birthdays, Thanksgiving and Christmas, were all special. We had wonderful traditions, presents, special food and most always spent them with my Dad's family. With five brothers and their children there were enough of us to have a party regardless of what the occasion. Valentines were sent very single year from my Dad to me. I still have some from as far back as the early 70's. Two years in a row in the 1980's he sent me the same card. For me that meant he purchased them for the words and not just for the color and decor. Mom was the cook of all cooks and so every holiday there were special goodies. We were allowed to pick our favorite cakes for our birthday and I loved the angel food cake. Since my birthday was December 30th Mom still never created a "Christmas cake" rather she decorated it like a New Year's Party! Thanksgiving was our traditional turkey with all the trimmings but Christmas was the "big one" in that she made potica. Easter with no potica wasn't Easter. As I write this in 2016, I can say that this Easter was our first without potica in my whole life. After Mom could not bake it, we purchased it from a Slovenian Market on E. 185th St., in Euclid, Ohio. Then my cousin Nancy Flemming would even surprise Mom and have some mailed to her.

Easter also meant going to the Cleveland Art Museum all dressed up. With little monies, we always had our Easter outfit and that outfit was our Sunday clothes for the rest of the year. But boy did we feel like we were "decked out." Dad would take us to parade down at the art museum gardens, pretty hats, new shoes, and the works. When we were married and left the house, Dad would watch out the window for us children to arrive. When he saw us he put the needle to the record and out would come *In Your Easter Bonnet.* Just another wonderful tradition I grew up with and loved. To this day I wonder how they managed these new clothes. There were no credit cards, everything was cash and cash was hard to find. My parents amazed me at how they always made the holidays so festive even though there were days during the year that were not!

Christmas meant we took a ride to the General Electric plant where they had a huge light display. Cars would ride through slowly as we strained our heads to share the windows in the back seat and see all the lights. And there were always presents. Not a lot, but always presents. There was always something we had asked Santa for, and later always something special. I asked my husband once "What was your favorite of all the Christmases at your house?" and he replied "I cannot remember any." They did not have any special traditions that I had guessed all those years I thought everyone did.

I had a very special Christmas one year. To this day I still thank my Mom and Dad and remember as if it just happened. I was 7 years old. My Mom was pregnant with my sister Carol. Mom didn't have a car so we would walk to the grocery store. Next to the store was a dime store, Woolworth. We kids would walk around in there and there was this doll, my little boy! It was a large doll with features of a baby boy. Short hair, clothes like a little boy would wear and I called it my boy doll. Oh, how I wanted him. I even had a name for him, Charlie. I talked about him, asked Santa for him and prayed to God for him! "Oh Santa, I want my little boy Charlie for Christmas." Since Mom could not shop a lot (Carol was born December 21) my Dad secretly came up with this idea. He said "Judy, the girl is your age, Louis, the boy is your age, and Kenny they have a little boy just like you!" So shopping we went. I had a great time picking out a hairbrush for this little girl. I remember the color and everything I picked out, because later I would find it under our tree for us! We also pointed out to Dad that there was a lamp there that Mom loved. It was very specific that she just had to have it and said "Can't we please get it for her Dad?" Dad would say we don't need it, it was expensive and that he would think about it. A couple days before Christmas Dad announced he had enough money to buy Mom the lamp. Yippee! He told us we could go with him to pick it up at Woolworths. While he was paying for it and having it wrapped, we were of course looking at all the wonderful toys in the dime store!! All I remember is him saying "OK, come on kids. I have the lamp." I looked up and he was carrying this big box on his shoulders.

Christmas morning was always the same tradition, no one went down stairs until Dad went first to light the tree! So just picture the excitement. Three children 9, 7 and 5 years old, with never getting toys except on their birthday and Christmas, running down to see what was under the tree. So we unwrapped our gifts. I really don't remember what anyone received and I don't remember even my sibling's gifts. We children all opened our gifts before our parents. I guess it was because Mom and Dad learned long ago not to make us wait. After oohing and aahhing over Santa's presents I don't remember at all feeling like everything wasn't perfect or that I did not find my little boy doll. I absolutely remember waiting for Mom to open her lamp! 67 years ago I still remember exactly how Dad pulled the big box from under the tree and said "Here Mollie, this is for you." I knew it was the lamp, and I was so excited for her! I wanted to make sure I sat right next to her to see her face. This was so exciting!

Mom opened the box. My heart was racing. I was jittery watching her and wanted to see her expression. Just before she opened the tissue she stopped. I remember thinking "Oh, my gosh, I hope Dad picked the right one," and she said "Oh Rudy, you didn't look closely at the tag. This is not for me, it says 'for Judy'." As I write this, I remember her voice, how she said it, how she looked at Dad with this expression of utter confusion. I could hardly understand what she just said. Yes, today I still hear these words and feel this emotion! For me??? "Yes," said Mom, "That's what it says." I proceeded to remove the tissue only to see Charlie! The box Dad carried was not Mom's lamp, it was Charlie!!! Think about the gift you purchase for someone as a special surprise and you will understand how I felt. Or, think about the gift you received that you wanted so bad but really never thought you would get and what it felt like. I am sure you can still feel it today. I can. These memories of the holidays and tradition and remembering how Dad was so tired from work but took us for the Christmas lights were probably just little things to him. To me, my brothers and my sister these little things are what we are today.

And, how we celebrated birthdays! The little gifts we gave each other and especially the memories that we can share even now with our parents is gone. Did they really understand just what receiving Charlie meant to me as a 7 year old? I think about how they thought up this way of giving him to me, the trick with Mom's lamp. I dressed Charlie in boy clothes and carried him everywhere for a long time. What I cannot remember is what happened to him. I am still looking as I wander through antique stores for Charlie! Charlie was born on December 25, 1948 so he would be 76! I told a friend once "We had a very dysfunctional family but at holidays we all came together to celebrate." It seemed like Mom and Dad took extra precautions to stay in the holiday mood. I don't remember one single holiday where we were not a happy family. Baking cookies, cooking Thanksgiving dinner, buying a fresh Christmas tree, picking out what kind of cake we wanted Mom to bake for our birthdays kept all in the spirit. I hope my Mom and Dad would realize and understand what those happy days meant to us, now over 70 years later. I also think these were special times for them because as parents you want to always celebrate with such tradition and happiness. Even my Mom remembers small gifts she got as she would say "Pa got to work at the railroad on the horse so I was never sure how he bought us presents, but he did!"

To My Wife on Valentine's Day

Just my way of saying, Dear,
How very much I care,
And how I'll only love you more
With every year we share.

Rudy

Chapter 16

A Promise Broken

Leaving home wasn't like in some families where the kids grow up, move away with a friend to an apartment, move to another city for a job or move away for college. My leaving home was an extremely emotional event because I felt like the caregiver, intervention, medium and press. It was like teenagers being left alone with no one to monitor.

My Mom went with me to choose my wedding gown and it was more than she expected to pay. She suggested I put it on and she would call Dad at work to come and agree to the beauty of it all, and pay for it! He saw and he did! I remember this moment because it's one a bride likes to remember of her wedding events. For Dad to close up the garage, knowing he was up to his neck in work, was really a surprise. I wanted him to see it before we made our decision but had no idea he would agree to pay for it. By this point in my life I realized how much work Dad had to do to turn a banged up car back to its original beauty. I knew to come to the store was not easy. Neither of John's parents nor mine really had enough monies to afford a Slovenian wedding, but being the first in my family to marry I knew that's what my Mom really wanted. I guess so did I. John's parents paid for the liquor and my parents paid for the food. The food? Wow! A Slovenian wedding was a sit down dinner beginning with 4 or 5 settings. It began with homemade chicken soup and ended with special homemade desserts. I remember seeing Mom walking around ensuring everyone was happy and the food was served hot. Of course this reception had to take place at a Slovenian home, a special venue hall for weddings, etc. John and I paid for rental of the hall, the band, which had to play polkas all night, church payments, gifts for our bridal party and photographs.

My Uncle Joe had a movie camera and came to the house before we left for the church and captured some wonderful videos. My favorite was Dad coming down the steps in a frizzy looking for his suspenders! Uncle Joe's daughter, my cousin Elaine, was in the wedding party, as was my sister, my best friend Judy Faber and my cousin Chickie. Aunt Mary's daughter was my maid of honor. The name Chickie always raises questions and yes, it was a nickname because her real name is Alvira. My Dad just could not see this little baby called Alvira so he called her Chi-Chi, which later turned to Chickie. Her check book and everything else was Chickie. Just like Mom, whose name is really Amelia, her debit cards and check book also read Mollie.

November 24, 1962 John and I said our wedding vows! It really was a beautiful wedding and had some very special memories! You are saying everyone's wedding has special memories, but did you hear of one where the Mother of the bride and the Mother-in-law, and some others, took all the presents back to the Mom's house, opened them and then rewrapped them so I would never know? When my Mom told me this, I was so happy. She thought I would be mad but we had most of the bridal party over a week after to open the gifts. It wasn't until after Mom revealed the "other opening!" She said "We made sure we rewrapped them perfectly!" I thought it was so funny! I wish I could have watched them! I am so glad they enjoyed this because Mom certainly worked so hard to put this wedding together.

In the back of my mind, I still wondered if I could count on Mom and Dad to enjoy the wedding, their dance together and maybe just think of good times and be patient with each other. At the wedding my Dad told me during our Father/daughter dance "Judy, I promise I will never hit your Mother again. I want you to enjoy your new marriage to John and not worry about Mom and me." His exact words to me. "Nothing changed" were the exact words from my sister who was only 14 and the only child left in the house. How could it? They had not gone to counseling, although I guess counseling wasn't a word used in the 60's? At least not in their vocabulary. I have no idea what went on, but I can only imagine. I think it was amazing I could visit with both of them and not see any pouting or irritability so I am not sure how they hid what was happening from everyone.

How could it be any different? Dad still drank. At this point he had no reason to quit drinking. My Dad did not think for one minute he was an alcoholic. To him it was something that was just a drink. I will say I never

saw him drunk. He could certainly hold his liquor. Mom was
Mom. Untrusting of Dad and over the years had not learned to let-it-go! They were two firecrackers waiting to go off and no one to say "Wait a minute. Think about what you're saying. Think about what you just did. Think about the child we still have living here!" Every time I worried I would remember Dad's words during the dance. I felt he would remember what he said and try to be patient.

Louis was in the Army. Kenny was working and gone all the time with his girlfriend Carolyn. All there was left to report any issues was my sister Carol. I cannot imagine her being left alone with them. She had some curt remarks about that once. Divorce was always out of the question and there were none in our family. Dad and Mom's family were very strong Catholics with Monsignor Kirby being the boy Dad grew up with and who got him the job at the church. Mom and Dad themselves were good Catholics. Never missing mass, observing Fridays, eating no fish and the sacraments. Four siblings on the Skolaris side and 6 on the Hoffart side and all raised good Catholic families. So to say I was shocked when the phone rang that morning the following summer. It was Mom, announcing she was divorcing Dad, and needed to hide since she was sure he would come looking for her.

What a surprise!

Chapter 17

Left Speechless

We were married in November of 1962 and in the summer of 1964 our life changed. Mom would have waited until school was out and therefore had time to deal with the situation. We lived in the top floor of a two family home. Ironically, it was a customer of Dad's who owned the home and she happened to tell him she was looking for a renter. John and I were planning our wedding and wanted a very inexpensive place to live. We did not want the apartments we saw since we really wanted to get a good financial start.

This home had two single story homes and a large attic. You would go through a private door to our second floor apartment and enter. Before entering, there were steps to the attic. In essence you could only reach the attic from outside the private door to our apartment. Upon reaching our apartment you still had to walk up a separate set of the stairs to the attic door which you could lock. We did not. We never used the attic so when Mom asked for a place to hide (No, we did not put her in the attic!) we said yes, for sure, but she would have to sleep on the couch. The couch was just about brand new and Mom actually said it was great to sleep on.

Dad got served but he did not explode. The opposite. He was shocked and sad. According to my Uncle John, "Your Father was extremely upset and I invited him to my house to calm down." After a few days when Mom needed more clothes, John and I went over to the house. My Dad was just coming home from work. To be polite we stopped the car and rolled down the window to talk to him. We had not talked to him at all since the papers were served. He seemed so lost. He said "Judy, please tell me where your Mother is. I promise not to hurt her. I just want to talk." I denied knowing where she was. These were terrible times. Remembering now, it is still a sad time in my life. John and I went to work and Mom stayed inside the apartment. One day, Dad knowing the only place Mom would go was to my house, he showed up outside. My Mom heard the car. She was afraid he would break down the door so she ran up to the attic to hide. Up in the attic she heard him come to the apartment door and try to talk to her through the door. When she did not answer, he quietly walked away. She then heard the car leave and realized it was safe to come down. In shutting the attic door behind her, she inadvertently locked it! Mom was locked in the attic all day. Remember, it is summer!

When we arrived home and opened our apartment door I called for Mom and then heard the pounding on the attic door upstairs. It was terrible. I cried. I felt so sorry for her. Did she cry? No! Mom was the pillar of strength. She had to know the road ahead was not going to be easy. Except for being very thirsty and tired, she acted like nothing special happened. Amazing! Meanwhile, Dad did not like staying in the house alone. Mom had gotten an attorney, who was also a friend. He was Mr. Voinavitch who was also a councilman. I am thinking Dad was very embarrassed when Mr. Voinavitch reached Dad and told him a meeting was being set up for both of them. I am not sure who Dad got as his attorney. I only remember Mom telling me at their first meeting Dad was very quiet. He told her he loved her. He told her he did not want the family broken up. He swore he would change. He also told her she could go back home and he was going to my Uncle John's to live. She did go home. He did go to Uncle John's.

It's easy for me to remember these words Dad spoke at the time. I am sure you readers are thinking that is what they all say. You will read just how sincere Dad was as you continue this journey with Mom and Dad.

So far this huge announcement the whole family received was turning out to be very amicable. I was wondering why they could not have handled issues like this for the last 20 years. But, remember they had a moderator. Two attorneys. Also, Dad was really shocked and did not want a divorce. Uncle John said Dad went to church every single morning before work. He told Uncle John all he wanted was his family to stay together. Uncle John told him to just be patient and attend the meetings with the attorneys and keep his faith. Much later, during my sister Carol and our nightly talks, I happened to say "I don't remember where you were Carol." She said Mom had sent her to Aunt Edith's. This was my first clue that Mom had shared what was going on with Dad and her with anyone outside our immediate family. I guess Mom did need someone to talk to after these terrible arguments. Why had I not thought of that? I did not think she would talk to her sister Mary because Mom told me Mary never liked the fact she married Dad. "He doesn't play cards or dance" Aunt Mary told her. For whatever reason, Mom was always closer to Aunt Edith.

So Mom went home. Dad was at Uncle John's and going to church praying.

Then, Dad was told the news...

Chapter 18

A Cold Beer on a Hot Summer Day

When Mom asked for a divorce from Dad, and the attorneys met to discuss what the next step was, my Dad discussed this with one of his best friends from childhood, Monsignor Kirby. Father Thomas A. Kirby was not only an extremely close friend of Dad's, but he said mass at the church Dad worked as janitor. As a young boy Dad would travel during summer months with Father Kirby as far as Canada. By now Father Kirby is a Monsignor and has been very close to Mom and Dad. Father Kirby knew my parents very well as friends and was the priest that performed their marriage ceremony. He realized quickly that the problems between Mom and Dad would be very hard to work out if Dad continued drinking.

Father Kirby knew the Hoffart boys and that they all loved a shot and a beer. Think about it. It's 1920's and there is no television so when you get together you have a drink together. He told Dad that the attorneys' suggestion that Dad go to AA was an excellent one. If Dad chose to not try this idea, and if there was a divorce, Mom would be allowed to stay in the Catholic Church while Dad could not. They did not condone divorce but if one party was not held responsible for the break-up they could, with approval, continue to receive the sacraments. This was a big blow to Dad. He had never thought this could happen. He absolutely wanted to reconcile and put his family back together so agreed to try AA. Dad never thought he was an alcoholic and I never saw my Father drunk. Not all alcoholics drink until they are drunk. Some just crave the liquor and can still hold their own. My Father would get in arguments with Mom and then go get a drink! My Father was told there are a lot of issues that can bring out his addiction to alcohol. Regardless, he had to quit drinking and AA was the best program to try and still be able to have proof that he actually was not drinking.

My Father said he was assigned a sponsor and he was to meet this person at the Friday Night AA meeting in Euclid. Upon arriving Dad saw many men going in with suits and ties and thought he was in the wrong place. Just as he was deciding to turn around and go home, this man came up and introduced himself and explained he was Dad's sponsor. It was then Dad said he opened his eyes to the fact that this problem affected many people of every gender and status. My Father crossed the line at that point on a journey that he would have to follow for the rest of his life, the journey called sobriety. I don't really know the day to day issues my Dad had during the next two months he and Mom were separated. I know he moved in with his brother and my Mother returned home. I was told he went to mass every day and to his meetings as part of a Friday group and a Saturday group as well as a monthly group in Aurora. I know my Dad had a spiritual experience. Realizing he was doomed to either the loss of his family or a death from alcohol Dad turned to his faith, his love for God and the AA program. My Dad grew up with a very religious background and I think he returned to what he knew was the only place he would find someone to help him. A place he could find the strength he would need to beat this addiction. God said "Ask and ye shall receive" and I know my Dad asked because his strength over the next 35 years was nothing short of a miracle. It was a miracle in which he participated in and prayed for every day of his life. My Dad told me once "I face the future with courage." He said "There is inevitably a trivial excuse for taking that first drink, and I understand the consequences but I still pray every day for strength." Dad also had a wonderful spiritual devotion to St. Therese. He had the book of her life *Roses Fall Where Rivers Meet* and a statue of her on his bedside table. He was very determined and he followed every step they suggested to be successful. I found his little black AA book *24 Hours a Day* in his bedside table after he passed. I have read it many times from cover to cover and understand the words that gave him strength. This all sounds good, but after almost three months apart, and having joined AA as the attorneys suggested, he wanted to leave Uncle John's and return home. He knew it would be very hard to convince my Mom to give him a chance so they could reconcile and put their family back together. He had proven to himself he could and would handle sobriety, but was that enough? Would Mom believe Dad could actually give up alcohol?

I remember the meeting that changed my life and that of Mom and Dad's. I still think of it every single day as if it was yesterday.

Mom called and asked if she and Dad could home to our home. Mom said "We would like to talk to you and John." They were coming over in 3 days and my stomach was so upset. I was sure this was the end of my parents together, all our family traditions and celebration of holidays. I had just found out I was pregnant. The thought of this new little child not enjoying the wonderful opportunity of sharing time with my Dad and my Mom as a family made me a nervous wreck. Dad and I sat on the two large hassocks, next to each other. Mom and John sat in chairs. Mom said "Your Dad has been going to AA and now he wants to come home. I have talked to your brothers and sister and they said they feel we should just decide for ourselves. So Dad and I decided to ask you and whatever you say, we will agree to do."

Agree with whatever I say? Why me? I have thought about that over the years. I think it was because I was the caregiver, the child that was there through the fights, the one keeping them from killing each other. I never left the house. I was in the thick of it all. I have no idea where my siblings were during the arguments or now during the time Mom and Dad are deciding their future together. You cannot blame my siblings for just wanting to move on and suggesting to Mom and Dad to make this decision themselves. Maybe it was Mom's idea since we had spent so much time together that summer moving into our first house. It was my turn to give them an option if I in fact chose to do so. I could have just said "I don't care," but I didn't. I had followed Mom's days after she gave Dad the divorce summons and I also knew what Dad had been doing while living with Uncle John. To me, this was an important decision for them. Dad looked at me and said "Judy, I promise you I will never drink again and I just want another chance." I can barely write this. I still see his face, this man who I saw so angry, now looking so pleadingly pitiful like he was pleading for his life. What did I feel? Total love. Don't ask me how I could after all those years, or why love, why not just some compassion or understanding. No. I felt love. I just loved this man sitting here. So, I turned to Mom and said "Everyone deserves another chance. Dad has done everything he can to show you he will not drink. Now he gets a chance to prove it." With that Mom said "Well, what if he comes back home and hurts me or drinks?" I said, "Well, then we will talk about that if it happens, but now he deserves to be at home as much as

69

you do!" I remember those words "He deserves a chance to be at home as much as you do". Today, just as I remember Dad's words, I also watched him keep that promise through some of the hardest times of his life. I have never regretted that moment, and for sure neither did he, and he deserved to be at home! It takes two. I was there, it wasn't all one person's fault. And true, one does deserve another chance if they have shown a sense of sorrow and a desire to change. It's really called "forgiveness." How can you be spiritual or say you love God if you cannot at least give someone who begs for it forgiveness and another chance.

My Dad kept his promise. Dad went to AA for 35 years. Mom never attended Al-Anon. I have no idea why not. My sister Carol, who was still at home, said life did change as Dad never showed any signs of aggression. However, what made it difficult for Dad was Mom, still bringing up issues of the past. According to my sister this created stress for her and Carol said she felt sorry for Dad. Dad stayed patient and refused to engage in these issues. October was Dad's anniversary date at AA. When we had the children we took them to the meetings, even little Todd our youngest in a highchair!! All Dad's children went to these special events at AA. We were all so proud of him. We explained to our small children exactly why we were there to celebrate, though at that time I am sure they did not understand.

I had a chance to just feel a tiny bit of what it had to be like for Dad, fighting an addiction and giving up something he really enjoyed. It was while saying some special prayers for a friend who was sick. I decided to give up chocolate to show God just how much I kept the faith and how much I felt my prayers were heard. As soon as I put the bag away I thought "Wow, I cannot have one of these tomorrow after lunch." Then the next day after lunch, as I would have had my two little chocolate pretzels, I thought "no pretzels today". Then this thought came across me as strong today as it was the day I thought it "I am going to miss my little treats." But then as I thought that, I thought "How did Dad feel the first time an event arose where everyone was having a drink, whether after dinner or at a party?" Think about it. Think about that first temptation, the first time you cannot reach for that drink, the first time you watch someone else drink and think "Why is it OK for him to drink and not me?" Then I am sure Dad prayed "I won't drink today." I think every

70

tomorrow is really today. He always had to be remembering his commitment to AA and is family. However, I could have a pretzel in four days. Dad could never have another drink. The program says "One Day at a Time." They know in their hearts if I want to stay sober I have to stay sober today. No excuses. Since I never was a drinker of even small drinks, I remember asking Dad one day "Dad, what do you miss the most keeping your sobriety?" and he replied "A cold beer on a hot summer day." Amazing. I don't drink beer but I have noticed how a beer on a hot summer day is a true "afternoon delight." He loved his fellow AA members. He never missed a meeting and never touched a drop, even with his brothers coming over for holidays. Dad had liquor for them and kept the wine my Mother loved in the same cabinet where it had always been. He remarked "Just does not mean everyone else has to stop." He even refused cough medicines. If you looked at Christmas pictures where Mom put out all the goodies she baked for the family gathering you can see the liquor bottles on the buffet. Again, Dad always provided whatever drinks his guests preferred.

My Father left a legacy for not just our family, but all his friends in every AA group everywhere. The changes he made are the reason I wrote this book. It is beyond comprehension how and what he had to do to accomplish his journey. He took the contract he made with God and his family very seriously but exactly how did Dad keep this contract with God? That is a story I wanted so much to tell and one of the main reasons for this book. His journey to sobriety was a true story of faith, determination and support. I mentioned earlier that to accomplish this feat, my Dad would be called on to make changes to his life that everyone that knew him, still to this day when we discuss it, were stunned. He taught everyone around him it was possible to do what is thought to be the impossible and he followed through with his promises to himself, his family and God.

Read on!

Chapter 19

Oh Happy Days!

Oh, how things changed after Dad began his world of sobriety! It was a new world for the whole family. We all felt the changes every time we were together. It was a wonderful feeling. Just happy. In June 1965 Dad experienced the joys of his first grandson, John Stih Jr. How he loved him. He took advantage of every moment with him and was there so many times I needed him!! Beginning when Johnny rode his bike off the porch and I had to call Dad to come and take us to the emergency room. Upon arriving they told me it would probably require a stitch and they would put him in a little straight jacket at which time I pointed to Dad and said "Dad, will you go with him, please?" At that time Dad was still working at the body shop. He had to stop and close the shop up, but he was there!! Then we have the first birthday. June 29th, all our friends and family are there in the back yard having a party. Liquor is plentiful. Where is Dad? He is taking Johnny for a walk around the block. He was very smart. He kept himself busy with Johnny. He was loving it and, at the same time, away from the liquor. Oh, he ate, he sure didn't diet, he just didn't drink liquor. I remember that because it really resonated with me how Dad was finding more important things in his life through sobriety. Then we have the second birthday with little Daniel. Again, the family is in the back yard having a barbecue. And where is Dad? First he was taking Johnny for a walk around the block pulling him in a wagon. The best part was when little Danny, who was put inside the kids' fence so we would not lose track of him during the fun time, started crying and crying. He wanted OUT! What did Dad do? He picked up a folding chair, swung it over the fence and climbed in and sat with Danny! It was a beautiful moment to remember.

There were continuous great birthdays, anniversaries and holidays. Mom put out all the goodies, including the drinks, and Dad never once told her not to. He believed others did not have to give up a drink just because he had. Dad loved his family. He had chosen sobriety to keep the family together and he was enjoying every day, every event. I know I was. I know my children were. I cannot imagine what it would have been like for the boys to miss having one of the best Grandfathers. Dad never even complained or made one single comment about "I am not taking a drink today." He never brought it up.

We have a wonderful picture of the family on Dad's 80th birthday in July (see picture) and there he is with his coffee cup in his hand! For sure he also had his Life Savers in his pocket! Life was good. The real sweet, loving spirit that was my Dad, that was hidden at times, showed every day everywhere. He was so thoughtful sending a valentine every year, remembering Mom's birthday and just so thoughtful of others. The whole family attended his Euclid Friday anniversary. That was where he went to his first meeting. With our three little boys in tow, we never missed these anniversary meetings. My brothers and their wives, my sister, the whole family was there every year.

As the grandsons grew up, papa was very important in their lives. They loved going to garage sales with him. When we moved to Albuquerque my parents came to visit and the boys just loved being around papa. He was so funny. He never lost his sense of humor. Like I said, kids loved him. I would hate to think of the relationship those boys would have lost if their Grandfather had not loved them so much and had learned to live with his addiction. It was due to his faith, prayer, strength and an unconditional love for his family.

Dad was worth saving.

Chapter 20

The Real Test of Sobriety

Dad showed his love for his family through sobriety. "I am content to face the rest of my life without alcohol. I have made the great decision once and for all. I have surrendered as gracefully as possible to the inevitable. I hope I have no more reservations." These are not only the words from Dad's *Twenty-Four Hour a Day* AA book but it is as if Dad wrote them himself. So what did Dad do to ensure he could keep this contract with God and himself? First, after moving back home, he let my Mom know she would not have to give up her wine that she so enjoyed. He expressed his firm conviction that this was his journey and not everyone else in the family. I know Dad must have struggled each day to continue his sobriety because he had temptations coming from everywhere. Remember, his brothers did not take the same path so there was still a lot of drinking In front of Dad. I am sure it was hard. He put on a good face going to meetings and showed he was determined to never take one single drink.

Being self-employed became a huge temptation. Especially since his brother, my Uncle Bill who worked for Pennsylvania Rubber, would stop by the garage even knowing Dad was in AA and ask Dad to go for chicken and a beer. I have no idea what he was thinking except a drinker loves company. My Uncle Bill died some years later of alcohol issues. It would have been easy for Dad to go. He could try not to drink and enjoy the air conditioned bar, considering the small garage had no air and there were many hot days. Going for beer on a hot summer day had to be especially tempting, but as Dad found out, there were many tempting situations. One was with customers who were picking up their cars and asking Dad to join them in a quick drink. "Lay upon God your failures and mistakes and shortcomings. Do not dwell upon your feelings of your failures by the fact that in the past you have been a beast rather than an angel. You have a mediator between you and God, your growing faith which can lift you up from the mire and point you toward the heavens." (Meditation from *Twenty-Four Hours a Day*)

Dad's color matching abilities were one hundred percent perfect so much so that the executives at the Fisher Body Plant down the street would bring their new automobiles to Dad rather than have them striped in the factory when they came off the line. He was certainly an artist and didn't realize it. All he knew is he loved doing it. He also loved his family and had made a commitment to God to retain his sobriety. This was number one on his list.

I could not believe it when I was told that Dad decided to sell the shop to my brother Kenny. Kenny had worked side by side with Dad, part time and full time for a few years. Kenny must have inherited Dad's creativity with paint and cars because they were two of the best auto body men in Ohio! I might be a little prodigious but I think Kenny, after over 20 years with one auto body shop, decided to retire with his company. They gave him a big retirement party. Also, when he had to take some time off for some medical issues he was told "You stay until you feel perfectly up to returning, regardless of how long it takes!" I think that speaks for Ken's auto body experience and the respect his employer had for him.

So it might be hard to believe Dad gave up the shop! Dad's next step was to find himself a job. Where? How? He was 55. He only had an 8th grade education. Dad continued his daily attendance at mass and his faith was as strong as ever. "I know that my new life will not be immune from difficulties, but I will have peace even in difficulties. I know that serenity is the result of faithful trusting acceptance of God's will even in the midst of difficulties." (Meditation from *Twenty-Four Hours a Day*)

Well, Dad was always a real handy man. There wasn't much he could not do. One talent he had was in air conditioning and refrigeration. He looked up many positions and found they would all require a refrigeration engineer's license. At this writing I do not have the exact license but it required school and passing a test. Dad decided this was probably his best route because he knew a lot about both and had even fixed a freezer for us a few years earlier. Part of the test required some problems which could only be solved if you knew algebra. Algebra? Dad only had an 8th grade education. I will tell you I have a college degree in business. In high school I took business math and in college a continuation of the same. I never had to take algebra. I also know that if I had to learn algebra at age 55 to get any license, I would say that would not work and would have to find something else to do. Seriously. I saw some problems in algebra and it was not for me! And I was not 55 at the time! But algebra did not stop Dad. This man was determined. He was on a path and nothing was going to stop him. My brother Louis graduated magna cum laude from Case Western Reserve University in Cleveland. I can remember coming over to Mom's and seeing Louis and Dad at the big round table in the dining room. It is the room where I used to see Dad and my Uncles with a shot and a beer, and now Louis was helping Dad to learn algebra. For all the sad happenings in my life, this sight remains one of the most beautiful and one I am most proud of for my Father. This was also my favorite paragraph to write now in 2017! This was a Kodak Moment. An answer to so many prayers. A miracle. God has a vision for us all. He believes in us. We must believe in ourselves. He will always help us, but we have to do the work.

Dad did the work. Dad did pass his test! Yeah Dad!!! And now he had to apply for positions using this license. One of them turned out to be at U. S. Steel, one of the largest steel mills in Ohio. When Dad applied he explained his background to the personnel manager, including the fact he was a member of AA. He even told him of all the AA meetings he was currently attending. I met this personnel manager many years later. He told me how the minute my Dad started talking he was drawn to his sincerity and did not doubt what he said. He decided to give Dad a chance and it was a perfect match. When Dad had open heart surgery years later this manager told him to come back to work and to retire whenever he wanted! For sure this was a true answer to Dad's prayers. He had a job. In his eyes he had a second chance and he was determined to do the best job regardless of the fact he was not the boss but just an employee. You have to understand the position. This meant early rising. He got up around 4am and drove the 40 minutes each morning. Dad had to light the boilers and take care of all heating and air conditioning units. He also had to get there early on snowy mornings and shovel the walk going up to the executives offices. I still have his lunch box with his name on it that he used to pack his lunch in each day! "God can be your shield. Then no buffets of the world can harm you. Between you and all indignity from others is your trust in God, like a shining shield. Nothing can then have the power to spoil your inward peace." (Meditation from *Twenty-Four Hours a Day*) Yes, Dad went from not just being in charge, and regarded as the best in the car repair business, to keeping walks clear for the executives. But he never looked at it that way and never even mentioned exactly what all his position required. We found all this out later after he passed.

Dad might have had a tough day at work, but he sure enjoyed his weekends. One was on Friday nights which found him at the Euclid Friday AA meetings. I have my most wonderful memory of one of those Friday night meetings. I had been traveling on the east coast and stopped at my parents' home on my way home to Arizona. I remember getting off the plane, hurrying to get the rental car and driving down the freeway while carefully watching the time. I knew what time the Friday night AA meeting started. I pulled up into the drive, ran in the house and confirmed with Mom that Dad was indeed at the meeting. I then zipped down the street, parked my car in the parking lot and knew this would be a huge surprise to Dad. I opened the door and looked down the steps. There was Dad!!!! He was smiling and wearing his favorite green jacket and shaking hands as people walked by. He was absolutely enjoying every moment. He was directly down at the bottom. After I reached the last step, I put my hand on his shoulder and said "Hi Dad." If you think this wasn't one of those Kodak Moments, you have to know how much I missed my Dad and how proud I was to see him at an AA meeting. The look on his face when he turned around was one of pure happiness. "Oh Judy, Judy, how wonderful to see you" he said as he hugged me. He then immediately said to everyone who could hear "This is my daughter Judy." I remember this so vividly that it brings tears to my eyes every time. With my Dad now having passed, I talk to him about this event and know he hears me. I know to him this was also very special. I did not get home that often and when I did it might not have been a night of an AA meeting. Yes, this was special for both of us. Remembering how he turned to me that special day and said "Judy, I promise I will never drink again" and now seeing each other at an AA meeting had a silent, wonderful meaning.

Dad worked at U. S. Steel until he retired at the age of 70. I could be wrong on exact dates, but it was about 14 years since he gave up his dream at the auto body shop and 7 years after his heart surgery. I have his refrigeration notebook which I treasure. It's filled with notes and special little papers. When I hold it I feel his urgency in making sure he was following the right instructions on his new journey. I also found his refrigeration service card! He was obviously very proud of this card. It says "member of refrigeration service engineer society!" I know he was very proud of this mountain he had climbed. "The higher power can guide us to the right decisions if we pray about them. We can believe that many details of our lives are planned by God and planned with a wealth of forgiving love for the mistakes we have made. We can pray today to be shown the right way. We can choose the good and when we choose it we can feel that the whole power of the universe is behind us. We can achieve a real harmony with God's purpose for our lives." (Meditation from *Twenty-Four Hours a Day*)

He did not retire totally. He kept going, as I found out later. This time for charity. Once I remember seeing a card that said something to the effect that "We are the best of friends and we don't look back." I gave that card to Dad. I wrote a note that said "Dad, we had to work at it." Dad told me he carried that card in his wallet every day. When he passed I went to his bedside table because I figured all he valued would be there. There was his wallet, his book on St. Therese and her statue, his hairbrush and a one dollar bill. In his wallet was the card! I took all of it!!!

Chapter 21

Those Wonderful Visits

When we think of Dad's sobriety keeping our family together we have to remember the visits Mom and Dad took to see us as John and I moved to Arizona and then to Albuquerque, New Mexico. I am sure they came to see the grandsons, but the boys loved these two so much it was wonderful to see them. When they made the visit to Arizona, Dad wanted to go by train. Leave it to Dad to want to experience something new. We arranged for them to take the Amtrak to Flagstaff so we could stay a day and see the Grand Canyon. I messed up the time of arrival for the train and when I called to check on the time the man said "Oh, are you looking for this older couple because they are just sitting here patiently?" What? Oh, my gosh! I was so upset that we had not written down the correct arrival. We dashed out of the hotel. When we arrived at the station there they were just sitting on the bench inside. I am sure they wondered why we were not there. They were probably so excited about getting off the train to see us, but you would never have known that. The boys spotted them and ran to them screaming "nana, papa." I think hugs and kisses made up for our being late. It was such an exciting time.

Dad, being the photographer from his early days, loved taking pictures at the Canyon and sometimes just standing there, staring, taking in all the beauty. We stayed 2 days and then went to show them our home in Arizona. It wasn't as big as our last home, but hey, as the boys would say "nana, we have a pool." Mom and Dad came for Christmas one year when we moved to Albuquerque, New Mexico. It was very special since we had such a tradition at home with my siblings and Dad's brothers and family. This was a real treat. I remember one visit where Dad told me "Judy, I need a list of things to do or I will only stay a few days." Dad had to be kept busy. He never sat! Dad was so handy. We had a new home so that meant we had to still find things for Dad to fix! After looking around we decided we wanted a light in the circular drive in front of the house. Do you suppose Dad could figure how to get electricity there and get us some light? For sure this would keep him busy for a few days!

My fondest memory of that visit was Dad always having to need something from Home Depot. My son Johnny was the only son of age to drive and had a little brown car. We lived up toward the mountains and there were twists and turns. On this one day Dad needed to retrieve something from Home Depot. Johnny, who was helping him outside, was excited to get papa in his car and show off his driving skills. I saw them on their return, not coming up the hill but flying up the hill! When they stopped and the passenger door opened, my Dad got out of the car and kissed the ground! Those were the days. Days given to us through Dad's sobriety. Something I never forgot for one minute.

Chapter 22

Dad Gave Us Back Our Family

Dad's journey with sobriety allowed us to continue all our holiday traditions. He gave us back our family. But Mom is not to be forgotten since Mom could not work in the factory. She continued working for the Euclid School System. As we read, she walked to work each day regardless of what she left behind at home the night before. She kept moving up in positions until she was named Coordinator of the Euclid School Cafeteria System.

I remember John and I driving her to Kent State University for some classes, obviously required for her new advancement. It was so exciting to drop her off and watch her go into college. If we thought it was exciting, can you only imagine how Mom felt as she walked toward the class building? My Mom, with no extended schooling, advancing to this position and now taking some courses at college! When she retired they not only had an announcement in the newspaper but a great retirement party! They also put together a big picture album. I have attached the paper announcement and some pictures. I am still in awe at all she accomplished. I am sure Dad's sobriety contributed to her being able to really concentrate on each and every position she had as she grew within the system.

This is just an example of what doing a job to the best of your ability every single day looks like, regardless of other issues going on in your life. You can fulfill even dreams you never thought of! Now, over 50 years later, I can honestly say I saw a respect and love I did not think I would ever see!

MOLLIE RETIRING...Mollie Hoffart, junior high coordinator for the
Euclid School Cafeterias, is calling it quits after 22½ years on the job.
Mollie retired officially as of last Wednesday. She was honored at a
dinner attended by 60 members of the schools' cafeteria staff, which
was held recently. Mrs. Hoffart began with the schools as a cook's
helper at the old Central Junior High, then worked as a cook-manager
at Roosevelt Elementary School, did pots and pans at the Senior High,
served as a baker at Forest Park and as a cook at Shore. For the past
11 years she has been the Coordinator of the Junior High Program
where she has been responsible for 33 cafeteria workers and meals for
over 2000 students per day. Asked about her plans for the future, she
simply said, "I hope to swim, play tennis and ride my bike, and enjoy
my four children and five grandchildren. I feel the past few years have
helped me to broaden my interests. It certainly beats staying home
and I enjoyed the professional challenge the job has given me.
Everyone here has been great." Mollie, shown here (left) attending to
final duties as   's bid adieu by Mrs. Libby Zimmerman, Supervisor
of the Eucl'*   Food Service Department. (Euclid Schools
Photo)

Euclid Board of Education

Certificate of Retirement

presented to

Mollie Hoffart

in appreciation

for faithful and dedicated service

to the Euclid Public Schools.

Superintendent

President, Board of Education

June 13, 1977

Date

Business Manager

EUCLID CENTRAL JUNIOR HIGH SCHOOL

Mollie Hoffart
1954 - 1976

Mary Black	Ann Kozlevcar
Kay Carmany	Marie Lipold
Helen Debeljak	Sophia Matuck
Doris Faragov	Viola Milite
Marlene Gross	Ann Mitkovic
Betty Hoffart	Martha Pesec

EUCLID CENTRAL JUNIOR HIGH SCHOOL

Mollie Hoffart
1954 - 1976

Mary Black	Ann Kozlevcar
Kay Carmany	Marie Lipold
Helen Debeljak	Sophia Matuck
Doris Faragov	Viola Milite
Marlene Gross	Ann Mitkovic
Betty Hoffart	Martha Pesec

EUCLID PUBLIC SCHOOLS
E U C L I D · O H I O

EUCLID SENIOR HIGH SCHOOL
711 EAST 222 STREET
EUCLID, OHIO 44123

SUPERVISOR OF FOOD SERVICE
MRS. ELIZABETH ZIMMERMAN
PHONE (216) 261-2900

January 6, 1977

Mrs. Mollie Hoffart
19380 Newton
Euclid, Ohio 44119

Dear Mollie,

There doesn't seem to be any adequate way of expressing my appreciation for your services these past twenty-two and one half years. But I do want to say once again thank you for your dedication, your loyalty, your hard work and above all your friendship as you've worked in our department.

It was a real joy to see you grow in your professionalism as the various chapters of your career unfolded. I'm sure this awareness was a satisfaction to you also. In many, many instances the success of our department these last few years came through your efforts and your cooperation in solving the problems that confronted us and we thank you for your help.

We are missing your sunny smile and your friendly conversation as well as your expertise this week but we all wish for you a happy, happy, retirement. Good luck and do stop in for a cup of coffee-- you know when coffee break comes.

Sincerely,

Elizabeth Zimmerman
Supervisor of Food Service

EEZ/cw

88

Chapter 23

Post AA Changes

So Dad returned home. There were many changes for him. My sister, who was still at home, said Mom and Dad sort of tip-toed around each other for a few weeks. But Mom and Dad always loved their children and showed it during these times as well. My sister captured one of these times in a letter she wrote to our parents Thanksgiving, 1960 when she was 12. Later in life my sister and I would have these nightly talks. During one of them I told her I had found the letter she had sent to them, which Dad had saved in his blue album. This made for a happy conversation considering those nightly talks were about our whole lives, which were sometimes diamonds, sometimes stones.

Now Dad had a whole new group of friends. He didn't join just one group, he joined many. Dad attended the Euclid Friday night AA meetings, while Mom went to play cards with her sister every Friday night. Amazing that Dad never ran out of things to do, see or go to! He was always in motion!

I remember once a month, on a Saturday, going to Mom's so the kids could have nana's pancakes. We all arrived as Dad was going out the door to Perkins Pancake House. What? Seems the Saturday Euclid meeting was across from Perkins and some of the men would meet there before the meetings. This AA group was called Night and Day. It was named that for a good reason because Dad was there many nights and many days! Dad was all dressed up. Dad was a dresser and he loved color. He had bright jackets and colorful dress shirts and, wow, he could find the wildest tie! Looking back I thought that he could not wait to get out of the house. Not just for AA but still taking every opportunity away from any potential arguments with Mom. When he was home he had a little bench in the basement where he fixed old radios. This was a skill taught to him by his brother Frank. Dad had lots of stuff in that basement. He collected old record players and so he had boxes of needles. He also collected organ records.

One of the secondary changes made was the move from Windward to Newton. This story starts on Windward but it's now 1971, 16 years later, and Dad has been in AA for 5 years. Should we call Windward "the beautiful first home" they owned or the "home sitting on an epic earthquake" or "that which held way too many memories for all of us?" Or should we just bite the bullet and say it was "just too large?" Going up and down the basement for clothes was tough and for sure they didn't need that little "teen" room we kids created way back when. I know it was Mom who wanted to move. Again, Dad just went along. Mom went house hunting and found a much smaller one floor home just around the corner. It did have a garage which our first home did not. Other than that it was much smaller. With my Mother being a gourmet cook I never could figure why she would purchase a home with a tiny kitchen but she made it work. Much good food came out of that kitchen! For Dad it also meant giving up some of his favorite toys. One of the hardest had to be giving up his Orthophonic, which he bought when I was somewhere around 8 years old and upon which he played all those old records! This was the end of the record collecting era but I think he found it easier because he was now so involved in AA. I am sure he realized this was part of the change that had to happen. He was determined to do whatever to keep his promise to his family and stay sober.

Dad joined three AA group meetings. They were on Friday evenings, Saturday morning, and one held in Aurora on Sundays with a brunch following. Mom did attend Aurora and once when I was home visiting I attended with them (see picture). The whole family attended his October anniversary date at AA. We were all so proud of him. Dad made the best of the changes, driving to work, going to AA meetings and meeting new friends. I think Dad's humming all the time was something I picked up. Today I can still hum to just about any music played on SiriusXM 40's Junction!

Dad also truly enjoyed his brother Frank. Today Uncle Frank would be considered eccentric! But he was loving and fun and a great husband and father. You just never knew what he would cook up and get Dad involved in. But when Dad had a project he would always call Frank. Some projects Uncle Frank dug up on his own like the Christmas tree. Huge! He began to drag it through the living room to the dining

90

room as Mom was screaming since the tree just about knocked over everything! The tree was way too big for the house but probably didn't look that big when he cut it down. Dad heard Mom scream and found Frank in the dining room, the tree knocking everything off the table. He then ordered Uncle Frank to "take it outside." I was laughing so hard. It was really funny. You had to be there to see the humor, for sure my parents did not! This man had a heart so big and never meant to have the tree cause all this trouble. Still today I think it was a lovely thought and a wonderful memory!

Dad and his brother Frank did a lot of projects around the house. This kept Dad busy, along with his Saturday garage sales and his AA meeting. Then, with life just strolling along, fiddling with his radios in his little corner of the world he thought he had worked out most of his struggles. Mom and Dad celebrated 50 years of marriage April 29. Life was good. Then, without warning, God handed Dad a bigger challenge.

Dad had a stroke.

Chapter 24

Forever Changes

Just when Dad thought he had his life on track, he had a stroke. It was April of 1992 and I was living in Arizona. Word came that he had a pain above his eye and had gone to the drugstore where the druggist gave him some eye drops. Two days later he had a stroke. I remember stopping at home in Ohio as I usually did when traveling for business to the East Coast. I arrived late and Mom had just returned from the hospital. She said Dad had some restrictions in his arm and leg and they would be starting him on therapy. The phone rang. It was Dad. "Judy, (He didn't even wonder or ask how I could be in his home but he knew my voice.) I need to talk to Mom!" Mom took the phone and explained to him she had been there all day, had just gotten home and he needed to get to sleep. She hung up. Two minutes later the phone rang again. I answered it. "Judy, tell Mom I need her to come and rub my back." (Again, never wondering what I was doing there.) Mom got on the phone and again assured Dad he would be ok until tomorrow. Two minutes later the phone rang again. Again, Mom tried to explain to Dad but I could see this was not working. So while she was on the phone I called the hospital, using my cell phone, and asked the nurse to go and "Take the phone away from my Dad" which she did! Poor Dad. He was so confused.

This was a huge traumatic event that had happened to him. He had no idea how to relax. Heaven knows he always walked a mile-a-minute. He awoke every morning with an urgency for everything he had planned that day. Now, he was in a hospital bed and realized half of his body was not responding like he wanted it to. Regardless of Mom being there all day, now, he was alone. I should have gone down to the hospital, walked into his room, taken the phone away and given him a hug. That is what I should have done. But at the time, I felt Dad did not want me to see him in such a needy position. He was always the strong one. How silly of me. So many regrets that we have to go through life with but we just have to tell ourselves we did what we thought was right at the time. Dad didn't miss me and he really didn't even acknowledge I was there. I think if he would have told Mom he would like to see me it would have been different.

As a stroke victim he was not himself mentally or physically the first few days. After taking into account what had happened to him Dad realized his world had collapsed around him. Since Dad had retired he really was enjoying his life; AA meetings, garage sales, and just going wherever he wanted, whenever he wanted. Now……

1. He would never get out of the house alone!
2. There would be no garage sale shopping.
3. There would be no fixing radios in the basement. He could not even walk down the stairs alone.
4. His visits to three of his AA meetings would now depend on Mom driving him.
5. Enjoying his favorite toys would require someone to help him, i.e. putting on one of his old records, puttering in the garage and just fixing the radios.
6. He had survived an addiction. Now he had to survive the loss of half of his body.

There were some very good times. Mom still had her Moments. But she loved him and now was her chance to care for him. For once he was needy and I think she looked forward to helping him. I began to wonder just how Mom was going to handle all his. I should have known she was strong and had been through a lot. If any wife could handle this, she could. I have a picture here of the day Dad came home from the hospital. I wonder who helped Mom move the table and chairs outside. On the back of the picture it is written "outside lunch on Dad's first day home from hospital." Mom had thought to move a table and chairs outside in the back and had made a nice homecoming lunch for Dad. (see picture) I wonder why they did not eat on the front porch. So many questions you think of later!

This still had to be very hard for Dad. Here he was, back home, to where his life stopped. Now he needed to try to first get his body back into some kind of shape so he could be a little independent and second to hopefully not look back and become despondent. I can imagine as he sat there that first day he was looking towards the garage where his car was and thinking how fast it was all gone. Dad came through this stoke the best he could and would take his cane and go walking. That was actually the only alone time he had, and at those times he felt somewhat independent. He needed Mom to drive him to his AA meetings and night driving was hard for Mom. I think getting him dressed and taking him out very early for Saturday Night and Day was also hard. I know there were Saturdays he missed. Mom was thinking of Dad and how hard it was for him to move around. What I think she lost track of was to a recovering alcoholic those meetings were important. I know his real problem was his feelings of not being able to continue with the life he loved. Going to AA meetings had been his life for 30 years.

Looking back I feel sad that I was not there for him. My brothers both lived so far away it wasn't a 20 minute trip to take Dad to AA meetings. My sister had left home and moved out of state. Mom and Dad were basically on their own most of the time. The kids were always there if she called and they would have come in a minute, but still, just coming over for a short visit was not going to be a daily affair. Even if one of my siblings had tried to get Mom help I think she would have refused it. Mom was very strict when it came to anyone even thinking she could not handle something like this. She was determined she would care for Dad.

Chapter 25

Two Lost People

As any person who has had a stroke can attest to, if you have your mind but not able to follow through with some of your hobbies or activities, it's a great shock and takes time to adjust, if you ever do. My Dad was so involved in communications with other collectors of records and radio. I even found an advertisement asking for old comic books that Dad had circled. Dad's collections and little work table were down in the basement and he was no longer able to take the steps down, nor in the beginning did he care to. My brother Louis went over to help him go down to the basement but in the beginning he seemed to not care about any of his favorite toys. He lost interest. I am not sure if he ever gained it back or if he accepted the fact he could no longer run to antique shows or communicate with collectors.

Mom was up to the challenge, as she always was. She decided caring for Dad was her first priority and realized she could not keep up the care of the home and yard. Together she and Dad made the decision to move to an apartment. She made sure they packed all Dad's favorite antique toys, radios, speakers, and even a pair of drapes with the Victrola dog picture on them. This move was one the biggest challenges for Mom who also had some very favorite items that this little apartment would not accommodate. But I never once heard her say she missed anything. She took care of Dad and still was able to select exactly what she wanted to take with her. Heaven knows there was a house full of birthday and anniversary gifts, along with items from her Mother and special cooking utensils she loved. I cannot even imagine how she accomplished this task and accomplished it so well!

An example of this are all the letters and pictures she boxed up from years of picture-taking. Besides some plates her Mom had brought back from Austria, Mom also had a commercial baking mixer, favorite small pitchers and even a plant holder she called "my little boy" that I bought her with my first paycheck when I was 16. She would have little room in this apartment so she had to choose wisely and she did, keeping all the old picture albums, favorite Christmas table cloths and even her silverware set. Oh, and let's not forget the big cardboard box of glasses Dad had purchased for her for their anniversary. The box looked like it had been opened only once. I am not sure if any of the glasses were ever used. These were glasses that held a drink Mom must have liked, martinis, yet I never saw her drink one. To tackle such a project I would think would have been impossible. Yet over the years I witnessed her repack, unpack and repack those same items at least 5 more times as you will read. It was my brother Louis who was left to accomplish the impossible, emptying their home after over 50 years of marriage. So where was I? Luckily I stopped on my way from New York on business and found they had moved! I spoke with my Mom almost every day and she didn't tell me she was moving or at least share with me the apartment she was moving to. Remember, their first real home, the Euclid Projects, where they were the 3rd to move in? Well, that is where they ended up, living in the senior apartments built on that land. I wonder if they ever thought "this is where we started nearly 40 years earlier." I doubt if either of them had time to consider that but I would not be surprised if they did. Another question I had years to ask them!

Now, at this point I am very surprised Dad did not get depressed. Since I was not there every day, maybe he did. But he seemed to try to do whatever they asked of him in therapy and took daily walks around the apartment with his cane.   His days fiddling with his radio, etc. were gone. However he still had all his AA friends and could get to the meetings as long as Mom drove him. I think these friends, friends for over 30 years, are what lit up his little world. He was always a history buff and took to watching all the news of the world. He also had his prayer book. I asked him once "Dad what do you do all day?" He answered, "There are so many people I need to pray for I can never finish all of them in one day."

Amen

Chapter 26

Mom & Dad Move On

There were two moves Mom and Dad made to Arizona after Dad's stroke. Mom and Dad were both dealing with something neither really knew how to handle. Does anyone, when life throws you this curve? The worst part of all this was she didn't realize just what she needed help with and what she could actually do as a 77 year old caring for an 81 year old with paralysis from a stroke. And if that was not bad enough, Mom was determined she would do whatever had to be done for Dad, and no one else. After Dad's stroke Mom would drive him to his AA meetings. I know with all my heart, not being able to go to all 3 places, it was difficult for Dad. That is where all his friends were. Dad loved to dress up, loved color, a bright green jacket and some spiffy ties. One side of his body did not come through the stroke as well as he would have hoped. He could walk with a cane but could not drive.

Here we have a man who was very independent, loved his radio antiques and his trading of such, and could not wait every Saturday for the garage sales, and once a year the radio collectors' meeting in Rochester, NY. He had a huge collection of radios and radio tubes. If, and that is a big if, he sat, it was only to watch the news on television and he would sit close (Yes, he did wear a hearing aid.) so he could hear every word. Dad also never missed a Saturday morning at Night and Day. I can remember bringing the kids over to nana and papa's on a Saturday for Mom's special pancakes and coming in as Dad was leaving. He was all dressed up. I never saw Dad in jeans or overalls unless he was working in the garage. I asked him "Dad, aren't you staying for Mom's pancakes?" to which Mom shouted over his shoulder "Oh no, Dad doesn't miss the Saturday meetings because they go to Perkins Pancake House first!" Guess Dad was used to Mom's pancakes but I think it was really after a week's work, he could not wait to get to his friends at AA and meet for breakfast. So those Saturdays were just one, but one special event that ended quickly.

One minute Dad was working in the garage and within a few days a stroke changed Dad's life forever. Now events like these meetings were just another disappointment for Dad. Both had to make huge changes and somewhere through that they both decided maybe they needed a big change. Like a move to Arizona? Yikes! For sure it wasn't they missed us, it wasn't that they loved Arizona, it was change. Change! Change! I am sure change was why both of them decided maybe a move to Arizona, with new places to see and a change of scenery, would help. I could not believe Dad would want to leave Ohio. He always said he liked traveling to see us and the kids, but he would never live any place but Ohio, his home. But of course Dad did not envision his life as it was now. It also could have been winter was coming and it would be hard for Dad to get around outside, go for walks and for Mom to drive him to AA meetings. Mom did call and said they would love to come and live near us. I think most of it was she felt there would be more help with Dad and also more company for her because they were both feeling the loss of their events with friends. I am sure Mom missed her card playing with her friends. I assured her the grandsons would just love to see papa and would help him and take him for walks. At this time, my sister lived out of state and my brothers did not live that close to give Mom some help every day. Dad's brothers had all passed but Uncle John and he was not well either. So, I searched and found them a cute assisted living apartment with a balcony, close to the bus line so they did not feel dependent on us. Also it dropped them right off at the senior center. I remember taking Dad there and while Mom was filling out forms Dad was watching the men play pool. I said "Hey Dad, you can come and play pool in the afternoon," to which he replied "Judy, I have never played but I would try it." Dad was always so open to anything. I never heard him talk about what he could not do now and he never had pity parties. Dad just seemed to accept his new life. I hope when it's my turn I can remember I have some DNA of Dad's, and be so patient and willing to change if needed.

I was working as was John but this apartment was about 2 miles from us. I would pick them both up for supper and found things to do together on the week end. It was not a long stay. I don't remember how long but it wasn't a year. Mom was never one to just walk up and talk to a stranger even if it was a woman where she lived. Mom was courteous and friendly but I don't think she ever made the first move. She always had her sisters, and for sure her friends at work, so making new friends was very hard. Again, she had Dad to care for and they both had to get used to being away from home and in a new environment. I know Dad was always out walking. Every time I drove up I found him walking outside, always with a smile. "Hi Judy," he would say and I could tell he was so happy to see me. He told me that Mom would like to go back to Ohio but if she changed her mind he was happy to stay. But for sure he never gave any indication that they, for sure, wanted to move back home. Just that statement should have been a clue. Moving out of state is extremely difficult. I know. I have done it.   I cried all the way on the plane from Ohio to Arizona 20 years earlier. Home is still home.

Consequently, one day she told me she thought it was better if they returned to Ohio. Dad really did miss his AA group even though I had found a new one very close to where they lived. But in their defense I think they really had gone through a turmoil in their lives and didn't know what to do and thought moving would help those days that, for them, were very long. It was just too much of an adjustment. They never did take the bus to the senior center or participate in any of the apartment functions. I have no answer for this except again Dad was outgoing but Mom was not. So, end of move one.

These two people didn't know it, but they were lost. They thought they had done well with this change and moving would just be perfect but they were looking for something that wasn't there anymore. To this day I can honestly say it was just too much of a change for them. Mom probably still felt more at home even though she said they did not feel "at home" in the apartment. How could they! It had to be strange, many of their favorite decorations were gone.   Maybe they had not stayed long enough. I called once to see if they were getting much company and they said "very few." It doesn't matter. They tried a change and they went back! I had to ask the landlord to let them out of their lease, based on my Dad's health, which was somewhat true and they were very nice.

So home to Ohio they went. At least they had missed the winter in Ohio and Dad had a lot of exercise here in Arizona walking every day. And so they lived happily ever after in their small apartment in Ohio!

What? You think so? It could have been six months, maybe eight, I have lost track (and you will see why later). The phone rang and a very unhappy Mother was asking "Please, can we move back?" This time I said they needed to purchase a place. They needed to feel like they were in their home and not an apartment. Maybe this would help.

I knew of a great 55+ community with a guarded gate, a great club house, pool, crafts, bingo, everything that this time she could get involved in. I felt they needed to stay put for a while to really give this huge move a chance. I took some pictures but was not sure what she would say. This complex was very close to our home, almost walking distance. I felt I needed to keep a closer eye on them to ensure they made it through the "homesick" stage. They were literally down the street. I could not believe it but she agreed to a purchase! John and I immediately started looking in this guarded gated community for a home for them. I was so excited when I found a two bedroom, with both a dining room and a kitchen eating area, a porch and short walking distance to that great club house. I sent pictures of the home, and clubhouse, and she became very excited to move...again! No hallway to go down to their "house," like in the apartment, just a nice porch where they could sit outside and see people go by. All the comforts of a home. For sure this would work. Well, we had time. The owners wanted at least 30 days. This gave Mom time to give her notice and make arrangements for movers. One day while talking to Mom she commented on how hard this move was because she was caring for Dad and trying to pack. Here, we again have an elderly women, packing linens, clothes, whatever and caring for her elderly husband with a stroke. I was surprised she even mentioned it because Mom always wanted to do everything herself. She hardly ever asked for help. So, I suggested she send Dad out here ahead of her so she would not have to worry. We would be so happy to care for him. At this point, I had no idea how we would care for Dad. I was working and my position required me to leave by 6am to attend meetings. But there wasn't any way I was going to miss having Dad with me for a couple weeks. The kids were overjoyed. I cannot tell you as I write this, what a wonderful blessing it was to have my Father all to myself for two weeks. In my whole life I was lucky to get a few hours with my Father, alone! By alone I mean without the rest of the family like at family events, or when he wasn't fiddling in the basement with his toys, there was always some distractions, now I had him!! We were so excited about the possibility. I immediately checked with my employer, Motorola, who provided a hot line for help with a parent or child. They gave me the name of a nurse, whose name was also Judy. After discussing Dad's needs, Judy told me she could be at my home at 7am every morning. She would help Dad get up, bathe, and dress, fix him breakfast and make him a sandwich for lunch before she would leave.

Perfect. Mom agreed this would work. The whole family was so excited. My Dad, even with his stroke, had not lost his sense of humor. He loved being as independent as he could, and he loved seeing the grandsons. If he did not want to come, you would never know because Dad, as usual, took one day at a time and accepted his life as it was. Dad was truly an example of strength in adversity and a member of AA. When we picked him up at the airport gate he was making jokes. He traveled on the plane all by himself and I was not surprised. Remembering he needed help with toilet issues Dad was open to everything required of him and he handled it all with a smile. So I was not surprised when the stewardess who helped him off the plane remarked that he was the sweetest man. The stroke did not take away his tenacity. We all met him at the plane and my son Johnny took hold of the wheelchair. He was excited about being back in Arizona and seeing his new house! I have no idea why they decided to take on such a huge project with Mom again having to pack the house, pack Dad and Dad leaving his AA group. Yikes! When I saw Dad in the wheelchair I realized this was a huge responsibility and wondered how my Mom did it! How did she care for him every single day? Dad for sure didn't look like he had lost weight or was sickly!! Imagine caring for Dad meant doctor appointments and just everything it took to care for a stroke victim. She had no outside caregivers or hospice help. Dad did not qualify nor did their financial status. Yes, they had been living here 6 months earlier, but I had not cared for Dad! Mom had. I did not know all of his disabilities nor his abilities. I knew he had one hand that did not work well, but I also knew Dad would not ask for any help! I immediately said to myself that I had to watch and determine when I thought he might need help!! Dad insisted he do everything when it came time for getting ready for bed. I thought maybe he would rather have John help rather than myself but he said he was able. The only thing he asked for was, after he had gotten into bed, he needed the little potty bottle by the bedside. That was it! I remember going to bed that night and thinking "Oh God please, please make sure the new nurse comes in the morning." I was sure my Dad did not want me or John to bathe or dress him. I was thinking, "Yes, I am so glad we contacted a nurse. Caring for Dad was serious business!" At 7am the doorbell rang and there was Judy, the nurse. I opened the door and could have kissed her! She was so nice, introduced herself and told me not to worry. She explained she knew exactly how to care for Dad. If he experienced any problems she would not leave him until she was sure he was OK and could care for himself until I returned from work. Dad was always very independent and that guy did fine all day by himself. He would pull up the stool in the family room and sit right in front of the television watching the news as usual.

I can still see him sitting there when I would arrive home from work. I was so happy to see him. I missed him! Now he was here, in my home for me to care for, a blessing I never thought I would be given nor that I would have the help to ensure we could handle his disabilities. I just could not wait to come home each day. One night I came home early and took him to the library. Dad loved the library. Dad loved to read and loved history. There was a special book he wanted so we asked my local library to order it through the main library and Dad was so excited. He was so thankful for such little things. We had a great two weeks! I remember asking him "Dad, what do you do all day?" He responded with the same answer he had given me before, "Judy, I have so many people to pray for, there is not enough time in the day." Exact quote.

I remember years earlier he had explained to me "You never pray for yourself, you always pray for the other guy." I remember him sitting on the porch, reading the paper, so calm turning the pages with care with one hand but not calling for help. What he did call for was "Where are those pancakes?" Great guy. Great sense of humor. Great example of faith and strength I felt so much love for this man. I thank God every day for the Father he sent me. He was worth saving.

Well, everyone was excited. Mom was getting ready to get on the plane and, wow, out of the blue the owner of the home we were purchasing called and said he changed his mind and did not want to sell. I was in shock. Mom had just called and said the furniture was on the truck. I explained to the owner he had signed a contract. He didn't care. There were probably some other homes we could look at, but furniture was on its way and we didn't have time to look for another place. The location of this home was so perfect and there were not that many homes with large front porches which Dad loved. So what did we do? Well, I cried! I did not know what to do. I remember putting my head down on the kitchen counter and crying. So what did Dad do? Dad prayed. I could not believe how calm he was. You would think a stroke victim would have little patience or get nervous when things turned stressful. Not Dad. He was so calm. He just went to his room and prayed while I cried! Can you believe this? Believe it! Calm. Praying! The next day the man called and said "Well, I will sign and get this home sale over with!" What? Oh, my gosh! Thank you God! To this day I have no idea what made him change his mind but Dad showed a great example of strength in times of stress! Even today when I think I cannot do something I will say "I am Rudy and Mollie's daughter and I can do anything!"

It is so hard to write this. I remember this so clearly. I have tears thinking of how Dad was so in control. When Dad decided to take on sobriety he took on more than that. He took on being a father. He was a parent you could go to with issues, was always calm and always had an answer. One thing I did notice that he brought with him was his AA black book! Oh Dad, I miss you so! Mom flew out, the furniture came, again, and they moved in to this perfect house in a very secure area with 55+ age group adults, walking distance from me just 1/2 mile down the road. John even gave them his little red car rather than trade it in on a larger one. Dad walked the neighborhood, the people were so nice to them, and Mom drove over to our house every day. The nice part was Mom and Dad were probably the oldest! With Dad walking with a cane, "The Wells" residents could not have been better neighbors. Unlike the apartment where she never really met anyone, these neighbors were there introducing them to bingo nights and asking Mom if she ever needed help. Everyone in the complex got to know Rudy! I even found a caregiver that would come three days a week to bathe and dress Dad to give Mom a break. Mom seemed so tired when she arrived and I knew taking care of Dad was taking its toll. Mom never liked anyone telling her what to do or how to do it and I wasn't sure she really wanted this caregiver. It was like telling her she could not do it all. I tried to explain "Yes, Mom. I know you can do it, but this gives you more strength to help Dad during the total day." Dad told her he thought it was a good idea and I think this created some feeling of insecurity for Mom. But just as I was thinking of cancelling this caregiver, Mom seemed to be making friends with her and enjoying her company. As you will read later, Mom had a plan. I never would have guessed what Mom was thinking, but leave it to Mom, when she gets an idea, no one could change her mind. So, here we are, all moved in, things moving well and Dad signed up for AA group. Whew! Everyone was so happy. One day after work I stopped by and they were in the pool! Dad was using a float and was holding on to the edge to talk to me. He loved the pool. I think it was because he could move his feet and felt like he had no restrictions. He looked so happy and told me he did not remember ever being in a pool. They also were up playing bingo once a week and everyone knew them and were so nice. The whole community gave them such a great welcome. So, life was finally settling down for them after two moves...

Don't you think?

Really?

Chapter 27

Regrets

Regrets, I have very few that I need to write about. As I wrote, Mom and Dad moved into their cute little house in Arizona and the neighbors were wonderful. There were many times Mom and Dad had the opportunity to get involved in seeing new places and participating in new adventures. Seeing Dad in the pool really was an amazing sight. Dad also admitted he had not had ice cream in years due to his heart problem 25 years ago!! We took them to ice cream socials at the church and at the clubhouse and all this was new to them. Their apartment in Ohio did not have outdoor functions and parties as they did here. I was working but each morning I would stop at their home and Dad would be sleeping and Mom reading the paper, usually about 6am. I would ask her what she planned to do today and we would just exchange little conversations. I would stop after work and find Dad walking around the complex with his cane. Dad was always busy, so now with the stroke he walked the neighborhood! Everyone knew him.

So what happened one evening was a shock. The phone rang around 7pm, John answered and it was Mom. "Dad and I are returning to Ohio." What? John was stunned. He called for me," Judy, it's your Mom, she says her and your Dad are returning to Ohio." For sure, I knew John had gotten it all wrong. Maybe Mom missed Ohio, maybe Mom was going back for a visit and wanted us to care for Dad. There were lots of maybes in my head as I took the phone. But there were no maybes in Mom's message. I took the phone and for about 10 minutes I tried to reason with her. "Mom, you can't, you own a home and there are payments." "Mom, I have done everything to make this move so perfect for you." "Mom, what about the house payments and what do we do with the car?" "Mom please, let us just have three months so we can put the house for sale and take care of loose ends." I tried everything. She would not listen. To every plea I gave her she would answer "Dad wants to go home." "Dad wants to go home." I was stunned. I was hurt. I was furious. I told her this was impossible, that she could not do this, and I refused to acknowledge what she was saying. She hung up.

What went wrong? What did we do? Did we not pay enough attention? Is Dad sick? Does Dad miss his AA members? I know I tried to get him involved in an AA group out here in Arizona. I told John he needed to go and talk to them. I was too upset and could not just sit down and talk with them. I had changed my whole life around when they arrived, loved it and it was like old times when we lived in Ohio ourselves with the kids. John went to the house but Mom would not budge on any of the issues. She was firm. Dad wants to go home, now! John said, for the first time, he yelled at them. Told them they were selfish, that we had done so much and that they had hurt their daughter, Judy, very much! When all our efforts didn't work, we then called in the deacon from our church to talk to her. She stood her ground. That was Mom. When Mom decided something she would never change her mind. This time, even with all I had done, Dad wanted to go home now! She had already called the movers! Can you believe this? She had called the movers! I had been there almost every morning, talked to her every day and she had made contact with movers and planned to move!

This next sentence is short and sweet. Within one week the movers came and they were gone! They really just picked up and left. There had to be a lot of packing to do but Mom did it all, she never called me, not even once. I had no idea she was leaving in a week! One week? Gone! I never went over there. Never! I did not talk to my Dad. I was beyond hurt and furious! Actually, I had planned to go and talk to them but I didn't know I had one week! I have no idea how they got home. Movers? Who? How did she and Dad get home? Plane? So she had plane reservations? It was March of 1997. Mom is 81. It is cold weather In Ohio. Mom had to pack everything, unless someone helped her. I have always felt there was someone and I think that it was the caregiver I got to help give Dad baths to help Mom out. Kim was her name and they became great friends. But yes, over the years I had plenty of opportunities to ask Mom how she did it, but I never brought it up. I would have if I had known my Father's favorite radios never made it back to Ohio. I found out years later. Moves out of town are tough. You can't just take a box at a time to the new house. You pack every single item you have! But she did it. She planned the move, hired the movers, packed the house and took Dad home. I never spoke to my Dad again at length. I did speak to him for 10 seconds when I called home and he answered 9 months later. He answered the phone and I said "Hi Dad," he responded "Judy, how are you?" I said "Fine Dad." That was it. Dad passed that December, less than three weeks after that phone call. As I said, I never spoke to him at length again.

The summer of 1997 I did not call him for Father's day. I did not call him on his birthday. The Dad I loved. The Dad I would have done anything for, I did nothing after he left!!! It took all summer for us to get the finances in order, sell the house and try to put our lives back together. I had spent every weekend and some evenings with them and I missed them, but I was hurt. I could not believe they left me. Of course, after he died and I thought the whole situation over, it didn't seem bad. At least not bad enough to never talk to him again. I felt like it was my ego, my selfishness. I felt I was so mad after all I had done for them and then they turned around and left. My Father, who I just loved so much and had such a deep love for, I didn't make any contact with because I felt he could have given us more notice. I never understood the big hurry. Is that being selfish or was it my ego? I would give anything just to give him a hug and wish him a safe trip home and that is never going to happen. I don't believe he was ever upset with me. But I think he missed my calls very much. He is all love. He loved me.

All that said, when Dad passed he had such a great funeral. I could actually stop and review everything that happened and realize that it was meant to be that he pass at home, in Ohio. It was in the Midwest where he grew up, loved, and with his close AA friends and family. It was an opportunity for all of them to have closure and to celebrate Dad's life. After all, Mom and Dad didn't move to Arizona because they were estranged from their family and friends, but rather they thought it would be a good change. They were looking for something that was never going to be. Sometimes we never know why we do what we do but we sure would like one more chance to think it over, just one more chance!

Chapter 28

December 22, 1997

Dad passed on December 22, 1997, one day after my sister's 49th birthday. He had the stroke in 1992 but for me this was still a surprise. My Mother called at 6:30am Arizona time to say "I think Dad is dead." Yes, that is what she said. I replied "You think?" Seemed Dad wasn't feeling good so they had a doctor appointment. Mom was getting Dad's clothes out and she heard a loud sigh! She said she was at the hospital waiting for my brother. I didn't want her sitting there alone so I called my friend Judy Falzone who lived nearby. She arrived minutes after Louis, my brother, and was able to communicate to me how Mom was doing and what had happened. My brothers Louis and Kenny made all the funeral arrangements. Louis called to see what date would be good for us to travel. I explained I thought we could get tickets and fly out that night with the visitation for Dad on the 23rd, mass and burial on the 24th and we would fly home late on Christmas Eve. I was devastated. Yes I know, I had been hurt and mad and everything else. And we had not spoken to him, except a 30 second phone call, but now this was different. He was gone! I would never have a chance to change my mind and call and tell him how much I really loved him. I really loved my Dad. To this day I think it was my Mom who wanted to move and I think Dad would have stayed. That said, the best way to honor my Dad was for his funeral to be in Ohio with his family and AA friends. My brothers planned it perfectly.

Myself, John, Johnny and my daughter-in-law Geri, flew out on December 23, and stayed with some old friends, John and Betty Attwood. John and Betty were always so gracious and helpful and this time they really came through. I was very distraught to the point I could not even sit up with everyone and talk about the old days when we lived behind them in Euclid where our last son Todd was born. I just had to go to bed. I was exhausted and knew the next day was going to be just horrible.

When we first arrived on the 23rd we went directly to Mom and Dad's apartment. I noticed how cute Mom had set up the table in their extra bedroom as an eating space and had the tablecloths she had for years on the table. Again, I was in awe of how she could remember what to take from the house on Newton with such little time to move. Still, with the pretty tablecloth and a small lamp on the table in the second bedroom, Mom had done her best to make it feel like home.

I had been there once before, right after they had moved from their home, but not in this exact apartment. While traveling for work I stayed there one night with them. I slept on the couch and had breakfast with them before Mom and Dad drove me to the airport. We stopped along the way at the Motorola Sales Office. Dad even sat down at one of the computers for a picture. It was so cute to see Dad at a computer, a technology he never learned to use. This visit to the apartment now was what I remember as an "emotional traumatic event." I saw where Dad spent his days and I realized how lonely he really was even though he was home with family and friends. We were too close for Dad not to feel the loss of the two of us not communicating. I felt it standing in his bedroom. I wanted to see the things that made him happy, the things that he thought were so important in his life. For whatever reason I felt they would be right where he could get them without asking for help, and that would be on his night stand. There they were. His statue of St. Therese, who helped him every day through prayer as he realized he needed to quit drinking and to join AA. Also, his AA black book, called *Twenty Four/Seven*. His hairbrush, as he as always brushing the little bit of hair he had. When Dad was 11 he was hit by a car and had a metal piece put in the top of his head. Amazing when you think of 1922 and such surgery that was totally successful. So hair didn't grow that well on top so he would grow his hair longer on one side and flip it across. So his hairbrush was important to him. There were also some funeral cards from some of his family and friends who had passed and one of his business cards as a collector of old radios, a copy of the life of St. Therese *The Life of a Soul*, and his wallet with $1 in it! I thought later of the fact Dad kept that business card. We can all wonder why. We might guess and we might not. Dad did not have any pity parties of what he could not do anymore, but obviously still remembered the important times. So what did I do? I took them all! Yes I knew these were not the important things anyone else would want. Dad had lots of antique radios, etc., and I was sure those would be what would be of value. At this point, I still had no idea those items were not even in the house.

Those few favorite items that I did take of Dads have remained special to me all these years. I value each and everyone one and have them in a special drawer. I take them out now and then and talk to Dad and tell him I love him. But now, with him gone, I realize how selfish I had been and how horrible it must have been for him not speaking with me for months. My Dad and I became so close and now I would have given anything to just call him and say "I love you!"

If you are reading this and have experienced the same issues, believe me you will regret all your life not letting all the regrets and issues of the past dissolve and have that one last conversation. I cry typing this. This book has had many haters that have made me cry but I am so happy I can share with everyone Dad's journey.

Chapter 29

The Viewing

My Father's viewing was held at Brickman Bros. Funeral Home December 23, 1997. My Dad would have been proud. Everyone that knew him, even for a day, as I found out, came to say goodbye. But it wasn't only goodbyes they said. Oh no, there was much more. I remember the two young men that showed up on their motorcycles with long hair and leather jackets. They seemed very young, I am guessing around 24. As I did with everyone I did not know, I walked up to them and said, "Hi, I am Judy, Rudy's daughter. I would like to thank you for coming and spending a few last moments with Dad." The one young man immediately grabbed my hand, which I had outstretched in a sign of welcome. He immediately began to tell me everything Dad had done for him and his friend. They were both in AA and said Dad had paid for one of their school fees and purchased a coat in the winter for the other. In grabbing my hand he immediately said "Can I touch your hand? Your Father was so kind, so caring, and I am proud to meet you, his daughter."

I also heard that Dad went at midnight on Saturday evenings to St. Vincent Hospital. It was to the center where the drunks were brought in. His purpose was not to convert them, but to let them know they were not alone. Many stories I heard about Dad, things we never knew he had done or was doing. Dad obviously did not spread the word of his good deeds. He would probably be embarrassed if he knew I was listing them now for the world to hear. I could not have loved him more, nor could I have been prouder. For sure I loved meeting these people who also loved him so much. He was worth saving!

It was a night to remember. It was also a reminder to me many times in the last 19 years that I should keep the special things I do for others close to my own heart and just enjoy the moments. The following morning when it was time to say our last goodbyes, everyone but the family left the visitation room. We expressed our love, cried and then left the room while they closed the coffin. But after I had exited the viewing room this little voice said to me "Judy, where are your brothers?" Looking around I noticed they were not there. I immediately looked into the viewing room and there they were, standing while the coffin was closed. I ran in. I walked up to the coffin and asked if I could cover his hands with the cover, and I did. I felt like I was putting him to sleep, covering him up so he would not get cold. I whispered to him not to leave me and that I would talk to him every day! I am a believer that spirits can hear us and that we should talk to them. My thought is, "What if we find out later they could hear and we did not talk to them?" Better to talk even if we found out later they could not hear us! At the moment of carrying on a conversation it brings so much peace.

In the years that have passed my Dad has appeared in my dreams twice. Once he was wearing his wedding hat, waving goodbye from a train. I am sure there was a message there. In the other, he was dressed in his wild shirt and trousers. I saw him standing in a doorway and I was sitting on a chair, talking to Aunt Alma. Yes, she had passed also. I screamed and said "Dad, Dad" as he walked across the room to me. His voice sounded exactly as it always was and he said "Judy, I have something to tell you" and then he was gone. I have always thought maybe it was something spirits are not allowed to tell, or if for some reason, I could not keep him in my dream.

Chapter 30

New Year's Eve

The funeral mass was beautiful with a short trip to the cemetery. I was shocked at how short the cemetery services were. Before I knew it, it was over! Over! Dad gone! Done! I cried on my cousin Chickie's shoulder and told her how much I loved him! I loved him! How could my Father, who was there for me more times than I can recall after his sobriety, be gone? Who would I call for advice and who would enjoy the old songs I had downloaded on my computer but Dad? Who always saw the glass half full and reminded you of your faith in any adversity? Who did I ask to pray for people when someone I knew needed a prayer because for whatever reason anything Dad every prayed for was answered? Who?

My siblings put together a little after-funeral get together like they usually do to try to calm everyone's nerves after all that has happened. We could not stay long. We had to catch a late flight back to Arizona. We had two sons, Danny and Todd, at home who still expected a Christmas the next day. Christmas traditions were always so important, most all of them handed down from Dad and Mom. When we moved to Arizona the kids wanted to keep all the things "nana and papa" did on holidays. Our Christmas Eve, following my parent's tradition, was we would stay up late and at midnight open our gifts. Mom started the food idea because she and Dad went to midnight mass and were so hungry when they got home. However, Dad started falling asleep during midnight mass, so we changed it to everyone coming to Mom and Dad's house around 9pm. Mom had more food than you could ever eat and we each brought something. We would wait until midnight and then exchange our gifts. As usual, wine and alcohol drinks were served. Actually, Mom just put them out on the buffet. I guess by now none of us thought it would bother Dad, as he had instructed us over 35 years ago, and we had become so comfortable drinking around him. But as a recovering alcoholic would tell us, it's a constant journey.

First, before leaving, we took Mom to Aunt Alma's house. For sure we could not let her go home alone. Mom was very close with Aunt Alma, who was Uncle Frank's wife. The two of them spent many nights up late playing cards together! I remember Mom saying to me "Judy, while I was waiting for Louis to come and take me to the hospital after the ambulance had taken Dad, Dad appeared to me in the living room. He was under this large arch and had on his suit and tie and he smiled at me. I sure don't understand how he could have had that suit on when I had not even taken it to the funeral home yet." My Mom said this matter-of-factly as she got out of the car. I could only think she was in shock at this death of Dad, her husband of over 55 years. I have never forgotten what she said.

This Year, 1997, found us in Ohio at midnight. We had to change the tradition and would open our gifts on Christmas morning. We arrived in Arizona at 4am. I remember we called and called the shuttle to take us to the airport parking place and no answer. Later he apologized and said he had fallen asleep. Understandable considering not many people come back for their cars at 4am on Christmas morning. We had our Christmas later that morning, around 10am. It was not the same. First thing we all noticed was how light the room was. It was day time which we had not experienced on Christmas Eve for over 35 years. Usually it's so dark out, we have Christmas music playing and you can see the stars out when you sit on the patio around the fire pit.

But the change in our Christmas tradition was for sure not the worst thing that happened to me in December of 1997 when my world seemed to stop. I could not seem to function as it all had happened so fast. A week ago he was alive. Two weeks ago I had spoken to him on the phone explaining Mom would knock on the window when she arrived home from visiting us so he would open the door. He said "Judy, how nice to talk to you, how are you?" I replied very simply "I am fine Dad." That was it. What the heck was wrong with me? So selfish. Still upset with the way he left me 8 months ago. I missed the most important call in my life! This Dad I so loved and I let my ego reign free! This beautiful man who took every day one day at a time, who suffered a stroke and had to give up everything he loved, and I could not say some nice words like "I love you Dad." No. Not me.

116

Please don't ever do what I did. As you read this, stop and think if you are being selfish. If there is someone you love that you have not spoken to because you cannot go and redo that moment!

Never!

Chapter 31

Just Hang On!

First move after Dad's passing, and second move and third! After Dad passed Mom went to Aunt Alma's for a couple of nights. When we arrived home early Christmas morning I was very depressed and miserable but Mom, I guess, was in shock. I never heard her cry or express loss until three months later. I am not sure how Mom was the first two months but obviously not doing well. She was on a mission of some kind. I think she was looking for something that did not exist, but she never stayed put long enough to really think about what she wanted and where she wanted to be. She mentally dragged me with her. It was March 1998 when she called and said she was lonely and asked to move to Arizona. I am sure she was lonely! Her partner of 55 plus years was gone. My brothers tried to find things for her to do and visited her but for Mom that would never be enough because Mom needed attention. Mom needed to be in charge of something or somebody and now there was nothing and no one!

So, Mom called. "Judy I am so lonely, can I move out there with you?" I checked with her apartment and found she was not intermingling much with the other residents and had little company visiting. Mother always wanted company and never really liked being alone. I think she finally realized the big family gatherings that had accompanied her ever since she met Dad and had a family were gone. She loved all that baking and cooking for our holidays. Gone. This little nondescript apartment looked very bare and lonely. She had never lived alone. Remember, this is her first time living alone plus she had to grieve the loss of her Rudy.

I proceeded to look for a senior apartment complex within a short driving distance of our home. I decided to try the same apartment she and Dad had lived in when they moved here after Dad's stroke. She had said the people were not that friendly, but when Aunt Edith visited Mom and Dad and we took her to see the apartment Edith was amazed. "Mollie, this is beautiful. I would have loved to have lived here" she said. I remember Mom sort of shrugged it off, later saying Dad didn't care for it! Now in March of 1998 I asked Mom if she would like to give that apartment another chance. It was near the senior club and other amenities. She agreed, and even stated that maybe it was just because she was worried about Dad she did not give that complex a chance. When I called to check on availability they told me there was one unit available with a balcony facing the fountain off the back bedroom. I went to see the unit and pictured Mom sitting outside, some plants on the railing, having coffee, looking at the fountain, watching the birds, and enjoying the weather. What? Mom? My Mom? The lady who never sat and always found something to clean. Sitting look at birds? Remember, I am trying so hard to help her with the loss of Dad. I am thinking maybe she will relax now without Dad to take care of.

Well, Mom packed again. What was this now? Third time? Remember she moved here twice with Dad, once to this apartment and then to the house they bought in the guarded gated community. Now, this is the third time packing up the house. She is getting older, it has to be getting harder. So I am thinking "This is it." The lease was for one year. I don't remember how long she stayed but I do remember during that time she wrote to my brother asking them to help find her an apartment back in Ohio. I thought "good luck." Get ready to help her pack again in six months! Well, he didn't find one, or chose not to because he knew what the consequences would be. Mom was beginning to get a reputation.

She was initially excited about having Christmas traditions with the grandsons because we had brought all the traditions with us. With Dad having a stroke and them moving, these huge Christmas Eve reunions, with Mom baking in the kitchen and decorating the house, were just wonderful memories. So, we really had a great start, again. She loved being here for the kids' birthdays and seemed to be really fitting in at the apartment. I picked her up and we would have our hair done and she also spent a lot of time at my house during the day. So? Well let's try to keep track of her, since she certainly was not counting! She was just packing! Just as she had done before, I received a call that she wanted to return home. She would be leaving this cute apartment with the patio and fountain outside to the same Euclid senior apartments she had lived in with Dad. Now I had to try to get her out of this lease, again! And, to make it worse she had already called movers and planned to leave in three days. I had to make up some emergency story! I would learn to become good at emergency stories.

Imagine, she is now around 85 years of age and packing can't be all that easy. Since she doesn't warn anyone she is moving, there isn't much chance to help her pack. I told you she never sat! I wasn't as concerned as I should have been because I knew she would be back and she was. Are you counting? Yep, the phone rang and it was Mom, asking, "Please can I come back? I really am lonely and miss everyone." I actually have forgotten which apartment I found for her this time. By now I am very frustrated as it seems my whole life is finding her apartments. I can't say I helped her pack and unpack, because she made plans without ever telling anyone. This last time though really broke my heart!!

Since my Mom was so close with Aunt Alma she had made some short visits to see her over the past 3 years, always coming back. So it was not unusual went Aunt Alma called and asked for Mom to come for a visit. What I did not know, nor did my Mother, Alma was dying of cancer. I wondered why she was so adamant about Mom coming. For whatever reason I helped Mom pack and got her plane reservations. Jimmy, Alma's son, always picked Mom up at the airport and Mom always stayed with Alma. They would drink whatever and play cards all night. This visit would change for two reasons. About three days into the visit I called to talk with Mom. My Aunt said she did not want to get into trouble, but Mom was not there at the moment. She finally spitted out "Your Mom is at her old apartment, washing the shelves to get ready to move back." I was shocked. I was mad!!!! I was hurt! How could she!!!! She had planned it all but I don't think Alma knew. Yes, I was mad!!! I told myself that Mom was never coming back to Arizona, never. She had made these plans and now she was going to have to live with them, no matter how lonely she got. Two weeks later, Aunt Alma died. That is when I realized why she wanted Mom to come so badly. Mom did remark "Alma was so tired we hardly played cards." So, Mom returned from the visit to Aunt Alma, packed up the apartment, and moved back to Ohio. The first two moves she hired moving companies. The last one I think she had a friend help. I have no idea as I was never there when she left. All I was doing was getting her out of rental agreements.

But, don't turn the page on Mom yet. Truthfully I have lost track of dates, nor do I want to go over it again. But yes, Mom wanted to come back again. My son Danny, who loved her, (We always called him the gentle spirit) could not turn her down. So she moved in with Danny in Prescott. I did not agree with this because it was in a location where she could not walk to anything and Danny would be working. I knew my Mother well and she did not like to be alone. Danny was wonderful and even built her a swing in the large tree on the front lawn. But Mom just could not be satisfied, no matter what any of us tried. We did not visit her every week. As it was a two hour trip we visited once a month. I felt she needed to learn to try to make herself happy, my being with her all the time just could not continue. I had involved her in whatever I did with the last moves and it didn't work. Besides, it didn't matter, if she wanted to leave, she would leave, and she did! In the end, my son Danny helped her pack and drove her across the country back to Ohio. I was not happy with Danny because I knew she would be back. They rented a large truck and Mom was anxious to tell me that, at one point when Danny was tired, she drove! Yes, 84 or older, I have lost track, my Mother drove the moving truck! She knew I was very unhappy with her moves back and forth. Even though I spoke to her every day we did not mention it. I felt she was still looking for what was not there. Trying to reason with an 84 year old woman who lost her husband was impossible. It would have just created a rift in our relationship. For sure I had learned a lesson with my selfishness with Dad and was not going to break my relationship with my Mother. Not even after 4 moves!!

Yes, my Mother broke a few hearts over these next couple years and so you're wondering how I could agree to a visit just 6 months later! Yes, Mom called and asked if she could come for a visit. She actually said "visit!" She explained "This apartment is lonely because there are no other single ladies here and I just would like a little vacation." Boy, have we heard that before!! I was caring for my first little grandson Nathaniel and also working out of my home in a new job. I really did not have a bedroom for her since we had only two bedrooms and one was an office. We worked out a program where she stayed a few nights at my

121

neighbor's home, since they were out of town, and a few nights at Johnny and Geri's, my son and daughter-in-law. Geri really loved Mom and had made friends with her after meeting my son years ago!

Years later, I found a small book I had bought for Mom to write about her summer adventure! It was found in a box with some of her cards. It described in detail that visit from 6/9/2000 to 7/11/2000. She writes about our shopping fun at an antique store and then to Starbucks. "I got a Frappuccino, new to me, a coffee with milk and blended ice, like a milk shake with whipping cream, out of this world."

Sunday, June 11, "I stayed with Johnny and Geri. We had dinner and then I got so bored I asked Geri if she had some ironing I could do. They were so happy that I would iron. I wish I had thought of it earlier." Yes, Mom was the best at ironing, I don't know how she learned to do it so well. I only know when she ironed anything for me, I hated to wear it and get it wrinkled! June 13th, "Judy had to work at Robinsons-May so I ran around checking out the mall. I loved it! Judy worked in the baby and children department and it was very slow because there was a big sale coming the next day. I loved looking at all the little clothes and folded them for her." This is so true. She did. She actually came to work with me, walked the mall and then came to my department and helped straighten. She asked to do that again if I was working while she was there because she had so much fun!

Remember, she is going on 85 years old. Sunday, Father's day she wrote "Had breakfast at Johnny and Geri's. She made waffles and I haven't had a waffle in ages! It was so nice to be with them. Later I went to church with Judy and John. So wonderful to attend a mass. Must get back to it at home. Then watched golf with Judy and got to see Tiger Woods win. Very exciting!" I can't remember when Mom gave up her car so this comment made me think she was not able to attend a mass as easily as before. I am sure the apartment she was living in had a bus, but evidently she had not learned to take it. No wonder she was lonely. Wednesday, "We went to see Cheryl, a friend of Judy's. She lives in a cement house!" (So funny because Mom did not understand or see much of Arizona architecture) Mom then writes "She had a new floor cover called flagstone. Seems to fit those type of homes and she is also very interested in cactus. She had a pool and many types of cactus surrounding the house. And a large motor home. I found this so interesting." This writing really amazed me at how much she not only remembered, but actually the name of the flooring! I am taking excerpts from Mom's every day writing just to show how busy she was while she was out to visit me. Also how descriptive she wrote! It was fun to see her reaction to what she saw and experienced. Who would have guessed! We were gone every single day and then, on June 30th, we left for our condo in California. She even writes how I thought I was going the wrong way at one point and missing an exit again. I am amazed at all she wrote and never realized it was so exciting for her. Saturday she writes "Went to Fiesta Island to an "Over the Line tournament." Seems like teams of three and they have to hit a ball over a line to score. Wow, I had never seen anything like that! We then went to Tijuana, Mexico and ran into a parade. They told me to look across the street and on a porch there was Mexico's president!!! I was excited!"

What amazes me about Mom's writing is I didn't' even remember any of this until I read it!!! I am actually thinking, "Wow, we really did go everywhere with Mom. No wonder she was lonely when she returned home!" This last encounter she had in California she wrote with all exclamation marks and for sure, Mom had a great experience. She writes "We went to Seaport Village and there was a man fully dressed with a beard and old shoes. I realized it was a statue and for a minute he looked real. Judy said "touch him." I was afraid to but finally I did!! And he moved!! He laughed with me and got off his perch and came down and hugged me. It was all so exciting!" This I do remember. It was just adorable the way he came down and hugged her!! As you can read by her experiences each day, she had a wonderful time.

I think the best part was just having family around every single day, something that my brothers, with work and family, could obviously not possibly do with Mom living 30 minutes away. Plus this was a vacation for Mom. I realized she would be leaving so of course I planned lots of things to do. If she lived here I thought for a sure I would not see her every single day. But as we know, coming back from any vacation, you have to adjust to everyday life and that was something Mom just could not accept. She always hated to be alone and now after one month in

Arizona, she just could not adjust. Her writing then continued in the little book which she took home. But she saved it, luckily, because it showed how much fun she had. Then on her 85th birthday, August 28th, she writes "I was ready and down stairs waiting for the apartment manager to take me to the airport and it is 5:10 am!! I am 85 years old today. My flight was great and Judy was there to meet me. I was so happy to see her!" Yes, Mom was coming for a visit for her birthday. I guess I just didn't take these little fun trips with Mom to be so exciting! I loved showing her around and was so happy for the companionship since most of my friends did not live near me. I never realized just how happy Mom was being with me. She writes with such excitement and happiness. Just to see that she even wrote her experiences tells me how happy she was. I am so glad I found this little diary because it really brought back so many wonderful moments together. September 9 was her last entry in her diary. "I have decided to buy in Senior Park, Mesa, here I come!!!" This was because when she asked to come for the visit for her birthday, I explained to her she could always come for her birthday, but if she ever planned to stay again, she would have to settle down and purchase a home. She needed to stay for the long haul. So that is what she wrote in this small book I gave her.

I think it's amazing a woman of 85 kept a journal, even though it was for just a few months. For me, looking back and reading it now, she left me a great present. With Mom accepting she would purchase a home I contacted my brother, who was in charge of her trust, and explained we needed the monies to purchase a small home for her. I proceeded to look for something before she arrived, something in the same community her and Dad had lived in for their short visit here. Her new home was in The Wells, McDowell Road, #5. God is good. To say God was with me this whole journey since 1997 is putting it mildly. But as far as I was concerned, she was home. This would be her home, and I think she knew it would be the last move.

As you are reading this you're probably saying "How many moves was that?" Well I think I lost track somewhere on one of the chapters. Don't feel bad. I also lost track over the years. She did use up all Dad's insurance monies. She would just pick up the phone and call a mover. A long distance mover!! She hardly ever even told my siblings in Ohio. A few times she only gave me a few days' notice here in Arizona. Remember, she is in her late 80's, alone and packing everything. It really amazes me 15 years later with all the stuff she packed and moved from house to house. Yes, there was the regular furniture but most of it was very special; pictures, magazines, albums, even special birthday gifts. Just amazing. How she chose this from the big move from their home when Dad had his stroke, and then carried it across the country for years is just incredible. Whew, I am tired thinking of it!

I guess that little vacation was a real turning point for her and as you will read, it was for me also!

Chapter 32

God Bless Moms

Mom the seamstress, baker and card player. Mom always dressed simple but nice. Every picture I have of her you can see her outfits always matched. She never had a lot of money for clothes but she knew how to dress. She was also a wonderful seamstress. She made almost all my clothes until I was about twelve years old. The projects where we lived were very small and I always wondered where she put her sewing machine. Another question I should have asked her because I don't remember. Mom also made potica as you have read! This is a Slovenian treat and don't call it bread. You would say "potica loaves"....Remember that!

So Mom was a seamstress, baker and everything you asked for. When we would move or need a babysitter, Mom was there and there were quite a few times. There was always a reason why we moved; smaller house, too small a house, retirement home, too small a retirement home! In each home, Mom was there. I was working and John was working but Mom was there to help unpack. In one home John was out of town. I had an out of town meeting so Mom came out and actually unpacked the whole kitchen. The whole time we lived there I never knew where anything was in that kitchen but I always had a warm feeling thinking how much fun she had arranging it however she wanted.

Mom never had a brand new home with a new kitchen although she was a gourmet cook. That was her favorite place to be and here she was, I was gone, and she had it all to herself. Mom was there to care for the kids when we left her during the storm of 1977. I remember her saying "I had to shovel that driveway every day!" Mom was there when we moved to San Diego. I was lonely and Mom was there with every move to help. I cannot remember one time I called Mom for help that she was not there, or to take care of whatever was needed.

When we moved to Arizona she sent the kids a big box. When we opened it inside were leaves! Yes leaves!!! Mom thought since we moved to the desert there would be no trees therefore no leaves. I laughed as I looked out the window at our maple tree! And, there were always cookies. Mom would make about 30 different kinds of cookies at holiday time and send a big box to the kids. Now as I look back I don't just think of how much she baked and how much the kids loved the cookies but how lonely she must have been because the kids were always there with her when she baked! Now she was baking alone. I ask myself "Why did it take all these years to get that perspective because I know for a fact, she was lonely?"

In earlier years she would call every time she baked and would ask me to send the kids over. Johnny knew how to make our first Thanksgiving turkey all by himself, at age 12, because nana taught him. I mention all these moves mainly because I wanted to give Mom credit for all the help. I would call her in Ohio with a need of some kind and she was always there. She was not just Mom, she was my best friend through a lot of out of state moves. Wherever we moved she and Dad always came to visit. Dad always said they would never have seen California or Albuquerque or even Arizona if we had not moved. Dad loved history and loved visiting. I think they missed the grandsons, but I missed them both.

I was very close to my parents by now and I really missed calling Dad. Mom was the one I always went to with tears, but Dad was the one who I went to for strength and advice. Our last move was actually to a bigger home because I found out when you retire you actually need more room. You have time for hobbies, grandchildren and guests! I was never one to sit and watch TV. I always had to have something to do. While I was working the long hours and with the travel it almost made it impossible to have a hobby. Plus I never even had time to think of what kind of hobby I would have, if I had one!

Finally we decided to look for a larger home. Mom lived just two miles away on McDowell and was so happily situated it limited the area we could look for a larger home. One of the reasons I pursued looking for a larger home was the thought that someday Mom might not be able to live alone. I had sworn my Mother would never be in a nursing home so we decided to just check around the neighborhood. John always bought new homes. We had twelve moves by this time and all but

127

four were new homes. We finally found a street of custom homes and there was one for sale. We had not even put our home on the market so I began praying! I felt if it were meant to be, we would get approved for the two homes until we sold the smaller one. I had already picked out a bedroom if Mom ever came to live with us. That said, I always said Mom would never live with us! But, already our lives were changing, Mom was 90, and I felt if it were meant to be, we would get approval for this new home. "Have a room for Mom" and in a second breath I would say "For sure Mom will never live with us!"

Did you catch that last sentence?

Chapter 33

East McDowell, #5 Mesa, AZ

This address was by far, over the next 4 years, my Mom's favorite place of residence in Mesa, Arizona. Understandably, she has been on a journey. Now, she feels she has a home again. It's been a hard road for her and yet, aside from moving here, and there, and here, and there, she has tried to make the most of the loss of my Dad. "Her Rudy," as she called him. Mom loved the home we picked out. The kitchen was very bright and it had a large porch. She also was a short distance from the clubhouse. This home we found was in "The Wells." This is a guarded and gated community on McDowell Road in Mesa, less than a mile from our home. It fulfilled all the requirements of safety and had a beautiful club house which held bingo and other fun activities, including a pool. Yes, you're right, if you remember, this is the same community where Mom and Dad bought their home in 1996. And if that is not a coincidence, Mom's new home was directly across from her and Dad's first home!

Mom made friends like I have never seen her do, and quickly. I must give a lot of the credit to the people who live in "The Wells." Once Mom met Joyce, a wonderful lady who lived down the street, Mom was never home. I remember having Meals on Wheels bring her lunch but they called to say they were quitting since Mom was never home. A requirement was the person had to be home to accept the delivery! Most times when I would go over, and she was not home, I would go directly to Joyce's and she would either be eating dinner with Joyce or Joyce was doing Mom's nails! I would say "Mom you cannot go to Joyce's every night for dinner" and Mom would say "But Judy, she is always inviting me."

One evening Mom even went to bingo. I called her, it was late, and Mom was not home. I was so worried I drove over and after a few minutes I found her at bingo! She wrote about this in one of her little books I gave her. She mentioned how happy she was to think she had missed her curfew and her daughter was so worried! All those years at home in Ohio I think the only friends Mom had, or should I say only people to visit, were her two sisters. One who she played cards with and the other who lived over an hour away, so it was a special trip. But did they go to lunch? Did they go to bingo? No, my Mother really didn't have a circle of girlfriends. My friends and I get together for the Tempe Art Festival. We meet for breakfast around a large round table in downtown Tempe. So I also brought Mom. She was so happy sitting with us and my friends were so sweet to her. What was so funny was watching her go from booth to booth, whizzing around with her walker. We would be walking slow looking at stuff and talking and Mom was just going. I think she wanted to be sure they did not think she would hinder their walking and seeing everything!

I took her everywhere. In the summer we decided to go for ice cream to get out of the house and do something. After about 4 weeks we decided we couldn't do that anymore. It was lots of sugar and no exercise. Mom, being a dietician at one time and a good cook, knew the elements of healthy eating. One afternoon around 3:30pm Mom called to say she tripped over the dishwasher and had a terrible cut. I picked her up at 4pm and returned from the emergency room at 4am. Yes, twelve hours. It was not a happy experience and I wrote to the hospital president about it, but never received an acknowledgement. Seems they were busy. I mean, busy. By 10pm they had yet to even offer this elderly lady a cold pack. I had gone up to the counter three times and each time I was told that they were sorry. Period. They moved us at midnight into the "blue room." I thought that meant they were going to finally take care of her but seemed it was just another room since the emergency room was full. Finally we saw the doctor. He stitched up the wound, but 48 hours later she had an infection! The year would have been 2001. I must say since then this hospital has not only improved but is considered one of the best. Maybe it was just a busy night, in fact, they now have two hospitals within a five mile range of each other due to capacity needs. With the infection I took her to our family doctor who told me she needed to go to the "wound healing center" at Arizona Heart Hospital. Wonderful place! You cannot just walk in with a cut, you have to be referred, and it has to be a bad cut. We went twice a week for 8 weeks before Mom's leg was totally healed! Then, at some point in the five years she lived in "The

Wells," she also developed a sore on her leg which was diagnosed as cancerous. We ended up at the Mayo Clinic for treatment twice a month. Mom received radiation on this small tiny sore. One time I took my grandson Nathaniel because he wanted to see just what radiation was so we watched through a small window. I have no idea who would have done this for Mom if she had stayed In Ohio. I can only be glad she happened to be out in Arizona with me as I was retired!

Meanwhile, living in this retirement community and also being the oldest at that time, I was amazed at how involved Mom became with bingo, birthday parties and events at the club house. I really had never seen her so outgoing, always on the run, hardly ever in her own home and happy! I had never really spent so much one on one time with Mom, but I never noticed she saw the glass half empty while I saw it half full. This showed me I needed to get Mom and maybe even myself some help if we were going to enjoy our lives together! I was always aware that arguments at home with Dad took two! But with Dad it was over money or time at work. Now I was seeing something totally different in her; depression, for sure no confidence in herself and maybe even some insecurity. In my prayers, I surrendered this journey to God. Heaven knows I had done just about everything I could do. I was at a loss for how to handle this lady who was in her 80's. The prospect of her seeing my perspective was little to not at all!! Then I got the idea to take Mom to a counselor, one that came highly recommended. She was very soft spoken and talked to me and Mom on the first visit. Then Mom went for two months of visits alone, and then us together again. It seemed Mom did perfect on these visits however in a minute she would still turn very negative. I have no idea just what it was Mom did or how she acted but after six weeks the counselor diagnosed Mom as extremely insecure and somewhat depressed. After hearing me explain Mom and Dad's background, she decided Mom's depression was more "situational" rather than just a depressed person. The counselor said that they would be sitting there and discussing Dad's death with Mom and her new move. Mom would be very cordial to the point of thanking the counselor for her concern, to quickly having a fit that she was even there and mad at "Judy" for taking her! Some appointments Mom was just as understanding of the situation and appreciative of the help, but the next appointment very impatient with the whole process. The counselor was not able to give prescriptions but suggested I take her to a doctor. She wrote on her notes to the doctor that she had diagnosed Mom as very insecure, lack of self-confidence and some depression. She suggested Mom go to a physician to get medication. I did. The counselor told me "Your Mother is always trying to do special things because otherwise you might find her useless." Along with that she said she lacked self-confidence. The counselor even mentioned in her report that she was very surprised Mom progressed to management in her position she had for over 20 years in Ohio. She credited it to Mom enjoying working with other women and having women friends, something Mom told her she never had all her life. The doctor even mentioned this was a long journey and it was not just from Dad's passing. She said she would not be surprised if this was a part of her childhood. She prescribed a very low dosage of a depression medicine. I began to slowly see some changes in Mom. For one thing Mom began to not just make friends but went to events and totally loved her new neighborhood. If she was happy, I was even happier because I knew how much both of us had gone through the past few years. I thanked God for bringing her some peace. Yes, I thanked God. My faith at times was all that sustained me through the moves, the getting out of leases, the worry of her moving back to Ohio and living alone again, her health, just everything. It could have been even more stressful but then I started just surrendering this whole journey to God. I remembered Dad's journey and his strength. I knew there was nothing, absolutely nothing I could do to convince Mom to see things my way. I knew she was just getting older and more tired and where this would end began to beat me down. After I decided to let God take care of this sweet lady, who by the way also had a lot of faith and who at 89 could still say the act of contrition, every word. He did. I finally felt comfortable with Mom in this lovely home in this beautiful, safe community and making friends.

While I am writing this in 2017 I reviewed the paperwork from Mom's discussions with the counselor. It was an eye opener for me, reading some of Mom's actual words. It seems she always felt very insecure and always felt she needed to do something special to ensure people felt she was worthwhile. She felt she worked so hard at making a nice home, something she always wanted. She said she just wanted to be a Mother but had to go to work. She said when she went to work that first day and the door slammed shut behind her, she felt like her whole life had come to a horrible end. She is quoted as saying "Rudy went to AA and everyone thought he was a saint. But my caring for 4 children, baking, cooking, cleaning and keeping a nice house and working eight hours a day was never a consideration of a good Mother. I don't think any of my children thought of me as a good Mother because of the arguments Rudy and I had." I was stunned reading this. My Mother held on to this thought all her life!! If me and my siblings knew this I am sure we could have explained to her we appreciated all she did.

For two of the meetings the counselor had Mom and me together. When Mom mentioned she didn't think she was a good Mother I remember leaning over and hugging her. I felt so bad for her, just her feeling that way. I told her I never wanted to hear her say that again. There was more. But for the first time, and it is 2017, I am seeing and remembering that she was right. There was always a birthday cake, presents, clean clothes and for sure good food, and for some years she even walked to work. I am wondering how long she repressed these feelings and if depression was her real problem in most of these arguments. If I ever did anything for my Mom, taking her to counseling was what I am most thankful for. Back in the 40's and 50's I guess we never really thought about people being depressed. Those were tough times, you were not allowed to be a wimp! We will never really know, so all we can do as a family is remember them for the most important things they both gave to us and that is love, unconditional love.

135

Chapter 34

In the Blink of an Eye

Yes things changed, both dramatically and quickly. Mom was enjoying every day. On August 28, 2005 Mom turned 90. I planned a party for her at the club house where she lived. A group of men who played instruments played "Hello Mollie" to the tune of Hello Dolly when she came in. They loved her. She loved them. I felt she would never leave this house. I was so close I could always care for her and everyone there looked out for her. I had never seen her so outgoing and so involved with the other members. Always out and about with her walker. I also surprised her and took her home to see her children and her sister Edith. I told her we were going to San Diego and while sitting in the airport I told her where we were going, Ohio!! We all got together at the country club, drove her to Geneva, Ohio where their farm was, and took her to see her sister Edith in the nursing home. Life was good. Then in a blink of an eye, it all changed.

One evening Mom called and said she had fallen. She needed help. I arrived to find her still on the floor. I called 911. At the hospital they diagnosed her with a fracture of the femur. Since it was not broken with just a bad fracture, it required her to stay off the leg for 4 days. Following the four bed rest days, she would then need to use a walker to protect her from another fall which could definitely result in a break. I could not believe the pain Mom must have been in, but in the hospital as I sat with her for 2 days, she never once complained. I worried with her dementia that she might try to get out of bed. The hospitals were not allowed rails on the beds (so they told me) and they suggested I have someone sit with her for 24 hours. I am not sure what they do now, but it's impossible to sit with someone unless you get a private nurse or you have friends and family. My family was in Ohio and my friends lived quite a distance and I would not ask them to come and sit for hours. They probably would have, but instead my husband and I took turns. At night they gave her some meds (with my OK) so she would sleep and feel more comfortable. Each day the nurse asked her if she wanted a pain med and she would reply "'What for?" Yes, my Mom as amazing. When I get hurt I always grit my teeth and say "I am my Mother's daughter, grin and bear it!"

When Mom came home I had to find someone to stay with her at night. Daytime I was there. I asked all around the complex but there wasn't anyone who really wanted to sleep at Mom's house and be responsible for her. So I called an agency. The caregiver came at 9pm until 9am. Mom was in bed and they had given her a bedside potty, no walking to the bathroom. This was very difficult for both of us the first day because I am not familiar with how to transfer someone who was not supposed to put any weight on the leg. Also Mom didn't feel she was that sore and she was not a good patient. That evening I was so happy to see the caregiver. Mom was so determined to get out of bed. I felt that since it was now nighttime Mom would be tired and it would not be so difficult. What was I thinking! I received a call at midnight. The caregiver was having a horrible time keeping Mom in bed! She was determined to get up, have her glass of wine and watch TV. (We had no idea until that time that Mom was a sundowner.) I told the caregiver to give her an Advil PM and it should help. I never heard back. The next morning at 9am I came to relieve the caregiver and she said "I am not coming back. I had a terrible time, and your Mother was hitting at me and swearing." What? Mom never said a swear word in her life. I was sure that this caregiver just didn't like staying up all night and Mom was for sure not good company. So I called Barbara who had already met Mom. She was a caregiver my friend used and was also a friend. When I explained what the girl had said, Barbara replied "I don't believe that. Your Mother is the sweetest person. I will be glad to spend the night with her". The following morning, again at 9am, I came to relieve Barbara. Barbara was standing out on the porch and when I drove up she said "I have had a night from hell." Yep. Just like that. "A night from hell." What happened? Barbara told me "Mom was determined to get out of that bed. I had a terrible time getting her on the potty so I cannot stay another night. I was scared to death she would fall again!" We think this was her sundowner issue. She was used to getting up, having her wine, and turning on TV, etc. but remembering nothing the following morning. I was stunned. What now? I had no one else to call.

Just as I was standing on the porch in total disbelief of the situation, the home-health nurse pulled into the drive. She was there to show Mom how to get on the toilet, etc. I told her of our experiences and she said that was typical for a sundowner. She said it was time to get Mom under controlled supervision for a few days so she could be watched and then given whatever medication she would need now that we knew she was a sundowner. She suggested a hospital in Mesa that had a great program called "Generations". If there is anyone reading this that worked with the "Generations" program or had a loved one in the hospital with this program you can attest to it is the best program for evaluating dementia patients and providing them with the correct medication. "Generations" acknowledges each patient has different problems and reacts differently to specific stimulus. You didn't just read a book on dementia and feel confident you knew exactly how to care for them. Like anything that is good for mental health it was discontinued a year later and the hospital itself was closed down. They told me there was a hospital that had a similar program. We will see about that one later. So here is the schedule at "Generations."

1. They have their own room and they get dressed every day.
2. They eat in a cafeteria style room all together.
3. They have activities, etc. and they are closely observed.
4. They are assigned a nurse, a doctor and therapist.
5. They set up a program where we would meet every other day.
6. They took in my input as to how she was acting before coming there.
7. They were diligently observing her reactions to different situations.

All of these were very important to finding the correct schedule for her. To me these were the most important steps for both the patient and the caregiver, and for me who had never done this before. You could not possibly have had a better program for your loved one.

Mom was beginning to get very good treatment at "Generations." I admit the first morning after she was admitted I arrived around 10am, giving her time to have breakfast with her new friends, only that was not what I found. Instead I found her sitting in a wheelchair, drugged. I was so upset. I called the doctor. He was very concerned with what I saw and said he would come over immediately and explain to me Mom's first night. I was so happy to see him and, to this day, I appreciate the fact he was sensitive to my concerns. He explained he will never drug any patient unless necessary and never to the extent they cannot get up in the morning. Are you paying attention? You will see how the other hospital discussed my Mother's situation with me. Not! However, the doctor continued "Your Mother was up at midnight and still up at 2am and very combative so we had to administer medication. I promise this will not happen again now that we know how combative she gets and the timeframe! " and it did not. My Mother was never, ever drugged again! A big difference from the other hospital program.

Mom's previous facility was where they shared a room and there is no cafeteria. I am not sure how they ate because we were not allowed to visit until 1pm. Can you believe that? Not even able to have lunch with your Mother or loved one. You had to leave at 4pm so no supper together either. There is no team of nurses, doctors or therapists to talk to. In fact the doctor that came at 6:30am every morning made medical changes based on unknown parameters. The nurse??? The nurse's station was towards the back. How could anyone see how people interfaced with others, although most of the others were either drugged or watching TV. There was absolutely no stimulation. This program should have been taken down. I don't know if people complained but they should have. What they did to these patients was as close to abuse as you can get! The fact I could never even talk to a doctor was beyond horrible. I don't think they cared about finding what drugs were really good for these patients. It was just a place to put them.

"Generations" personnel were wonderful. Mom seemed to be accepting it even though she wanted to go home. She did like all the people around her. After 6 days they diagnosed her with dementia and being a sundowner. Neither are a good recipe for her to be living alone. They suggested I try to find an assisted living home before she was discharged. This threw me for a loop as this happened so fast. I had not even thought about an assisted living home for Mom. The first thing I did was ask around the park for anyone who knew someone that would live with Mom, free board plus a monthly payment. But there was no one really interested and time was running out. I just could not believe Mom would have to leave her cozy home, with all her friends nearby, and Loeke, her beloved cat. Now I was supposed to find her an assisted living home!

I could not do it.

Chapter 35

The Decisions We Make

I had heard of this happening to other seniors and I was determined it would not happen to Mom. Now as I write this, please think about these decisions before just taking action. The doctors scare you to death. Looking back my Mom was just fine in her house. Yes, she fell. Yes, she was a sundowner. Yes, she had dementia. Well, she was 90 but not severe dementia. Taking my Mom out of her home so soon was not a good idea. I deal with it every day. So you unhook the stove and put cameras in the house. Home health, which is paid for by Medicare, would check on her at least 2 times a week. Mom was in a gated community where every single person knew her but I was so scared when they told me she could not be alone I immediately went into action. You need to have time to think about this. I wish someone had told me some options. If you can't visit enough set up a village of friends so that someone can go each day. Maybe have lunch with your loved one or introduce them to other neighbors. Visit different times but remember these people really want to be in their own home. They need to see some old faces. Some don't sign up for activities and need some help.

Mom was totally able to care for herself and she loved eating breakfast by the window in her home, with her cat! Joyce, her friend down the street, had her over for dinner almost every evening. If she knew my Mother needed watching, she would have gladly taken her under her wing. I never called her. But with a lot of prayer and searching I did find an assisted living that would take her cat and was large enough for every stick of furniture. She would not miss one thing! This would be just like she moved to an apartment. This move from a home to an apartment would be hard, but the place was really beautiful. Everything she had, every linen, every piece of furniture would fit. Note how I describe what I feel is a wonderful place; so pretty and nice furniture because as I will realize later there is more to the right home than a white table cloth at lunch!

141

My Mother is amazing. I remarked earlier about her strength and determination because in cases like this it came in handy!! She seemed to just go along with the change. I am not sure I could have been so accepting. She was introduced to her new friends, had a great group at her table and there were many activities. In the beginning the lady said she had to knock on Mom's door to get her to attend some of the activities. I can understand that. It still had to be a huge change for her. To this day I am amazed at how she accepted all that had happened. Many years later I found a small diary of Moms where she wrote for just a few days. One of her comments was to her friend Joyce who was her best friend when she lived in "The Wells." Joyce lived right down the street. Mom mentioned how she missed their coffee days. I was sick at heart. Reading this, if I had known about the coffee days, I would have been glad to have taken her over to Joyce's house. My Mom never mentioned this in her new placement. I think even though she never said much, she was homesick! How did I miss the signs? Everything she had at home fit in this assisted living, even things off her desk, cards, address book, even her scribbled notes. But how did I miss the personal part of the move? Her feelings in leaving her home? I hope if you're reading this you take these personal feelings into consideration. There is more than pretty walls and a bright bedroom.

Each month they would hi-light one of the members and put their name and information on the board by the dining room. I remember the day Mom saw hers! It was April and the month of her and Dad's anniversary. So I had a beautiful picture of the two of them hung on the wall and the *Spotlight,* which was the inside newspaper, called her sweet Mollie (see picture). She called me. She said "Judy, I just saw my picture on the wall. I was so excited!" I saved that phone call on my answering machine for 8 years until it was accidentally deleted. I wanted to remember it because her voice was so happy!

This assisted living home was very expensive but mostly it was just too far from my house. It was suggested because it was next door to my grandson's school. Also my daughter-in-law would be there every morning and she would stop and see Mom. I think this was a bigger move for Mom than we thought and I think the week days were long and lonely. I liken this to a child's first day at day care. It would have been nice for me to be there while Mom met some of the new people, maybe even get her to attend some of the activities by going with her. Instead, she woke up the next morning with no one she knew. They called me and asked me to come by more often so I started coming for lunch or being with Mom for a new activity. I realized I should have found a place closer to my home because I could have gone over more easily. Maybe even every day rather than depend on my son and his family, who had 3 little children and school activities. But after one year, I realized Mom wasn't that happy. She told me later that "This one lady wanted her to do everything she did." I was upset because again this was an example of Mom just accepting her fate rather than speaking up and saying "I don't like it." But Mom never ever said that about anything I tried to do for her over the years. Never. This assisted living was extremely expensive, coupled with missing seeing Mom every day, so I decided to move her closer to me. When I told her she was moving, she was actually happy yet she never spoke up about wanting to leave.

I moved her to the Grand Court in Mesa, about 20 minutes from me. Now I could really stop by and take her shopping, to church, or just bring her home for dinner. This apartment was different. It was not on the first floor but it did have a balcony and they did take Loeke, her cat. So again, all of her furniture fit. She had a separate bedroom and I set her chair up so she faced the TV and the balcony. If you visited you would always find Loeke sitting on the arm of Mom's chair. She was so devoted. But no one came knocking to invite Mom to daily events. The people who sat at her table talked to each other but Mom, even with a hearing aid, had a hard time hearing so she never entered the conversation. I noticed this when I went to spend lunch with her. It was very disheartening! I started going over there more often to see her and I introduced her to all the events attempting to get her interested. I asked the activities director to try to get her engaged. I had also asked her to change Mom's seating in the dining room, to no avail.

Mom was also one who loved attention and hated being alone. She never learned how to amuse herself. Television was not her "thing" but she played solitaire all day, and I mean all day! Mom had made such great friends at "The Wells" when she lived there. I just expected she would make new friends now. I realized later that it was the people at

"The Wells" who reached out to Mom. They did not have dementia like some of the people at this new assisted living. They were just retirees enjoying retirement and loved helping Mom, who was 89 at the time. So Mom did not walk up to someone and introduce herself, which is what I felt would happen. I then realized I needed to be more attentive to her needing to make new friends all over again.

I really don't think you can ever do enough because they really don't want anyone else but you! The other side of the coin is you cannot move your loved one to a home, nursing home, or elsewhere and not visit at least 3 times a week. I don't think three times is too often. I think it's needed. These elderly people really want family. Can you blame them? Going to nursing homes now and seeing elderly people asleep in their wheelchairs due to boredom, with some due to meds, appears lonely. I have talked to staff working in those homes that say it's not unusual for a patient to not have a visit for two weeks! I thank God I was as attentive as I could be. If my Mom was able to go out, I stopped and took her with me everywhere I went! Let's face it. This poor lady had two moves in 2 years yet I never once heard my Mother say "I don't want to go," "I don't like it," or "Why is this happening?" She just accepted everything as she had done all her life. Then there were events that showed her dementia was getting so much worse.

One night I received a call from the desk that Mom had chased this man down the hall until he could get into his apartment and lock the door. She was screaming "Rudy, Rudy it's Mollie. Rudy, Rudy wait for me." She would also go down to the desk around 11pm (sundowner) and ask if she could go for a walk. One night she called here at 9am begging me to come and take her shopping. I went and picked her up and we went for ice cream. But the calls started coming more frequently, way too frequently. Even when I had been with her all afternoon, it was never enough. Mom was just not happy. Time for a change. If Mom was not happy I was not happy. I really wasn't. I felt there had to be something I could do. I realized being on the second floor at the Grand Court was probably not the best because it was easy for her to isolate herself. If she had been on the first floor there was much more activity, but there were no rooms available when Mom moved in. I had tried for two months to hold on to the hope a first floor would open but it did not. By now Mom was at the end of her lease so we had to move her. But where? Always look for first floor! By this time we were running out of money. The first apartment was $3500 a month and the Grand Court was over $2200 so I needed to get her approved for state care. This became a huge stress for me, along with caring for Mom and picking her up almost every afternoon. I now had to take on the journey of getting her approved for Arizona Long Term Care and this meant dealing with the state.

SPOTLIGHT

We all Know Mollie Hoffart as one of the sweetest ladies here at Grand Court I'd like to share our special friends story. Mollie was born on August 15, 1915 in Cleveland Ohio she has three sister and one brother. She described her parents as wonderful people. As she remembers her father worked on the railroad. She has very fond memories of her family. Mollie attended her days of school at East Geneva in Ohio. During this time she absolutely loved playing basketball and baseball. Her and her teammates won a tournament after 2 years of playing basketball. She said that she played baseball with the boys and could keep up with the homeruns. Mollie's love was definitely for sports. When it came to her studies she enjoyed math and history the most. After high school Mollie became a maid cleaning homes. She told me that it was not a bad experience and she really learned a lot by working in two terrific homes. She explained that the women that lived in these homes taught her how to cook. It was very worthwhile. Mollie was married on April 29, 1939 she met him while attending a church activity. They fell deeply in love. Her husband was great at restoring cars once they had been wrecked. In 1940 Mollie had her first child and 3 more followed she has two boys and two girls. Mollie worked in a school cafeteria while raising her children. She loved her job with the school. It made her day to see the children and especially when they would say " Whatcha got good today Mollie?" When I asked her what hobbies she enjoys the most she was quick to answer playing cards. Mollie moved to Arizona once her husband passed away she loves the weather here in Arizona and being so close to her family. Mollie moved to Grand Court July 20, 2007. Please stop by and say hello to our special friend. Maybe you kind play a card game or two.

Chapter 36

Arizona Long Term Care Program

After spending just about every penny from the sale of Mom's home, and paying for two assisted living arrangements, I was running out of money. In fact, there was less than $4000 left in her bank account from the sale of her home. If I had known what I know now, I would have accessed this program when I moved her into the Grand Court. What I don't understand is why the personnel at Grand Court never asked me if I knew about the program. They didn't even tell me they accepted Altec patients. But, I had forgotten one of the requirements Mom did have which was one of the most important if you are applying for help from the state. That was to have no liquid assets in your name for 5 years. My brother Louis spoke with a senior attorney and decided it was best to put all Mom's assets in a trust in the names of my siblings. Mom still had her debit card and she never even realized this had happened as it did not take away any of her independence in shopping, etc. So now, its 7 years later and I am applying for Altec.

1. You can own a home and a car.
2. You must be totally dependent on needing help for dressing, eating, shopping and have a doctor's diagnoses of Alzheimer's, severe dementia or other medical issues where you cannot care for yourself.
3. You agree to have the state receive all Mom's income, i.e. pensions and social security.
4. You are allowed an allowance for personal needs, clothes or food.

This program also comes with insurance providing 100% coverage which includes hospital costs, when needed, but you do pay some premium based on your income.

This would mean Mom would now be on Arizona Long Term Care which means she would get some caregivers to help her. If she had a house and elected to stay there then she would have had to pay over $800 a month for insurance and caregivers. Also the state would have gotten all of her income less $100 for her special needs. I have to say at this point, caregivers do not come from Medicare. If I had not put Mom on the state program I would not have gotten the caregivers when I needed them. You must make an appointment, receive the forms and that is when you begin this journey of paperwork, paperwork and paperwork. It is understandable to some degree. I was told the state had over 1,000 applicants a week as of 2017. I knew someone who was put on a program but they paid an attorney and got though the red tape in 30 days. I checked and the cost was over $3000 so I decided it was probably not so bad for me to do the paperwork. Each time I thought I had everything filled out, with all the forms in place, I had gotten a message "Your file is now being reviewed." I could breath. Then there would come another call with a request for another copy of her checking account, her actual pension contract along with her husband Rudy's pension information. This was frustrating because all this had been copied and attached to the form! Some things I felt they never needed. But they asked and you have no choice but to provide the information.

It was time to move Mom and the clock was ticking so my stress level was very high. I remember praying and praying. When we applied they gave us a list of homes that accepted Altec, because at this point I was sure I could not care for her in my home. Mom was as alive and on the go as she always was. Aside from the dementia she was very healthy. Mom never took a pill for anything physical and nothing kept her down. Because she was a sundowner I was not sure how to keep her from leaving the house at night. But this time, I knew what I was looking for. I felt smarter and was determined to look harder and find exactly what I felt would be good for Mom. My dream home for Mom was a cottage type with no more than 6 people and hopefully none that were sickly and wearing oxygen. I wanted people who Mom could talk to and converse with since she was not to the point she could not carry on a conversation. I had heard of these type of homes and so this time I was on a mission! I immediately proceeded to check out every single home on the list and was shocked to see how small the rooms were. Basically just two beds, one dresser and a drape in between. The assisted living homes were on the same list. I eliminated all the nursing homes immediately since Mom was never going to a nursing home. That was fact. Just not going to happen. I was really looking for a "care facility" but let's face it most of these are nursing homes. You have to specifically look under "assisted living homes." I knew there was a difference and they might be extremely hard to find. Assisted living is where she was previously but needed more care. I was looking for a setting where she had her own room, could walk around and participate in some activities, and was similar to the assisted living homes she was in but more coverage for dementia patients. Mom's sister Edith had a dresser and a TV. It was a beautiful home, clean and very nice personnel, but Mom was not ready for a bed and a drape in between. Mom was still playing cards and doing activities. Mom also loved the outdoors and loved walking with her walker. The perfect place would be with a lot of outdoor space to walk, yet be secure.

Checking off the sheet of homes, I was becoming very worried but was determined to check every single one out. I used myself as a check off sheet. "Where would I be happy living if I had to be under special care?" Believe it or not, I was down to the last place on the sheet. It was called Copper Village. You entered down a long driveway and I could see all the grass and small cottages. As I drove in I said a prayer "Please God, help me. This is my last chance for Mom!" Yes, I remember my prayer, almost pleading. After two other places I was so worried that this might not work for her. Remember, our loved ones have different personalities with likes and dislikes so you have to try to find the place that suits them. As I drove to the office I noticed the fencing around the grounds and I knew it would be safe. I noticed a swing in the back yard of one cottage and each cottage had a large front porch. It was explained to me that there were nine cottages, all by level of dementia. When I finally sat down with the marketing agent and manager I found out there was only one space left. It was in cottage four, which is the cottage they determined was best based on my description of Mom's dementia. I had to reserve and pay for it and hope the Altec program was approved quickly. So I paid with the last $4000 that we had. The monthly bill for this cottage was $4000!!

We made it. We found the perfect home! Mom was scheduled to move In July 1st but Altec approval can take 3 to 4 months. I knew John and I would have to dip into our savings, but I was going to definitely sign her up. This was the place for her. It was beautiful. Everything you would want for a dementia patient was here. You could bring her own dresser, bed and chair but we could not bring Loeke, Mom's cat. Each cottage had a kitchen but the food was prepared at a larger building. All homemade food was provided. Mom could get coffee and small items during the day and I would be allowed to bring in cookies or whatever was approved for her diet. What I really needed was Mom's approval. I had to pay and reserve the bedroom but they knew I would want my Mother to see her new home first and they totally understood. For a lot of reasons I was hoping Mom would be approved. For the last 3 years Mom was one of maybe one resident of fifty or more and I always felt she had to tend to herself and get involved. Now, as she got older and her dementia was getting worse, I wanted a place where there would be more attention paid to getting her involved but small enough to sit around in a living room watching TV with other residents. I felt she needed contact with other people and the last place did not fill that need. I don't feel they tried enough and Mom wasn't good at making new friends.

I felt totally responsible if this did not work. I know, you're thinking we cannot be responsible for our loved ones' happiness when there are huge changes. But you still love them and you want to do everything to try to make it work. So to ensure it would work, I surrendered this finding a home to God. I know if I work, God rests. If I rest and feel confident, God works. So the following day I picked Mom up and could not wait for her to meet some of the ladies in the cottage. Being that this was just dementia and a level 4, they could converse. There were no oxygen tanks or special needs patients, just some elderly ladies that could not remember what they said yesterday! Mom thought the small home and grounds were beautiful. When I showed her the inside of the cottage I explained that this could be her bedroom and we would decorate it in pink. She loved the idea. She even decided where her bed would go. Each bedroom had their own bath, which she liked. We stayed for lunch and this gave her a chance to talk to some of the ladies. Realizing she has dementia and would forget some of the visit, I took her back 3 times. Three days in a row! The second time we visited where they cooked the food. Since Mom always worked in the food industry for the school system she really enjoyed the visit. Mom still loved being in the kitchen anywhere she went. We also went back (the second day) after supper for the bingo games. So as you can see, this was not a quick trip or a surprise move. We took our time. But I knew if we did not get state approval soon we would be in trouble. I knew we would be paying $4000 a month out of pocket and I would have to choose from one of the other homes I had visited, which in my heart I knew that would not happen! Never. She would then come home with me before that happened in which case it was meant to be. John and I were really not ready. We felt we would need more training and more information on the help we might get at home but, I would not think of that. I knew I had given this issue to God. He had never failed me. I must admit this decision for Mom was one of my most intense, but one of the most important. I really thought that Mom, with her dementia, would forget this "beautiful pink room of mine" which is what she called the cottage. Each time we went I would take her onto the big porch, out to the swing in the back yard and swing. She loved it. I now had to get the paperwork finished and most of all transfer Mom again to a new home. I was sure Mom would accept the new home since she had accepted the changes in the past. I had paid for July and hoped we would be approved so payment for August would come from the state. Everything seemed so perfect. In all of these moves I felt we had found the right place at the different stages of her diagnoses. I truly felt that all that was left to do was to move her clothes and furniture and introduce her to her new friends. Yep! That was it!

Mom had other plans!!!!!!!!!!

Chapter 37

If at First You Don't Succeed...

When the day came to move her furniture in and fix up her room, we took her to my son's home for the afternoon. She did not see us move anything from Grand Court. Then, I picked her up and told her we were going to her new home, the cottage we had visited three times. But with her dementia, she could not understand what I was talking about. "A new home?" she said, with a very worried tone. That is when I realized this was not going to be the same as the other moves. Mom's dementia was decidedly worse, which we acknowledged. I guess we never realized exactly what impact this was going to have on this new move. We drove to the cottage and went in. She saw her bedroom where everything had been moved in, pink blanket on the bed, etc., but she refused to stay. She told them she was not moving in, rather she was going home with her daughter, Judy. She then walked out. This was our first mistake, letting her just walk out. When we tried to tell her otherwise she became upset. We had to remove her from the premises since she was upsetting some of the people on the grounds. The marketing person there was so helpful. She told me to call her doctor and get a strong medicine that would work in three hours as we needed to calm her down. This was a Saturday and if she was not admitted today it would be Monday. Taking her home was not an option as her bed and all her belongings we had moved into this pretty pink room. Her recliner chair was sitting in the living room! I realized I had to get ahold of myself. This black cloud was growing over me. My heart was breaking for my Mom. When I prayed all I heard was "Keep the faith."

I did call the doctor and he sent the prescription to the drug store within 30 minutes and I took her home. I tried to be calm. I explained we needed to have something to eat since we had been upset and had no lunch. She agreed. We ate lunch and I snuck in one of the pills. One hour later, nothing! During this time she talked about the home we had just left and she said it was nice, but not exactly what she wanted! Oh dear!! She said she would be glad to move from where she was but she would like to

"Look around a little." What?????????? I laugh writing this, how cute, how like Mom, but I remember this so well. Now I might be laughing, then I was not! She had no idea. None. Of course she didn't. How could she? She was in her own little world. Of course I talked about how wonderful this new home was and went through every detail. She would just reply "Yes, but I am not sure." I explained we had visited three times and she had agreed this was a lot better than the second floor of an apartment where she never saw anyone. Most of what I explained about the home she had forgotten. We waited one hour and gave her another pill with some dessert. She then became somewhat sleepy. Then she says "I think I will take a nap." Oh no, Mother, we have to go and pick up John, which was an excuse. I could not let her fall asleep at my home. "OK" she said, "let's go get John." Mom loved John. Anything John needed Mom was right there to do. She doesn't ask "Where is John?" She just gets ready to get into the car.

Meanwhile, I am watching the clock and realizing we are running out of time. I cannot afford for them to close the office on Saturday. As we are riding, she is slowly slipping off. I kept trying to keep her awake. We pull up in front of the cottage and she immediately realizes where we are going and starts to scream. "I am not going. Please Judy, don't take me there. Judy, how could you do this to me? Judy I love you, please don't do this to me."

I still remember those words. Even now, 2017, I feel those words! I ran into the office to get help. Meanwhile, Mom locked herself in the car! The attendees came out to help me. They tried to unlock Mom's door but she would relock it. She was half asleep but still able to scream and try to fight back. It was then I started crying. I felt so horrible. I knew this was the best, but Mom was scared to death. It was July. It was hot and I had kept the car running for the air conditioning. I called my sister Carol and I was crying. "Carol," I said, "what am I doing to Mom? She is crying and screaming for me not to do this to her. It would be so easy to just drive off but I know this is the best for her!" My sister was so calm and said "Judy, don't worry. Ron and I are on the phone with you and we want you to know this is the best for Mom." She told me to let the people do whatever they had to do to get her in the cottage. Finally, two personnel from the cottage came out. Mom was so drugged she could hardly fight back. I still remember them carrying her into the home. They told me not to come back for a few days. She would probably wake up for dinner and they would introduce her to everyone. They would then put her in her own recliner that we had moved and make her feel at home! If she saw me she would not try to adjust. I knew her bedroom done in pink, and the nice people she would meet, would really help her adjust. I had no choice so I left.

This is a tough memory to write about. You try so hard to do all the right things, but when the family member has dementia or Alzheimer's they cannot understand. I was so hysterical I could barely drive myself. Seeing them carry your Mother into a home is extremely traumatic. I call it the most emotional traumatic moment in my life. But I knew in my heart, Mom would adjust. I knew without a single doubt this place was so pretty and so perfect and she would get such good care. I was worried that even if she was at my home there was only me to talk to. I could not take her many places because she would start to roam and I had to keep an eye on her. The new facility had other women, and best of all, clustered together. People her age to talk to, eat with and activities. For sure, I did not have the activities for her at my home.

I did not see Mom for 4 days. I cried myself to sleep and asked God to forgive me for being so concerned when I knew he was in charge. I even thought maybe they were wrong in not letting me see her. What if she thought I had abandoned her? I was overwrought with grief. The morning of the fourth day I was on the phone at 8am sharp. "Hi, this is Judy, Mollie's daughter. She arrived late Saturday and I am calling to see how she is doing." I am thinking "I am going over there regardless of what they would say." The woman from marketing answered the phone and was very nice and actually extremely excited to hear from me. They started explaining how she loved her room and loved going to the kitchen for her coffee. They also explained they allowed her to pick her favorite TV programs and the other residents were happy to mingle with her! It turns out the other five ladies were so gracious to see a new "friend" as they called her. And here I was hardly walking!

We must all remember moving our family, and trying to do the best we can, is not always easy for us. For us! We always think it's the

154

dementia patient but sometimes they adjust easier. In Mom's case I had not just picked "another place." I had not listened to what worked for others. I had not listened to doctors. I prayed and knew in my heart that we would find exactly what would be perfect for Mom. I think she was to the point where she actually was capable of forgetting more than we thought. She never mentioned her apartment to any of them, rather she actually acted like she lived there forever. There was no talk of previous homes. Amazing as it sounds, she never even asked about Loeke, her cat. About three months later we brought Loeke to see Mom and she would hold her on the porch. Mom did realize that "this cat" as she called her (not by name) looked familiar. I think Loeke suffered more than any of us. She was so devoted to Mom. Of course she did not understand where she was and she mourned for a long time. There was nothing familiar to Loeke in our home, so she did not have a place that reminded her of Mom. But we gave her a new place and put one of Mom's pieces of clothing in it.

My Mother did so well in this new environment. I think it was because she was surrounded by other people rather than alone in her apartment. She loved talking to them, going to bingo, all having lunch together in the kitchen, and especially all the areas to walk outside. Also the big porch where I sat with her many nights eating strawberries. I even brought the whipping cream with me. It was a very homey atmosphere which was the best for her at this point in her life. I don't think I had ever seen caregivers that truly cared for their patients like those in this cottage. Every time I visited, Mom was clean, dressed and above all, happy! She was not to the point where she could not explain a little of what she did that day or what she ate. She always had such nice things to say about the "girls" as she called them!! You have to understand just how great a place this was. First, it was not a nursing home. There were not two beds in a room. There was not a sheet drawn in-between them. She had a small chair in the room, her chair from home. There were two caregivers for five, sometimes six patients. Not one caregiver for eight! The caregivers did not have to make meals. The meals were cooked in a big kitchen on the property. Good meals. And this big kitchen eliminated the time a caregiver would have to spend away from the resident cooking meals. I could write a book about caregivers. In fact, later as I write about caring for Mom, I write in detail about caregivers.

Mom was now in a situation where there were fabulous caregivers. I did learn quickly just how important caregivers are in the life of our loved ones who most of the time cannot express what happens during the day. We were lucky to have the best of the best. Mom's cottage was managed by a caregiver named Linda. Linda not only cared for Mom, she loved Mom. This was truly a gift from God and an answer to my prayers. But as you will read, God always answered my prayers and there were many sent!!

There was a large porch however she could not go out anytime she desired. Doors were always locked. If you wanted to go one of the caregivers would take another and they would all sit together. They had a plan to help each resident be able to have choices and involvement and yet be safe. The premises themselves were locked and there was security. There were nine cottages and people did move around. It was so much like a home. Dad had made Mom a card table which sat on her lap so she would sit in her chair and was still able to play cards. She went to bingo but someone helped her because she did not hear well.

Mom's approval from the state came four months later and then the rent was paid by the state. We were done! We made it! Thank God! I felt Mom was finally safe. Mom was happy. All was well. A year went by and her wonderful grandsons would come and swing her on the swing and take her for walks. I was there at least 3 afternoons since I was then doing substitute teaching. I also went in the evenings where we ate strawberries on the porch. I mean, it could not have been better.

And then, life happens.

Chapter 38

Seven Years of Journaling

During the next few chapters I will write directly from notes in my journal and will identify them as such. There might be some notes in between on my thoughts now versus 7 years ago. But that is exactly what I want you to read because we sometimes look back and wish we had made different choices. Also, my journal does not go into as much detail as I want you to know. There could be a whole chapter taken from one day in my journal. For example, Mom's second trip to get her medications changed. Mom wasn't on a lot of drugs but, with dementia, things change. Many times I am sure you have found it very frustrating asking your loved one what happened because they probably forgot what they ate 10 minutes ago.

We will begin my journal writing with August 2009. The entries follow Mom's fall described in detail. I remember writing all this and feeling totally helpless and angry. I also filled 5 pages of writing. I think I wrote to help myself relieve some of the stress because I was terribly upset. As you will read, I took everything that happened to my Mom, good or bad, very personally. I would go from guilt to a pat on the back in one day. I have to remind myself these words in the journal are 8 years old and reflect how I felt at that time. As I read these words now many feelings return. I still feel, as much time as I spent with Mom, it was never enough.

Here are the writings from my journals.

Chapter 39

The Fall That Changed Mom's Life Forever

Mom loved her pink room and life was so good for her until August 3, 2009.

August 3 I received a phone call that Mom had fallen. Seemed the caregiver told Mom not to go outside while she was helping the others go to bed. Mom went to bed later so usually she would sit in the living room and watch TV. This night she went outside! How she got out I am not sure because the doors are always locked. This night they were not. Who forgot to lock them? Luckily another caregiver from another cottage found her lying on the sidewalk. She was rushed to the hospital and they said she had broken her femur. She needed surgery. She is 93. When they called me I was beyond scared. I prayed she did not break a hip because, as most elderly people break hips, it seems they give up. But we had been warned when she fell at home, that if she fell again, she might break the femur. She did! The femur is the largest bone in your body. At her age surgery was scary but they said she slept like a baby. That's my Mom! I stayed almost all day with her because the hospital had no special set up for a dementia patient. My Mom could try at any time to get out of bed. In nursing homes they put the bed down low since they are not allowed to put rails on the beds. I even visited a nursing home where the mattress was on the floor. Of course this won't happen in a hospital but you still have to be there to watch her. Through all this I do not remember my Mother crying. She had to be in pain but I never heard her complain. It was like Mom always went with the flow. She had such strength. I know she saw days of struggle and change throughout her life. Maybe that is what gave her such acceptance of all the changes and issues these past 3 years. I am not sure I could be so adaptable.

August 9 After she left the hospital she was taken to a rehab facility which was horrible. Horrible! She was there for therapy. I visited her every day and on the first day I found her still in bed, with no food and not cleaned up at 10am. She said "Judy, help me." When I went to complain all they would say is they were doing their best. Seems all morning they have meds to distribute and other patients to wash. Those that made a lot of noise, and could care for themselves somewhat, got taken care of first. Mom, who was so weak and I am sure was in pain, could hardly talk let alone find a buzzer to call the nurse. Remember she is 93. The fact she said "Judy help" meant she needed help and was not receiving it. I immediately got help. Mom desperately needed to use the potty. She never did wet her pants. Later she would wear diapers and still, until 2 days before she passed, she would tell you when she needed to use the potty.

Then I asked about the therapy! They explained her insurance had not yet sent over the approval! What?? The hospital social worker is supposed to set that up, or someone is supposed to ensure all this is in motion. I can't believe an insurance company could approve rehab with no therapy. The paperwork was obviously not done correctly. Mark that down for something to watch for! These things can slip through the cracks. As it turned out Mom only had one therapy session before she left on the 4th day. The three days she was there my Mother's care continued to be a case of neglect. I might have expected better, but then don't we all want the best for our loved ones? At least I expected her out of bed and in a wheelchair when I would come around 11am to have lunch with her! I had to ask for everything for her. When her therapy was approved she would not walk. Not even try. She would have 30 minutes with a therapist and then was returned to her room. They finally moved her to a room with a roommate. At least now there was a chance a medical attendant would come to the room for the other patient and see my Mother's needs. I still did not trust them and I would come every day to help feed her lunch and ensure she received help when she needed it. Finally, I had enough. I told them I wanted her out of there. She had one or maybe two days of 30 minute therapy. That was it. They said the home she was going to had to agree to take her in her condition. So I called them. The manager came down and visited Mom and knew right away this was not good accommodations and agreed to sign the papers to bring her back to Copper Village. Imagine, I have power of attorney and I could not have her released! Think about it. Copper Village created this problem with their negligence. I still don't know why the door was unlocked so that Mom got out that night. I was very thankful they were willing to take her back. To this day I hold them accountable for the problem, which by the way left Mom in a wheelchair the rest of her life. Not just due to the initial break but what happened next.

When Mom returned the caregivers, who I have said all along were wonderful and loved her, would help her get up and try walking with her walker. I took her to the therapy appointments but insurance only approved this specific location. They did not have the railings where the patient stood and tried to walk with help. They could only lay her down on a table and assist in the moving of her legs. I thought it was ridiculous as far as therapy. Mom had a fear of falling and had a fear her leg would not hold her up. This was totally understandable, so this type of therapy did not help her. I still could not believe how Mom tried to walk with her walker. But Linda, the manager, would get Mom out of the chair, hold her with a belt and get her to take one step at a time. She was an amazing caregiver but she and the other day caregiver were upset with the night caregiver and felt this should never have happened. Mom did complain of pain and was anxious to get out of that wheelchair. Everything seemed to be working perfectly. Did it? Read on.

September 28 See Mom. Call Mom's dentist. Call Mom's doctor about her Wednesday appointment. Call dementia clinic for appointment. I like writing. (I wrote that?) I can see words in my mind but as soon as my hand goes to the paper I can't get the words out and my mind goes faster than I can write. I lose the whole thought. So guess writing isn't in my future! *Amazing what we write. Even more amazing is what we think when we read it 8 years later!*

October 2 I get a call that Mom has fallen again. They have no idea when she fell and Mom does not remember to use the emergency cord tied to her wrist. She gets up and has no idea she cannot walk. I am furious that my Mom was at the hospital alone, without me. The hospital report says my Mom wanders around at night and fell. Of course they would say something like that. Who would know the difference? Well, she is still in the wheelchair and afraid to take a step without help or her walker, so it's possible she forgot? You might think so, but even when it was time to get her out for her exercise with Linda she would say "I

160

cannot walk." I think she needed to go potty. She refuses to wet her pants but they probably didn't hear her and she probably tried to get up. This was also in the evening. I read this and wonder why I didn't realize something had to change, either the night caregiver, the cottage or even the home itself. I am thinking that I did not want to move her because Mom loved it there and the caregivers during the day loved Mom! I write: This is the problem. Mom forgets. Doesn't anyone realize that? Guess not. There are only 6 women in this cottage and 2 caregivers and the day caregivers are excellent. They watch very closely. There are no other women in there who cannot walk. Most need care in personal hygiene, medicines, eating, etc. I am there almost every day. There was one who could not remember she had just eaten. There are all levels of dementia but most were like Mom but just not able to live alone and needed some help with personal issues and meals. But other than that, cottage 4 did not have any very severe dementia. The hospital report mentioned Mom did not have severe dementia. I cannot believe she would put her foot on the floor and walk around. The problem is Mom was just fine until her fall. Now they need to pay more attention, due to their own fault. They wrap her wrist and the following day I take her to the dentist. This is my life. Very hectic. There is not much room for extra planning between Mom and substitute teaching. Both are always last minute calls and crisis. Reading this, I begin to see my frustration and tiredness of it all. I had spent every single day with Mom since her fall and felt so sorry for Mom. She did not deserve this.

October 4 We had an appointment for the dentist. Mom's arm was still wrapped. We were trying to get her dentures fixed to fit her mouth better as Mom's weight declined.

October 6 Went to see Mom after dinner. We sat on the porch and ate strawberries with whipping cream and fed the stray cats. I needed to find some time to spend the night at the cottage. I would like to see just what the schedule is since I know Mom goes to bed last. So at 3:30pm I went to see Mom. We are going away for just 3 days and I am going to miss her! Two falls in 2 months. The other women are somewhat able to care for themselves although they also have dementia. But cottage 4 is not for severe dementia. My Mom's hospital records also say dementia, not Alzheimer's. So she qualifies for cottage 4.

October 10 Kelly the caregiver asked Mom if she went to the dentist and she replied "Oh no!" But she did and it was hard for her. So I took her some strawberries and we sat on the porch after her supper. They said she ate like she was starving and she forgets when she does eat. But she loved sitting on the porch eating strawberries and feeding the stray cats.

Wow, only 2 months and I realize I am going to be 69. Time to make some decisions on what I would like to do with my ideas on continuing creating journals for the Phoenix Children's Hospital. I think back on some memories with Mom. Thinking of all the things she would do for me, clean out my kitchen drawers, iron, and all things she just loved to do. Now she sits in a chair babbling about nonsense and I can't make out what she is thinking. I ask Mom a question and she answers "Well, windows are clean, good to keep them clean. I washed them all day. Is Dad coming?" Then as quick as she says that she says "When can I live with you?" Sometimes I have what I consider real conversations with her, but to her, they just seem to go over her head. For example, I said to her "Mom, when you finally go to see Dad you and these memories will stay with me, in my heart." Her answer "Oh good, Judy." Very calm, like she didn't even hear me. *Amazes me that I can write this at the end of a day and remember it all. I think back now and realize how lucky I was that I even wrote and kept a journal! What I don't understand is why I trusted they were only giving her meds that I approved!!*

October 15 I visited Mom last night as I do about five times a week, sitting on the porch and eating strawberries. She is just going further and further into "never land." Words that come are all jumbled and make little sense. There are some moments she knows exactly what is going on. She is looking for Dad and she says "I am very upset that he is leaving me." What Mom???? "Yes, he is not around as much."

Well, my life almost changed forever. Driving home from the art meeting, going exactly 45 miles an hour in my Tahoe SUV, a driver crossed in front of me, a big wham!! The other car was totaled. My SUV flew. I saw these white clouds and thought I had died. My favorite cousin Marlene died in a car accident in 1967. I realized then that the white clouds were actually the airbag! How funny. People ran to my door, opened it and I could hear them asking about the airbag. You're saying what???? Not a mark? In fact, the chair I was painting and took to share with my group was still laying perfectly in the back storage of the SUV. I went and sat on the sidewalk. My car from there looked perfect. Then one of the bystanders said "Have you seen your car?" I said "No." At that point the police arrived as I was sitting on the curb. The policeman asked if I was the passenger. I told him that I was the driver. He said "This car saved your life. Have you seen the front? It's gone." Years of Catholic school and a lot of faith has carried me through all my life. Even now I tell God to "Whisper in my ear what you want me to do or say or see." The worst part of tonight is I won't have a car to go see Mom. That is what I am thinking tonight after this horrible experience. I think "Well, it wasn't my time."' I now know why it wasn't my time. I had someone who needs me and who I needed. I am blessed.

October 17 I went to see Mom and brought her chocolate. She is truly old. Mom was never old. Mom was never her age. Mom was never so quiet, accepting and so affectionate. I am getting to see a side of her I have never seen. She told me she can't live too long without Dad. She thinks he is at work or at his AA meeting. She says she knows she sleeps alone, then the thought passed! I realize she is not there long enough to dwell on it. Thank God!

October 18 I had a dream that went something like this, written exactly as I wrote it in my journal. It is pouring rain outside. I have no car. I have to go to work. So I walk in the rain. Of course I don't recognize anything, never do in dreams. I find solitude in some apartment, people in and out. Then I am leading a group somewhere. Mom is in the line with me so are Marie and Louis (my brother and his wife). I am asking Mom if she can walk this far, need to find a shorter route. Then I think this scenario is all about me wandering. Wandering here and there. Wandering in the rain, I wake up! I write that but reading it that night I told myself I didn't feel like I was wandering!! I feel I have a path. I have a direction. I just need to get started. Put all these sad events I am remembering, such as Mom's falls, etc., behind me. I realize I am doing my best. I cannot keep questioning myself. Our art group has picked a box to embellish. I thought of a toy box because I have so many little toy embellishments and maybe I need to start reading. Creating is good for your health. Creating is something we were all created to do. Maybe that was the message. Get to your art!

October 21 On the porch with Mom a lady stops to talk to us about her Mom. She says "One day Mom just forgot to walk. She fell 18 times and now does not know my name. She forgets to breath and almost died three times and she is 90 years old." Wow, I am thinking my Mom is now 94. I begin to think of the pain in store for me and Mom and then I stop and thank God for where we are right now. One day at a time. I put my arms around Mom as we sat on the porch and I was thinking "This is the last day she will know me." I am not sure, but somehow it was like she knew what I was thinking because she turned to me and said "Judy, I love you very much." It's moments like this, writing this book that are gifts from God. Reading this, writing how she said she loved me, is a special gift and a gift I would not have if I had not decided to write. As you will hear me say many times during this story "write in a journal."

October 22 Mom's appointment at the Alzheimer's clinic. Took Mom today for her appointment and later to her walking therapy. There is such a place in Phoenix, Arizona. I had read about it and made an appointment. I knew it was time for me to find out as much as I could and have them evaluate Mom. For Mom, six weeks of not walking plus dementia, equals loss of ability to tell the brain to walk. Dementia alone can rob the brain of the ability to walk, so they tell me take her for walks. Doesn't matter if she shuffles, even bent over, just walk. This is what those wonderful day caregivers are doing for Mom. It's sad because this did not need to happen, but, they continue to try to help her. They do give or suggest medications at this clinic. They visit with her, ask her some questions to see where she is and to give you some reading material and some ideas of what could happen. Even though every single patient is different they tell me not to expect anything but realize Mom will be at her own pace with her own issues. They do not diagnose her with Alzheimer's, but rather severe dementia. They knew her medical records so they did not suggest changes, so guess that is good. Well, Mom is still in the wheelchair from the fall and I am concerned as to what they said about not walking for a while. Mom is still not walking so this was definitely the turning point. If you had told me she would never walk I would not have accepted that. Caring for someone with severe dementia requires changes but it's not impossible as I will describe later in this book. But now, in my journal at this point in time, I did not have to worry about that, since God does not give us the ability to see the future which in this case was a blessing.

October 22 Mom also went to therapy today. She did a little therapy and did whatever they asked, but I am sure tomorrow she won't remember. The therapy is terrible because they do not have the bars for her to stand and practice putting weight on her legs! They just lay her on a platform and do some muscle strengthening but Mom needs help to stand and try walking. This is the only therapy the company allowed under Mom's insurance. Terrible.

Halloween 2009 We go to Johnny's every year since the grandkids were old enough to walk for Halloween. So cute. I would never leave her at home since I know she loves Halloween. She sat at the front door and handed out the candies and said something nice about everyone's costume. She was so nice even remembering good words with her dementia. I was amazed. We took Mom there every Halloween since she came here. She loved it!! It seems being nice is just Mom and it comes naturally. I would like Mom with us on all holidays.

November 2 As usual Mom and I are on the porch. For some reason she was very confused and didn't even realize she was on the porch. Tired? Worn out? Something! Each day is different. I brought candy and she throws it out and yet there is no one there! We used to throw it to the kitty so I am thinking she is doing this from habit. When we came out on the porch she didn't have a clue why, yet we sit on the porch almost every night with strawberries and feed the cat. The day before she seemed so perfect. I took her for a walk and she even talked to Ron, my sister's husband, on the phone and made perfect sense. I look at her and think how old she is getting, or is it because they don't put cream on her face? I think tomorrow I will bring some cream for her. I did bring cream and continued to always put some cream on Mom's face.

November 8 We are leaving for San Diego in a few days. This is horrible for Mom. No family to see her for a couple days, but this is a black tie event at John's Company. We fly out and back so this will at least make it somewhat a shorter time away from Mom.

November 13   They showed slide shows of Arizona at the black tie event because the new president of the NAR (National Association of Realtors) was from Arizona. The pictures were of the state and the new president is from Tucson. The pictures were beautiful. I am sitting there thinking that I would love to travel and see this and then I remind myself, "I live in Arizona!" I called and Mom was fine.

November 15 The cottage asked me to come and help decorate their Christmas tree. I am so excited because now Mom and I can decorate a tree together.

November 19 There is a flower on my cactus!! I have been going to Mom's later in the day. She is now sleeping longer. I try to get her out by 3pm. There is an orange orchard next door and we walk down the street and enter through a long driveway. This is a regular walk for us. I love to point out the flowers and we eat cookies that I brought. They also do weddings and have a walkway with arches. Today I pushed her under the archway and we talk about how the pretty brides love this. I say "Mom, pretend you are the bride," and I sing *Here Comes the Bride*. Today she says "Judy, it's so nice out here." I had waited for her to say my name because I am never sure if she knows me or not. When she does the whole day is so much brighter. I felt I could just skip down the street pushing her! I put a big star next to this writing in my journal tonight so someday I can go through and pick out all the very special times, even though every time is special.

November 23 Mom fell. Broke her collarbone! Now for sure, she cannot use her walker to practice walking since she broke her femur. She has not been wanting to at all and has been in a wheelchair most of the time. The caregivers were doing so well at getting her up and walking using the walker. This is unbelievable. The caregiver was the same one on duty when Mom fell and broke her femur. I am furious, both with myself and the cottage. I must admit the day caregivers are exceptionally careful with her and love her. The evening caregiver should have been changed. Now I wait to see if this is a setback in her recovery to walk. This was the time I should have removed her from the home or insisted the evening caregiver be either transferred to another cottage or let go. But I didn't. It was at bedtime, but I was not told until the next morning. I was not at the hospital with my Mom.

November 26 I spent the day with Mom. She is so black and blue I have no idea how she sits but she never complains. She cries out if you touch it, pulls her arm back and sometimes even she forgets until she tries to use it. Mom absolutely refused to walk after that fall. I cannot blame her. In her situation, with severe dementia, she had no idea she could walk!

Thanksgiving Went to Johnny and Geri's. Poor Mom, she sat in the wheelchair and looked so tired. I am trying my best. This poor lady is in her 90's and just broke her collarbone yet she tried very hard to eat and respond to all of us at the table. But she was very tired and very confused. At this point I am not sure she will come to our house for our traditions on Christmas Eve.

December 2 Mom's memory is really going down. Today she knew me. They think we might have to start giving her some meds for her outbursts. The problem is she sits and talks and is very loud. In the small living room the other ladies cannot even hear the TV. Right now all she receives is vitamins, her Zoloft (given years ago) and her Namenda. *Reading this now in 2017 I realize they did give her some meds. Knowing what I know now, her outbursts were dementia related. Being in a cottage they probably could not take all that noise, considering the others living there. I had no idea just what they gave until much later, but now it explains a lot about her behavior. What about the fact all meds were supposed to be approved by me?*

December 7 It was raining so I did not go to see Mom. Saturday we are taking her to get her hair done, even in the wheelchair with a broken collarbone. I want her to look nice for Christmas. I plan to get Danny to help bring her here for Christmas day. It's hard to get her in and out of the wheelchair. She is dead weight and does not understand. Between Dan and John Mom will be here for Christmas.

December 14 What a day!!! Mom has a cough. I see her every day. One day she acted at lunch like a drunk, waving a spoon in the air saying nothing, groans, and small yips. Are they giving her drugs I don't know about? They are supposed to ask me about anything they give her. Whatever I think, it's too much, but I will wait and see how bad this gets.

Saturday   I did not ask them what meds they were giving her but I told them I would appreciate them lowering the dosage. Today we took her for her hair. They said it was too cold to take her out but I wanted her to look good for Christmas. My Mom always looked good. She dressed so pretty and with her hair always in place. I took her to my hairdresser and she was perfect! She remembered the place which we have gone to every 6 weeks for 12 years! She even mentioned to Charlyn my hairdresser "How short are you cutting this hair? I am going to look like a man!" Then when we put her under the dryer, it all changed!!! "No, no, don't put that thing on my head" she said, and then all of a sudden she started singing "No, no, no," while under the dryer. She was singing a song, she was not crying! She was not screaming! I think their mind gets stuck like a record! She is so cute! Maybe it was not the drugs, just dementia. Every day is different. This was so cute I still remember it. At that point I remember thinking "She is God's child and only He knows what she can or will be able to do. We just went with it."

December 21   I dialed my sister, who lives in Ohio. It is her birthday. I put Mom on the phone but Mom does not even realize it is Carol. She talks and talks, and says "Oh, it's been so long since I have seen you." Then we hang up and Mom says "Who was that?" This was a very funny moment. I remember my husband stopped in his tracks as he walked by her and heard her say that!

December 26   Of course, Mom came home for Christmas! She seemed to enjoy herself. She loved seeing the grandkids although I don't think she really knew who they were. I think she knows what she wants to say, but different words come out. She is still not walking! Still in a wheelchair. Mom said "Oh, I don't walk!" Then, in the next minute she says "I like to go for a walk, I like to run, and I ran all day today!" Another funny moment. Amazing I had a chance to see just how this dementia works!

December 27   Went to Mom's cottage to have dinner with her. She does not remember being at our home on Christmas day. She is alert and well. She is amazing. She is talking again like Dad is around which is new because she has been looking for him for weeks! Now she thinks he was here. *As I read this now, while writing this book, I am amazed at just how mixed up she was in December. You will see why I say that as you continue to read this journey.*

December 30 I told Mom today is my birthday. She then says "I wish I could spend it with you." I said "You are! We are having coffee together." To which she repeats "Oh Judy, let's have my birthday. I spent my birthday morning with Mom." I said "Hi Mom, it's my birthday." Again and again she repeats her previous words. So we went on with this for about 10 repeats before I gave up! I said "Mom, it's Judy and it is Judy's birthday." Then, as if she just woke up, she says "Oh, it's Judy's birthday! Can we have some coffee together?" Then we went for a walk with the stray grey kitten following us. I recorded 10 minutes of Mom's repeats on the walk. Even though she just had gotten up, she was so tired so we put her in her chair. Again, the caregivers Linda and Susan are so sweet. The best! I asked if they were giving her drugs and they said no. I guess she is just tired.

Chapter 40

The Real Goal

As I write this book and read my journal, which I have not read since it was written, I have had to look back at all the many mistakes made in this life and all the changes we have made for the love of our family. We know we are not perfect. But everything is possible with faith. All through my upbringing I was introduced to more and more ways to look to my faith, even in times I thought my parents had to die for life to get better. Instead, my prayers and my parent's real love for each other, along with Dad's true belief in prayer and his strength and love for his family, here we are. It is December 2009, finding ourselves on a journey, requiring us again to keep with our faith in God and help from friends and family. One of the things I do not want to do is look back. Sometimes we are sure looking back will ensure we don't make the same mistakes. It depends on how far back you look and what you're looking at. One of the things you don't want to do is dwell on those mistakes.

I removed Mom from her home because the doctors said she could not live there alone. Way too fast a decision! Looking back, I know she could have stayed. I will write later in the book how she, and many with dementia, can stay in their homes. I don't think we realize what it's like to wake up in a new home, your friends gone, your pets taken and you can't even make yourself a cup of coffee. If I would allow myself, I could have a pity party every night, especially after reading my journals written over the past 7 years. Boy, would I like to try this over.

The hospital I sent her to for the second review of her medications would certainly not be in my new schedule nor would some of the drugs Mom took! I have written a whole chapter on that experience as you will read later in the time frame that it happened. Also, I might have not listened to the professionals so quickly but rather looked up every single medicine they were recommending. For sure the "This is what dementia patients take," or "This is what we recommend," would be researched in more detail. As I remind myself we each react differently to drugs. I don't think there is one drug we all take with absolutely no side effects. But we should not dwell on the mistakes or failures of the past. Pray to get rid of any remorse and develop a feeling of peace knowing at the time you did the best you could. Isn't that all any of us can ask for? You stumbled and now you just get up and live the life God created you for. There is a wonderful life planned, I am sure.

I read a great sentence from Dad's AA book: "Do not stay to examine the spot where you fell. Only feel sorry for the delay that prevented you from seeing the real goal sooner." I wish I had taken Mom out of Copper Village when she broke her femur but there were some caregivers there that did watch out for her and loved her. I also thought another move would be really hard for her as she was in pain as it was. But if I had, she probably would have gone to another home and the journey God had planned for me might not have had a chance to be fulfilled. Well, there is a lot more to the journey than you have read so far. I think you will be shocked at what happened to Mom. I was not prepared. I really thought I was watching Mom very closely. How could some things get by me!!! Another reason I wanted to write this book.

Chapter 41

Nightmare!

I experienced a nightmare I can never wake up from during Mom's stay at Copper Village. Her only medicine, the tiny bit of Xanax prescribed by "Generations" almost 3 years earlier, needed to be changed. "Generations" had such a great program that when it was suggested to try this other hospital, because they also had a "behavior" program, I thought it would be perfect. It was March 27, 2009 when my world fell apart. I remember Mom being with us while we went to fill out the application. She had such a pretty top on. She would walk around this large office using her walker. She never touched anything, but we were doing paperwork for 30 minutes. They didn't exactly lay out a program, but assured us Mom would be watched for her behavior and they would report back to me. Either I didn't read the fine print or I was too trusting after "Generations," but as you will find out, it was elderly abuse at its worse!

After Mom was admitted I was told to come at 1:00pm the next day. I could understand that because, even with Generations the first day was always hard. What I didn't realize was I would only be able to see Mom from 1:00pm to 4:00pm. No meals with Mom. Strange, huh? The first couple afternoons I visited Mom she was bored. There were no programs, no bingo, nothing. Just a TV was set up with some people sitting and watching it. That's it! I would walk with Mom, just around this large room. Believe me. That was it!!! I kept thinking that maybe while visitors were not there is when they intermingled so they could watch their behavior. Boy, was I wrong. I began to notice Mom seemed very quiet. I know drugs when I see them. I asked the nurse why Mom was so quiet to which she replied "Well, they all go through a few days where they get depressed and want to go home." Then the whole thing fell apart!

I came in one day and I had John with me. I was now worried so I wanted him to see Mom. When we arrived she was walking with her walker, head down and barely able to take a step. I ran up to her as I was afraid she was going to just drop to the floor. Later she did! By law they had to take her to the ER to get checked out. Obviously there was no one watching her but at no time did I see one single attendant, just the nurse behind the counter. I was furious. I said "I want to talk to the doctor." She replied that he comes in at 6:30am so I told her I would be here. "No, you won't," she replied. "You are not allowed until 1:00pm." Then I said "I want him to write and tell me why my Mother seems more drugged each day." Her reply was "Well, she was probably combative." "Excuse me," I said. "Does she look like she is combative?" The nurse replied, "Not now, but she probably was when she was given a sedative." Plus she went on to say "There are no hard drugs of any kind being given to your Mother."

Now I am really concerned. I arrive the next day, John with me. I am now feeling like I am going to have a heart attack. My heart is racing, I cannot wait to see her. There she was sitting on the chair. She looked like a dead person sitting up. She was not moving. I went and got a blanket and wrapped it around her. She could hardly talk. Again, up to the nurse station, and now I am mad! I said, "I am not leaving until I see a doctor," to which she replied "If you don't leave we will have security walk you out and chances of getting back in will probably not be available." You cannot imagine how I felt. When John and I left I cried and cried all the way home. Oh God, please help me, what have I done? What are they doing to my Mom? My mistake was not letting them call security and calling the state adult abuse hot line. At the time you don't think like that. You take on all this guilt, hysteria sets in and you can't even think straight. So I went home and called three other hospitals and asked them if I could bring my Mother there. No. I found out hospitals won't take a person who is under sedation or a program at another hospital without the confirmation of the hospital they are in. Also, because they don't want the responsibility if the person doesn't come through this ordeal. As you can see this was not at all like "Generations." No team of doctors to talk to you and give you daily updates. I had no updates of any kind on any day! Not one! They didn't have any plans of getting the patients together to see how they acted, i.e., anxious, depressed or hostile. Nothing.

173

The next day, as I went up the steps to the doubles doors, I could barely walk. I think I only made it because my Mother was in there. I had to be there for her, but I was also now getting braver as I wanted her out of there. Are you ready for this? Well, I found her in bed. So drugged she had not even had a change of pants or sleep wear and its 1:00pm in the afternoon. I knelt by her bed and cried. I sang to her. I combed her hair. She never moved. There was a man sitting with his wife in the next bed. He introduced himself as a professor at the college and he said "Get her out of here." I went to the nurse and said "You had better get me an appointment with the doctor. I will have the state and anyone else I can find here tomorrow at 1:00pm and we will get her out of here."
Remember when I wrote about the "Generations" program? The doctor said they did not know she was a sundowner so the first night she had a lot of drugs, but he promised it would not happen again? Well obviously they knew how to handle a sundowner. This group obviously didn't know or care she was a sundowner. I am guessing they used a lot of meds.

I have yet to see this 6:30am doctor that comes. Don't you wonder how he can decide what to give her since he only comes in early morning? I am sure she is not walking around, talking or eating. So, who is giving him the advice or does he not care? What kind of animal is this that my Mother wasn't moving yesterday and now she is comatose? Got a call that evening. They set up an appointment for John and me for 10am the next morning. I had a chance to go into Mom's room before the meeting and she had not even moved. Same gown. Second day, laying there. We went to the meeting and there were about 5 of them; the nurse who I saw every day and a doctor (Not the one who came at 6:30am but someone on the staff.) He told us that "We always start with the largest dose of meds to see what they can handle and then we go down!" Ha. Joke, huh? He went around the table and asked the others how Mollie was acting. Why did he have to ask? Didn't he have her records? I really don't remember their answers as my mind was going 175mph. I knew that none of what they said could be true. Then when he said "We try very hard to not drug our patients." I put the 3 pictures on his desk! Thank you God for telling me what to do, for giving me and Mom this day, as this time we were in charge! Too bad I didn't get a

174

picture of his face. He was shocked, I am sure, but calmly he handed them back to me and said "Well, she is just dehydrated." Did he think I was stupid?   I said, "I am coming to get her tomorrow." I stood up and he said "She will be ready."

She was so doped up when we came. She was sitting in what looked like a highchair with a tray. She was trying to find the French fry with her fingers. And no one, no one, was there to help her. You can't believe all this? Well believe it!!! I lived it. I saw it. I asked God to take away these memories. I have no idea why I need to remember this. I can't even write this without loud bouts of crying! I went to the desk to sign her out. They gave me an RX for her. I said, "Oh no you don't. I want them all. I want every single RX that you gave her!" The nurse said "That's all we gave her." No, not this time. You are not getting away with this. I said "I am not leaving until I get them all." She made a call. I was standing there. I heard her tell someone that I would not leave until I got them all. Sometimes you cannot just stop a drug that has been given to someone so quickly. She hung up and called someone else repeating the request. She hung up and said they would be sending the prescriptions up shortly. We waited.

Why didn't I sue them? First, all I wanted was Mom home. Then I worried I would get in trouble for taking the pictures. These people have big lawyers and they will find some way to shut me up. So, I let it go. Mostly because I was in such a weak condition mentally I could not even deal with it! So I did not mention their name in this book. If anyone wants to tell me how I can at least present this whole issue to someone and use the hospital name I would love it. I would only do it to save someone else. After all this time I cannot even believe the program exists because they had to know there was no program! Someone had to change it and maybe it was another family. I probably will never know. Does this help you make decisions on where you put your loved ones? If you cannot visit them for meals right away there is a problem. Simple as it might sound!

I remember while sitting with Mom, all wrapped up in the blanket, she said, "I saw ma and pa today and ma said I was a good girl." Well, God answered all my prayers. I asked Him not to let her die. I wanted to take her to church for Easter! Guess what? To this day, I remember walking into the church on Easter, seeing the altar all decorated with yellow drapes and flowers and me wheeling Mom down the aisle. It was the happiest day of my life!!! The only good thing about what happened is that Mom never knew what hit her. The best thing about this ordeal was I had the wherewithal to take pictures!! The bad thing is every day she was there.

Yes, I have tried never to look back, remembering my Dad's words from his 24/7 book. I have a real appreciation for those in AA. How could a daughter who took such great pains to do the right thing make such a horrible mistake? I do tell myself that there was no way I could have known what would go on behind those doors. Did I ever think for a minute a doctor would come in at 6:30 every morning and you would never meet them, or even get an update? I believe you learn something every time you go through sad and difficult journeys like this one. I can say all I learned was to "Keep the faith." God will never let you down. Something could have happened to Mom that would have prevented her never coming home, but she did, and we did go to Easter Sunday together.

God is good.

Chapter 42

The Alzheimer/Dementia Clinic

October 22 I took Mom to the Alzheimer/Dementia Clinic in Phoenix today and later to her walking therapy. I found out they were much related. Six weeks of not walking plus dementia equals loss of ability to tell the brain to walk! Mom shuffles, hesitates and is bent over. Mom was good at therapy and she did what they asked. It was amazing. But at 94 I am not sure she remembers. In fact, I am sure when I go tonight at 6:30pm she won't. I brought some food for the stray cats. I have food from our cats at home Abby (named after the queen of the fairy's Abandancia) and Mom's cat Loeke. Again, we sat on the porch together. I just love these moments. I realize someday there will be no porch with Mom sitting on it with me. All I know is God has known me from before I was born and he will always take care of me. I went to bed reading this new book that tells you to ask the question "What is my life purpose?" In the book they give examples of monetary, success, etc.
None represented me, so I asked myself "Which one am I? I am not in this book!" Then I realized I don't ever think of a life purpose. Rather, I wake up and say "What do I have to do today or next week?" I always just thought my life was meant to take care of Mom, to pray for the end of Dad's alcoholism and to keep them both alive and not kill each other. Now, there is the question. "Why didn't I ever have a dream for myself?"

October 25 Went to Mom's fall festival at Copper Village. They have a beautiful grassy area where they hold some events for the members and their families. It was so nice. Later we went back to the porch at Mom's cottage. Mom, who usually doesn't make much sense says "Judy, I see more of you now than when I lived alone in my own house. I did not take issue with it because I knew we did everything together." Then I said "Well, I like coming, feeding the kittens and sitting on the porch with you." Then she says "Why? It's very boring!" It's so funny she can go two days and rattle on with no sense to it and then she will say something that actually lets you know how she feels.

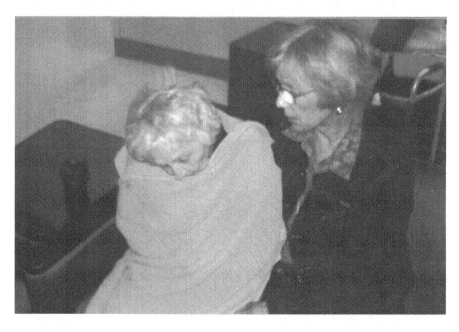

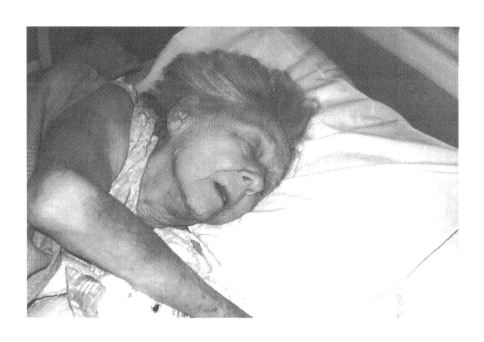

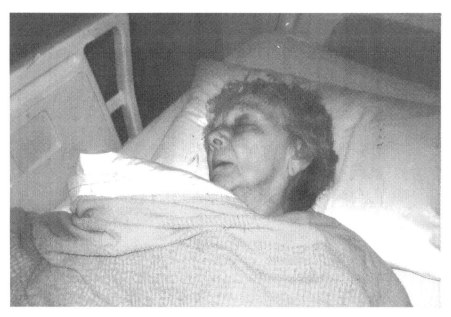

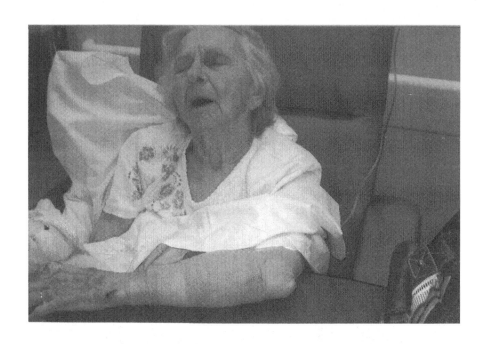

Chapter 43

Mollie's Journal

In 2006, I created a journal for Mom thinking maybe she might write in it and give her something to do. I was not sure she would ever write. Now, in 2017 I found it! You would think with the few things she brought with her I would have found it sooner, but it was tucked inside the large album her employees had made for her upon her retirement from the Euclid school system. I have decided to include it here, exactly as she wrote it, with the dates she put down. It might sound a little mixed up but she was 96 writing in this journal.

It begins:

Today is Thursday 1/14/06 I spent the night at Judy's. Tomorrow I have a doctor appointment. Today is December 6. ***Originally she wrote today is Monday, scratched that out and wrote Tuesday then scratched that out and wrote Thursday. So hard to determine what day she was writing this.***

I am having a little trip to a mall with Judy. I am now waiting for her, sitting in a comfy chair in the mall. Very busy! The weather is beautiful today and we are expecting Danny for Christmas. Will be great to hear how his job is in New Mexico. ***This makes me think the date was really the second one she wrote, December 6.*** So I am waiting for Judy in the mall it is quite busy! Well we will see how this day goes, we just got here.

4/24/07 Our Mothers and laughter day. It was such a wonderful day. Judy treated me to a lunch and style show put on by the women at John's company. It was a beautiful show, the style show, lunch, etc. It was endless. Real show. Many dresses. It turned out to be a wonderful day with John. What a wonderful Mother's day treat. The money went to charity, how nice. ***She even taped to the page a photograph.***

5/12/07 My trip to California with Judy. I left the house with John to the airport at 11:00. Plane did not pick me up until 1:00 arrived in

California at 1:30. How happy I was to see Judy! Saturday we went to 5:30 mass. It was beautiful. The church and the service. I loved it! Then we went to Judy's. I love her place. It is furnished so beautiful. I had a great night sleeping. *I am amazed reading this how much she remembered about the flight, the church and the condo.* Amazing. Dan's birthday at Amazing Jakes. We spent the afternoon bowling. I found out I cannot throw the ball too old! But I was happy being with the kids and Judy and John and Danny. *No date but Danny's birthday is 4/30.*

5/13/07 Today is Mother's day. I spent it with Judy here in California. Happy day. We went out for waffles, strawberry waffles! First time in my life. What a nice breakfast good waffles and with Judy. With Rudy gone no one else could take his place. Judy served the breakfast, good. Best. Then we walked the beach. Great. Then we went through a house on the beach that was for sale. Oh what it takes to have all of this! A Mother's beautiful day with my Judy. P.s. Error: we had breakfast at home, waffles and then out for lunch later. We went to Mimi's. Judy and I both had chicken pot pie, very well. Very nice place. I hope someday I can take John and Judy there. John is not with us today and I do miss him. *Wow. How much she remembers. Somewhere in this book I wrote about taking Mom to California for Mother's day, and someone took our picture and luckily I still have it. But I never thought she would remember so much, even to how to spell Mimi's!! Remember, in 2007, in August Mom would be 92!! I am remembering all the dementia medicines they said she should take! Luckily I monitored them!*

5/14/07 We went to see bathroom fixtures. They were beautiful. Wish I could afford them but I really do not care for black. Then we went to the tile equipment, so many new things. Then went to the post office and then we went for lunch. Judy is trying to get me to remember something. Very exciting, we were asked to take the communion up to the altar! Taking communion up to the altar is so exciting. I am 91 and to have the great pleasure of taking the communion up to the altar with Judy. One of the #1 days of my life. The opportunity to do this is the very best thing I could ever dream of. Thank you dear lord. I feel so grateful to have the opportunity to do this. *Oh dear, what can I say!! How she writes. She amazes me! I knew she loved it but until reading it now in her journal I guess I didn't realize the depth of her excitement. This was at the Mission de Ancala, the first mission in San Diego, walking distance from our condo.*

Tuesday 6/07   A great day. Another great day. Judy had doctor appointment for a shot. Then we went to Zinc Cafe. Such exciting adventures and very interesting place...We both had egg salad sandwich. Absolutely delicious on the way home we stopped to get our Carol a card and I got knee high nylons. Haven't had a pair in years. In the evening we went to church, a very special mass for Rudy Hoffart. I was so sad thinking of Dad but it was so exciting to attend the mass for my Rudy. We had the privilege to take the wine and the host to the altar. All I could think of was Rudy was watching us. A day in my life!! *Well I didn't write about this. I remember taking up the wine and hosts but guess I forgot I had made the mass for Dad. Now I remember setting it up knowing Mom would be with me. But I had to read this to remember!! Can you believe she even remembered the egg sandwich? Also, I wrote the word privilege from her writing!*

June 14 thru June 17   I would like to straighten our dresser drawers. Well I got something out but it's going to take some time because my back is killing me. 10:00 am

Friday June 22   Today is Nicolai's birthday. He is now 6 years old. Last Friday we went to Marie Calendars for lunch. We had banana cream pie! Judy and I are getting our hair done today. Saturday June 16 we went to a movie and saw pirates. *Yes, the dates get mixed up. But now we are back home. Mom was at Copper Village during this time, she arrived there in February of 2006. So this means we took her places. I am so happy I did! I read this with tears of happiness but I sure never realized just how happy she was. I am sure she told me but, wow, she really was excited.*

July 5 2007.   She writes 2000/07! Ha. Today is Thursday and I wanted to see Judy so much so I took a flight to California. To their house in San Diego. I am so happy the trip came up. I was so glad to finally get out here with Judy. She has her apartment so pretty. Redid the bathroom. What a wonderful room. She did great. The weather here is beautiful. We took a walk through a condo it was lovely. We took a stroll through and I got to see more then I have before. I have had a very relaxing time. I am so happy to be with Judy I will be staying until Sunday. It is so beautiful here a very relaxing time and place. *I have a picture of Mom sweeping the front walk. She would come down when John went back to work, then she went home and John came down. It worked. I would go play golf, she would iron. She loved it. She called it an apartment but it was a condo. Yes, we redid the bathroom and it was a mess, but my friend Cheryl came down to help me which is why I didn't want Mom to come until it was over. Again, she even remembers when we went through some models. I loved going through models and Mom was the perfect companion!!*

7/7/07 Today is Saturday. I arrived at Judy's on Friday. I love being with Judy. We had a snack and talked. We went to Pat's shop and then to Judy's shop to check it out. Pat has quite a shop! *Another amazing writing. Yes, I had a small booth in the antique mall in La Mesa and I have a picture of Mom there. But Pat's was a shop my Mom loved. It was huge with everything, almost like a Goodwill, but not organized. Very eclectic and the furniture had been repainted by helpers and was gorgeous. Everything in there you wanted and everything in there you would see nowhere else. She went out of business when they redeveloped the area and we have never been able to find her since!!*

7/8 Sunday I love it out here in California. We went to church last evening. Today being Sunday means there is only one more day!! We went to the flea market. I got a big black clock, now I will finally be able to see the time! I loved the flea market and had Dad in my mind all the time. *How appropriate! Dad was always at every garage sale on Saturdays and would get up at 6am to get on the road!! No wonder Mom thought of him!!*

7/9 Monday I have to go back to my small place. Well, Loeke will be happy to see me. But really love it here in California and I am loving being with Judy. Sitting on the patio having my breakfast. I have seashells for Nathan and Nicolai. I have a caterpillar book for Brandon. I love these boys. They are 3 gentlemen and I am missing them. **Everything Mom wrote is true. Mother's day in California, etc.**

No date: I have no idea what day it is. Judy is in California. I wish we were back in Cleveland. I wish Kenny would take me to visit Dad's grave. Oh, I miss him so much. Rudy, why did you leave me all alone! You really were a wonderful person. God knows and you are an angel in heaven. Pray for me Rudy. I want to be with you. I am so lonely I wish I had stayed in Cleveland. Kenny would take me to visit you. I wish I was with you. I do not understand why Judy is in California. She has a husband, children, grandchildren and family, so the rest of us are here. Oh Rudy, you know I always loved you and still do and miss you. *You can see how great she is with people around, going place with me etc., but the minute she is alone, she cannot handle it. This is why she moved back and forth so many times. She did not like being alone.*

No date: It was the first morning I woke up and could not get out of bed. I fell asleep and two hours later I struggled to get up. I don't remember what I did next but I got up at 10:00am. Had no energy during the day I opened the door but when the girl came in they would close it. I could not see a reason for closing the door. It was a terrible feeling. *This has to be still in the summer, because she says I was in California. So you can see the change. I am not sure what caused this. Absolutely aware of everything with me and then changes as she goes back to Copper Village. Now the whole journal changes. The way she writes, the writing all over the page (see picture) beginning with Friday, Saturday, and then Tuesday.*

Fri I went to Judy's today loved it! Stayed overnight in "my" beautiful room and bed. Being with Judy and John. Left on Saturday.

Sat Had a nice stay overnight and went home I love being with Judy and John. I feel like different person.

Tuesday Here I am. With Judy. Love it. I am so happy. I came for breakfast and spent most of the day see you next time. Love *No dates on these days but seems now we go from July to 3/22.*

Saturday 3/22 Today is Saturday 3/22/08. I had come to Judy and John's house. I am so happy to see my 2 dears, Judy and John. *It seems she might have lost track of the journal and then found it again.*

Now in 2008 Easter Sunday spent the night at Judy and John's and we went to Johnny and Geri's for Easter Sunday. Met Tina and Bobby. I got several items for my Easter basket. One of the many items was a new purse and a bunny. I got new purse and blue bunny. *We always brought Mom home for the holidays. I typed the names exactly as she wrote them!*

No date   When my mind gets worse I call Judy and believe what Judy says. Judy is my mind. *You can see from picture of this page that her writing is really changed. And this was the last page she wrote. But as I wrote from my journal I saw my Mother's demeanor really take a downturn. This could have been written right after she fell. We have no idea. It has been very emotional reading this. I guess I knew how much we wanted to see her, but just how much she absolutely loved being with us and remembering all we did with her was beautiful and yet brought back a feeling I should have done more. Why do we always want to beat ourselves up? But we do the best we can at the time and we try to show our love. But Mom, now gone, has left behind something for me to know how much she loved everything we did together and how much she loved us. I always said she was the best companion, always willing to go and do things with me!*

WHEN My Mind gets
WORSE
I Call Judy a Believe
BELiEVE.
whaT Judy
Says a
Judy is my Mind.

EASTER SUNDAY

Spent the night at Kelly's & John's + we went to Johnny's for dinner for Easter Sunday. Met Linda and Bobby + Johnny + Gerry + their Mom + Dad came - picked peanut + got several several items for my Easter Basket one of the many items was a new purse (big)

Purse + a Bunny!

I GOT NEW PURSE AND BLUE BUNNY

Chapter 44

Carol Hoffart Silvernail

December 21 December 21, 1948 was the day my sister Carol was born. My sister, who was a great support for me while caring for Mom. I was eight years old on December 30th. Mom would bring her to my bed and I would change her and feed her since I had rheumatic fever. She was like my little doll. Many years later I moved to Arizona. We did not talk very often so when she called one day it was wonderful to hear from her. We seemed to pick up where we left off. She said "Judy, I need your help. Mom is calling Ron (her husband) three times a day and I don't know what to do." Ron was wonderful to Mom and would never not answer her calls. So I told her I would go to Mom's telephone book and just pull out the page with his work number! Problem fixed! We then began an almost nightly conversation. Carol was always up very late so she would call at midnight her time and 9:00pm my time. We would discuss my daily issues with Mom. Mom was living alone just down the street, but I saw her every day.

Over the next years, until her death, the phone would ring at 9pm. I brought Mom home here to live with me. In the beginning, until I set up some sense of structure, the days were busy and tiring but around 8:30pm I would get ready for bed so we could talk and not interrupt anything else going on in my house. She was always up late, and the first thing she would say is "How are you?" not "How is Mom?" We both read the same books, followed John Edwards and compared notes on what we heard on TV. She was my lifeline. As sisters I could talk to her regarding issues with Mom like I could not talk to with anyone else. One of our discussions was we had both discovered Mom never had anyone to talk to or share ideas and events with, only Dad. For sure not her sister Mary. Mom had one close friend, Charlotte, who she met through Dad. Charlotte, her husband George, and Mom and Dad had a lot of fun together. But Charlotte, as Carol pointed out, passed very early in life. So who did Mom have then? Mom grew up in Geneva, was on the basketball team and had lots of friend. Then upon graduation she moved to

Cleveland. All she had in Cleveland was her sister, Mary. She also had her sister Edith, but for some reason Mary was always like the Mother. It was Mary who told Mom the color to wear for her wedding! So, with no friends to discuss everyday issues with, like we might do with our friends, Carol surmised that Mom was very lonely. I agreed, because Mom told me she felt very intimidated by the sisters-in-law and that is why she learned to cook so well. She felt she needed to feel needed. As much as we could gather, she never had a real close friend, which made for a very lonely life at times. However, I think that is why Mom loved her job. That is where her friends were, the team at work. She obviously arrived every day ready to work and I doubt anyone realized the pressure she had at home. So with no close every day friends, we both wondered if that was part of her and Dad's problem. Dad was at work and had people around to talk to. Mom, for many years, was at home with small children with not even a friend to call. We did not see her sitting down, taking a break and calling a friend. Carol was very intuitive. She was also the last sibling left at home. She saw and heard a lot. She said "I don't think either of them ever learned how to communicate. They always seemed to do it with anger." Good observation!

Again, how great it was to talk to not just a sister, but a friend. And not just a friend, but a friend who knew Mom and Dad very well. She was the youngest and was still living with them after my siblings and I married and left the house. By then Dad was in AA, but Mom would bring up past issues, which was always a lot of the problem. Carol heard them all. I really felt sorry for Carol because she was so young when most of the arguments took place and now listening to Mom and Dad, she was reliving them. But we both agreed they really loved each other. There were these small instances where Dad bought Mom a beautiful bracelet for one of their anniversaries and Mom made Dad his favorite meal. We did notice these times. We agreed it gave us faith in our family. There was a chance we would wake up and the house would remain quiet, quiet, quiet! We also agreed we enjoyed the big family with Dad's brothers. This is where much of our tradition came from. We talked about Aunt Alma. Carol called her a saint. She was married to Dad's brother Frank. The memory we both laughed at was when Uncle Frank brought this big Christmas tree he had cut down to our house. And then there were the car tires he stored in the pantry area in their home. Aunt Alma never complained, even though they also lived in the projects and there was little to no room in the kitchen let alone a pair of tires! Oh, how Carol and I laughed. I remember this so well because it was a night she was not feeling well, and she laughed and laughed. I felt so happy for her!

Looking back we surmised that communication was a big issue with many of Mom and Dad's arguments. They came through some tough times newly married. They had two children in two years and yes, experienced the depression years. Carol and I, after many nights bringing up the subject which had affected our lives so much, came to the conclusion they were two people who never gave up. They were frustrated and scared at life but didn't know how to share their fears and feelings with each other. Carol and I also talked about how, when living in the projects, the morning after Mom and Dad had an argument, Mom would go next door and sit and smoke a cigarette! I also have a picture of Mom sitting in the house on Windward smoking a cigarette. I said to Carol "Do you think that was after a big fight and she did it on purpose?"

Yes, Carol and I had many midnight talks. She was my lifeline with Mom. She played a huge part in mentally helping me cope with the issues with Mom. Then one day the phone rang, Carol had passed unexpectedly. The phone never rang at 9pm again. To this day I have not seen her obituary or her funeral card. I could not function for two days. I had to put the phone away since I saw it next to my bed knowing it would never ring again at 9pm. When I received the news, which was unexpected, I went to my studio and began to paint. I had no idea where the brush would take me, I just pulled out a canvas and grabbed some paint. I started painting a heart, and painting the inside dark black. Then I stood back and looked at it. It was very dark and obviously not a color for a heart. I didn't seem to care but then I thought to add some red, so the middle of the heart has red paint. I realized I was angry, upset, crying and not really thinking like the colors an artist would paint a heart. Then, I remember saying to myself "Judy, if you continue to always see the dark, you will never find the light." At that point I picked up some gold paint, and finished the painting! It hangs in my studio to remind me of always there is light thru adversity. We just have to find it, in this case paint it.

I had spoken to Carol on Thanksgiving. She told me she didn't feel well and did not go to Thanksgiving dinner at my brother's house. Since this was Thanksgiving night and she had always called at 9pm Arizona time, she did not realize we were in New York. John and I had gone to New York for our 50th anniversary and so it was midnight. I explained and told her I would call her back Friday. I did call her, thank goodness, and she said "Judy, so glad you remembered to call me back." Thinking back now I would never have forgotten to call her back, but the excitement in her voice has left me knowing she also enjoyed those nightly talks. They were not just for her to help me with Mom! For me, this loss was a terrible setback in my journey with Mom. And for her husband Ron, it was the loss of his beautiful angel!

To My Loving Mother and Father,

Dear mom and Dad, on th[is] ksgiving Day, I want to thank for the things you have done me. With my deep appreciation to for letting me be born to such derful parents, you my mother father.

So on this day I want to k you for your sacrifice's for and show my love for you. of the times you have helped me, ed nights with me when I s sick, when you wanted to somplace. But no, you stayed th me instead. The many us you bought me something. n you wanted it yourself.

So I want to give you anks on this day. Dear om and Dad. Lovingly Your Daughter Carol Hoffart

194

Chapter 45

Another Christmas with Mom

December 24   We brought Mom home for Christmas. She loved the big tree we had. It was 15 feet tall and hit the ceiling. She loved all the decorations. Mom always decorated. She just loved holidays and tradition. It was so wonderful to have her home for a couple days. She was actually very aware of everything! She noticed the presents, talked about Santa and we were absolutely amazed. She really did not have severe dementia at this time. She just seemed to slowly get worse.

December 30   I turned 69. This has to be the only birthday where I felt time was running out! 30 didn't bother me. 40 was most memorable with the cake my sons made for me. I had taken a very unusual trip to the mall, alone! I also splurged purchasing three turtleneck shirts at $5 each! When I returned there was a huge banner and a beautiful four layer cake! Seems they started to bake and realized they needed more frosting so they sent Todd, the youngest, to the store. He had to walk quite a ways. When he returned they decided they needed more frosting and sent him off again. You have to picture this four layer cake floating in frosting. Looked like the Tower of Pisa! I think I was so proud because I left three boys at home. Rather than tear up the house, they did all this for their Mom's birthday!! 50 went fast, even 60 didn't bother me. I think, because at this point I really had no real purpose in life, my everyday world was just having things I had to do. So getting old and taking care of a husband and sons was just fine. I thought 65 would bother me, but then found going on Medicare wasn't so bad. But!! 69?!!

Next year I will be 70. In fact I was already starting my 70th year. But now I have a purpose. Mom needs me more each day. I want to learn about paint as much as I can enabling me to be close to see Mom almost every day. I can use my painting as something Mom and I can do together. At that point in my life painting was not at all important. I had painted and distressed furniture and it was a great time, especially with Mom visiting my shop. But now I did not want to miss lunch with her and I began to feel every day with her was important. As we all know we don't know anything about time!!!

If you keep a journal and you read what you have written 7 years earlier I hope you read it with a smile. I read this and thought "Boy, if you had known then what all would happen beginning with age 69 you might have wanted to get to 70 quicker."

69 was going to be a year to remember.

Chapter 46

A Brand New Year!

Script from my journal: I am thinking this is going to be a wonderful year. I have lots of plans with art and I want to go through Mom's clothes and buy her some new ones. She had a new Christmas sweater but she loves all her old clothes. I also want a bow for her hair and some pretty stockings. She was always dressed so nice but I love dressing her up now. She knew how to dress, simple, inexpensive, but always perfect! Reading this, of course, I have no idea of 2010, only optimistic plans. As you will read, 2010 was a year to remember for many reasons.

January 3 I went to see Mom. She can't remember I am there each day which is sad because I don't want her to think her family has abandoned her. She thinks no one comes. She thinks she sits there all day. Today was a beautiful day and we sat outside all afternoon. She said "Beautiful, beautiful" at least 10 times until I asked her a question to get her brain out of wherever it was. Now as I see her in the wheelchair I know she will never walk again. It's too long. Breaking her collar bone during her therapy just finished off any chances of her walking. Her muscles are weak and her brain tells her she never walked! But it was a wonderful day. I love her so.

January 4 I went to visit Mom but did not stay long because I have a cough. She showed no expression, sitting comfortably in her chair eating a cookie. She said "Hi" like I was a neighbor. I helped her open her cookie which she said was a "bar." It was amazing because she was right! But there was no "Judy, how nice to see you" which is her usual. I could not stay or get near her so I said I would see her tomorrow at which she off-the-cuff said "OK!" I called later to ensure she was OK. They said she was. Linda, the manager in the cottage, loves Mom and takes such good care. Now writing in 2017 I can see she was probably on pain pills since her broken collar bone still hurt her. If she was on any pain pills, I was not asked. Yes, I would have approved but then I would have realized her demeanor. And, I would have liked to have known exactly what pain pills they were giving her. I was absolutely watching every pill Mom was given.

January 9   It was a day full of memories. I was getting something out of the drawer and missed Mom, remembering how she would come over and clean my kitchen drawers. Mom was living her dreams every time she was in the kitchen. Writing this now memories come and it hurts down in my stomach. I think when Mom is gone I'll plant another rose tree and watch it bloom as Mom bloomed in the kitchen. Then I got emotional and thought, "I cannot do that because every time I look at it I will remember Mom." I won't be able to not picture Mom in the kitchen. Not just any kitchen, this kitchen. So I am thinking I will miss her. Yes, more than I am capable of even thinking of it now. How will I find life every day and make my own day. I will make my very supportive husband understand my grief. Does not mean I don't love him. It's just that Mom was always there, somewhere; kitchen, phone, baking my favorite birthday cake, sewing. She was just "so there." I realize each day that every day is a true gift from God. As I read this in 2017 I am taken aback by how I felt then. It's 2010 and I was already thinking about dealing with loss. My thoughts have not changed one bit. I was just amazed that I felt how I would miss her because I enjoyed the time with her. You will read how I continue worrying about how I will do life without her, getting very specific about what I will lose and miss. Later you will read just how much time I did get to spend and how I accepted her death.

Chapter 47

Ahh, the Orange Grove!

These updates are taken word for word from my journal, dated 1/2010 to 2/2010, while my Mother is still at Copper Village. Looking back, I should have removed her after her falls, but she loved being there and loved her friends.

January 10   Today after seeing Mom and taking her for our daily walk in the garden next door at the community church I was wondering if Mom isn't really here for me considering she can't:

- Help me in the kitchen.
- Can't call me ever, considering she would call me 15 times a day.
- No companion for ice cream or shopping.
- No more help in my studio.
- Now she just "is."

When she goes to heaven, as she should in my mind, she will be my Mother. Actually there is no more Mom, as I knew her. When I see her she will be a beautiful spirit but our life as we knew it as Mother and daughter will be no more.

Those words are taken, exactly as I wrote them.

January 11 Yesterday, Mom was very awake and alert, even remembering Loeke, her cat, and today barely awake. We went for a walk anyway. I feel she is leaving me day by day.

January 17   This is about the fifth time where I witness sallow skin, not eating and didn't even know I was there yesterday. Today I got her up and had her eat some soup. No idea how she just sits all day, no food, sleeping. Then today much more alert. I had lunch with he, took her for a walk and she picked an orange from the tree. It was hard to pick it off, but she did!   Later I came back with a rubber ring since she says her butt is sore, and found her again sleeping in her chair and not wanting anyone to bother her. There is no walking even with all the work with the caregivers. I am sure they are not happy that she fell at night. I wonder if they were on duty if that would have happened. But silly to think about it. It's done.

January 18 Did not see Mom for a couple days due to rain and my cough. So today went to see Mom and they ask "When you do think she will walk?" You're asking me? We skipped her orthopedic appointment due to rain so maybe her orthopedic doctor knows. Her knees crumble when we stand her up and she isn't well enough mentally to understand. She knows she wants to stand but loses all sense of listening and trying when we stand her up. No idea! I am not a doctor but will see what they decide.

I have to stop and tell a funny story about Mom and her visit to the orthopedic doctor. Mom was in her wheelchair. The doctor was sitting on a small stool in front of Mom feeling her leg and asking questions when all of a sudden Mom says "Oh, I dropped my contact." So the good doctor pushes back his stool to look down and I immediately tap him on the shoulder and say "Doctor, Mom doesn't wear contacts. She never has." He smiled!

January 20 I had breakfast with Mom. I took her a scone and found her sitting alone in the kitchen chair since it is 10:30am and everyone has eaten and gone. I am guessing she got up late. She has been sleeping the last couple of days when I arrive. But this morning we had a nice time. She was surprised to see me and we talked. Some of the other ladies came in to talk with us and I made Mom acknowledge them. "Say hi to Liz." "Say good morning to them." These ladies are nice and they do converse with each other. It is a small kitchen to have everyone get around, whereas in the living room it's larger and they don't face each other. I think what they all need is more interface with each other. At 3pm I went back and found Mom sleeping in the chair! I tell Mom we are going outside and she says "No." I tell her we are going because "You cannot sit here all day, eat, and sit again." So, the wonderful day caregivers and I dress her in her heavy coat, scarf, hat and we go out. She seems to come alive and talks. She loves the oranges in the tree and is very verbal saying "It feels good to get out." I feel there is more in her brain than she shows because she has little opportunity to exhibit it.

January 26 Foot sore, butt sore, sore arm. Maybe the collar bone has not healed. Need an x-ray. Butt is sore from sitting so she needs to get up more, but hurts. She sleeps until 10am and is tired by 12pm so I took her for a walk. Sometimes we sing, but today she could not sing. She says "I hurt." We went to the orange grove. She says "Can I get an orange? I want to take it home and eat it with Dad." Maybe if she could remember Dad is gone she might not hang on to seeing him. Now she is afraid he will come home and she will not be there. I left later because there is absolutely nothing, not one thing, I can do for her. She wants to rest and quit hurting. There is something wrong here. This is not the way it is supposed to be. I am caring for her, she should not be hurting. I did allow them to give her pain meds. I need to see if they are giving them to her. Plus, she has arthritis pills. She should also not have a sore on her butt and they should walk her more. This whole stupid fall has really created a terrible life for her. This is not a cheap assisted living home.

January 28 Was with Mom last night. She was at the table, but so lost, tired, alone. Thank you God for keeping me safe so I can be with her. She was excited to see me! I smoothed her hair and hugged her and asked her where she hurt. She says "Everywhere" and then she says "I don't know." I said "Mom, you look so tired and it's only 7pm." Mom usually went to bed at 9 or 10pm. This was later than everyone else, which is why she was alone months ago, went outside and fell. I still don't understand how she got outside! I said to Mom "Do you want to go to heaven?" I felt it was time to have some pity on her and not think of myself. She said "Yes, I would like to go to heaven." Getting her into bed was hard. She hangs on to her chair like she is afraid you're throwing her off a cliff. With her dementia she might think that. In bed she curled up. John tried to straighten her legs and she screamed. I said "Yes, it hurt." and she said "No." I asked her why she screamed and she said "I don't know." So now she slept but at 7am they told me she called for Rudy. I went over and looking at her I thought "My world has stopped, there is nothing I can do for her." She says "I am going home." And after a pause says "I'll miss you." Then she cries out in pain when you touch any part of her, especially her leg. I cannot understand the pain in her leg. She cries even if I take her hand. She gets startled like she doesn't know what is happening. Is it time to take her home? God has never misled me. Somehow it feels like Mom is meant to pass. I need to listen very closely to God and get the right instructions.

January 30 They called in hospice. They said she is 94 and giving up. I said she isn't going to die here, I am taking her home. I told them I wanted a couple of weeks to see if she responded and if she did I would bring her back. I told them to hold her room since it is still paid for. I thought of this at the last minute because when I asked a caregiver if they were giving her too many meds she rolled her eyes. Then, as we were leaving, one of the caregivers told me my Mother almost choked on a piece of meat at lunch yesterday as if she did not have the energy to even chew. I again asked if they were giving her meds I did not approve. I could not understand why she was in pain if she was given the pain pills. So are they not giving her pain pills but some anxiety pill that is making her so sleepy? I never was in favor of just one doctor for every cottage. They had told me we did not need her family doctor anymore. This way many patients don't have to be transported. I am wondering if he gives them all the same medicine and forget. With me, he is supposed to ask. I for sure did not authorize one. But whatever, I just decided to take her home and check it all out for myself. Hopefully we would be back in two weeks or less.

January 31 She is home! Mom is in her room here. I am not sure she understands. I think you could take her anywhere and she would not know. She talks to herself. She slept with knees up and wanted to hold them together and lean towards the right. I put a pillow in between or else we can't get them unlocked or straightened. They hurt but so far I cannot figure out why. I am hoping by having her here I can have some quality time with her. Eat together, have coffee. Now she is a captive audience. She is talking to someone. I told her to go to sleep. She has an alarm and I hope I hear it with the door closed. We have to separate the kitties. Abby, our cat, does not like Loeke, Mom's cat, which we also had to bring home with Mom. I am thankful for this opportunity and should decide what to do in two weeks. She may be fine. I doubt it, but she got so much care at the cottage. But, it was they who created this and it's a lot harder and painful for Mom than for the caregivers. They really love her and try every day to get her to walk. Thank you, God for everything. I know you are with me and Mom. She is home. The angels need not worry.

February 1 Oh, my gosh, who does she talk to all day? She is asleep at 7:30pm, exhausted. I noticed a med on her list that I did not approve. I am wondering if that is making her worse. Mom is sleeping in the guest room in a regular bed so it is somewhat difficult to get her up but we are doing fine. Hospice came and changed her. She talked and talked all day. At one point even clapped. Said "1, 2, 3, 4. I'll take 4, yeah," and claps! I ask her who is she talking to and she replies "Dad." The first day wasn't so bad but I had the nurse who changed her at noon. I didn't because she didn't want to get up and was content to lay in her bed. She is dead weight so I waited until the nurse came to wash her and get her up. I have no help. Will see how this goes. The most important thing is to see if Mom is really dying or if it's the meds. She was very loud and angry so I called the nurse. She said to increase that one med. John said "If you give her more I am leaving." So, guess what? I actually decreased it and I am not sure why she is even taking it. Was it given when she fell and just never cancelled? I did not question the meds the hospital gave her. I know she was not on any meds at all when she fell and broke her femur.

Wednesday Mom took a nice nap today and was still awake at 9pm. That is good! She has complained hardly at all of pains since she has been here. Eats like a bird. John helped me transfer her from the wheelchair to the bed. John has been a big help even though he is at work every day. I wonder how people who care for loved ones manage their relationships! I wonder why I write at night when "Morning pages are just that, morning pages!" **The journals I write in are from the Artist Way Journals, a companion to the Artist Way Book. They are titled The Artist Way Morning Pages Journal.**

Thursday I think we are doing well. No crying. Very strong in my conviction to see these two weeks through. Mom seems well, even less pain. No leg pain, no butt pain. I have no answer for that. She even has some very sane moments. I did have a hard time the first time getting her from the bed to the wheelchair, but hospice then showed me how to do this. It's really not bad because Mom's legs are still somewhat strong and she can help. Her cat Loeke is something else! She sits on Mom's bed all night and sits on the arm of the lounge chair when Mom is in it, all day!! Such devotion. I have to admit caring for Mom is not what I thought. But here we are having a week we will never have. Mom knows I am here and I have to believe she feels good because she seems better, just seems. Not sure yet if that is for real.

February 4 Mom is really just existing. She really wants to just go home. Tonight she asked God to take her to heaven. No matter how tired she is, she still talks and talks. I am getting many nice emails from friends. Amazing. I am sure I did not have to do this and I admit it's not what I thought. Mom is more helpless than I thought.

Friday She talks to? Like a child in a playpen, so engrossed in whatever place she is at. She talks, waves her hands, doesn't cry out, is not angry. Even when you move her, if there is any pain, she will say "Thank you" when it is over. I find this experience watching her amazing. She seems calm and has discussions with her blanket which is on her legs in the wheelchair. I went to a dance with John and a volunteer from hospice came and sat with Mom. I hope I can reciprocate someday. There is much I am seeing in this short visit. For sure she is not dying. She has no idea where she is or where she was yesterday. She says "Oh Judy, how nice to see you," when she has been here four days. She does not cry out for a blanket even though her legs were cold. Instead, she pulls up the blanket as she talks and talks to it as if it were her purse or her coat. She is someplace special.

February 8 Mom had a good day yesterday all things considered. John and I dressed her and noticed her pain is not long lasting. All cleaned up and sitting up in her chair she was in a very calm demeanor. She looked at Dad's pictures, ate great, and guess what? I chose not to give her the morphine this morning. I called her regular doctor and explained the morphine I noticed they were giving her. He thought it didn't seem like a lot, but maybe for Mom it was. He said I could take her off and see what happens. At 2pm she was by the window in the kitchen and she even said "Look at the birds outside." We put her to bed at 8pm and she was still in there talking at 9pm. I am not giving her the night meds she was being given. Another med I do not remember approving, but I really can't blame them because they are allowed to give "emergency" meds since Mom is a sundowner. Maybe that is why she was so out-of-it during the day. So far I have taken her off the morphine and have seen a huge change in that she is more aware and actually less pain. I have no idea how this works, only that it has. It is time to let Copper Village know we are definitely taking her back to her pretty pink room with her friends and great caregivers! I think she knows something is wrong and she cannot walk. She is still in pain, I think from the collar bone break. She talks to the sky, the air, the blanket, the kitty. Loeke just sits there with her all day.

February 9 Today was unusual. I took her in my studio and she said "Judy, what can I do?" like her mind is here. She will say "I am so sorry, for what I am not sure." She talks to the kitty, but tonight she was exhausted. This could be because no matter what we do she will not take a nap and she talks all day. I am wondering if it's the talking all day that creates some havoc at the cottage. So did they give her meds? Meds I am not told? So, God "Where are you? I think Mom wants to go home. If she isn't thinking it, I am for her!"

February 11 Today was Mom's last day here. When I called two days ago to tell them we were coming back they informed me they had changed her to another cottage. I was furious. Come to find out that is against the contract. You cannot move a patient without the permission of the family. When we arrived at the cottage we were told it was cottage nine. All her furniture had been moved. Her pretty pink bedroom was no more but that was the least of the problem! Cottage nine is for the worst of the worst!!! Mom is not ready for cottage nine. Mom still plays cards, talks, understands, and feeds herself. These people have no idea of how to do any of that. Mom loves sitting in the living room and listening to everyone and eating a cookie, etc. Not in cottage nine. When I arrived one lady was taking off her bra in the middle of the room. It was obvious Mom was not going to have the same level of care, there would be no helping her walk. To me, right now, at the stage she is in, helping her walk is of the utmost importance. I stayed with her while she ate supper. She sat at a bar type, not a table. In cottage four they all sat together at the table and made conversation. There would be none of that. They showed me her room. No pretty pink room. I went home crying. I told John to go and see! He did. He said a man in a diaper followed him to his car! I said "Mom cannot stay there!" I went back. Where was Mom? It was 6:30pm. They said "Well, we put them to bed at 6:30pm." What? Seems they get them up early and they all go to bed at the same time, 6:30pm. I went into Mom's room and found her, she looked at me and said "Judy, what did I do wrong?" I told her she did nothing and to be patient, I would get her out of here!!! When I left I was crying. I ran into the manager and she saw me. She had the nerve to say "What is the matter?" My answer was "How could you do this to Mollie?" When my husband checked, we later found out, they were not allowed to do this without informing us!! But here she was.

February 12 We are going to San Diego for the weekend. I went to see Mom. I was sitting with her next to her chair when two men came in. One slapped her on the knee and said "Hi there." I said "Who are you?" to which they responded that they were the weekend crew. I said "You don't even know her name. Do you know anything about her?" to which they admitted they did not! I knew right then, if two men tried to take Mom's pants off she would have a heart attack!!! Mom never wet her pants, she always knew she had to potty. She would be scared to death. She was not a "cottage nine" resident. They were not even told her name!!! So began two hours of calls. I called everyone, from the manager of the caregivers to the manager of the cottages demanding that a female caregiver be with my Mom this weekend or I would sue them. I had plenty of reasons to do so!!! When it was resolved and they changed some caregivers around there would be a female caregiver. We left but I did not leave until everything was settled with Mom. I am beginning to wonder what happens to these poor people when their families only check on them once a week, once a month.

February 13 I am sick. I cannot eat. I am vomiting. I am crying. I am in total distress. How dare they treat Mom like that. When I did ask why they moved her they told me she was too much trouble now being in a wheelchair for the caregivers in cottage four. Excuse me! Who put Mom in that wheelchair? They had already rented out Mom's room. Can you believe this? With no notice to us. John finally located the owner who lived in Colorado. After speaking with him he said two things. One, he would find out just what happened and two, we could remove Mom with no 30 day notice fee. Are they kidding?

February 14 Valentine's Day! My Dad sent me a Valentine every single year for years. I have one from 1985 and wish he had written the dates on all of them. But this day was good and bad. It was good because we are coming home and getting Mom out of that nightmare! I thought of her every minute. I know exactly what they were doing for her, nothing!!! The fact she even said "Judy, what did I do wrong?" made you realize she knew this was not her old home. You think a dementia patient doesn't realize that? After almost two weeks with Mom I came to realize there was more Mom could remember and do than anyone thought possible. John told them to have the movers have her furniture on the truck and ready to come home on Monday. Monday Mom comes home!!! To begin with she came home without her teeth. I called them and they said they didn't remember her teeth. So I went over and found them in the dresser drawer, nice place to put your dentures at night, for sure they were cleaned, right??? Today was just short of an out-of-body experience. I have absolutely no idea how I was going to care for Mom. Just getting her out of bed was hard. I know my life was going to change but for sure I am not turning back. The best part was Mom was out of there. I am crying now as I write this knowing she is safe in our home!

Tuesday Amazing God! I received a call today from the caregiver assigned to Mom from the state. I guess I forgot all about the fact she is on a state program. The girl informed me that with this program I would receive much help. I would receive 28 hours of caregiving and assigned a state caseworker to answer any questions. She told me I would be receiving a call from the caseworker within two days. Oh, my gosh, you have no idea how happy I am. If that was not enough, today hospice came over. Mom was put on hospice when they said she was dying. Well, now I also will get help from hospice. The first thing they said was "We need to get her out of this double bed and into a hospital bed. It would be much easier to feed her, bath her and transport her to the wheelchair." What? They told me Medicare would give the bed, a tray and a potty. Oh God, you have come to help us after all!!

2017

As I am reading this and writing it all down I still remember those moments. I remember my thoughts of exactly how I felt, that Mom was never going back there and the joy and unbelievable feeling that came with the help I was going to get.

Hope your day
  is like a Valentine
Designed for you alone - -
Colored with happiness,
  laced with love - -
The nicest day you've known.

Happy Valentine's Day!
Happiness Always!

Rudy

210

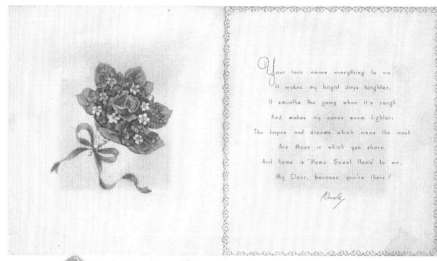

Your love means everything to me,
It makes my bright days brighter,
It smooths the going when it's rough
And makes my cares seem lighter.
The hopes and dreams which mean the most
Are those in which you share,
And home is "Home Sweet Home" to me,
My Dear, because you're there!

Presley

THE *Soul* IS NOT WHERE IT LIVES BUT WHERE IT *Loves*

Chapter 48

Some Days Were Diamonds.....Some Days Were Stones

Some days are diamonds some days are stones.   In
the beginning, I only had twenty eight hours a week of caregiver help. This
amounted to four hours a day. I had to choose which four hours because I
could not get them to schedule two hours in the morning to help get her
up and two hours in the afternoon. I am sure some caregiver companies
will do this, but unfortunately the one I chose would not. They felt it
wasn't worth the time for the caregiver to drive (sometimes 10 miles or
more) to our home for two hours. Hospice of the Southwest was also
covering my Mother and they came three times a week to bathe her. This
was wonderful as it left me with seven days to use the twenty eight hours
and at least three mornings a week I did not have to use any of those
hours to get Mom up and bathed in the morning. So I had a few extra
hours to use in the evening to help put Mom to bed. This would not have
been so bad except it left me with many afternoon hours of no help. My
biggest problem was in transferring Mom from the wheelchair to the
potty. In the first two years Mom could help me a little. She knew how to
hang on to the potty while I picked her up and turned her around. Later,
she could not even do that as she became totally dead weight. She also
refused to wet her pants. Amazing.

Hospice provided all the diapers, solutions, cleaning material,
meds and a nurse that came once a week. Medicare provided the bed,
wheelchair and potty. That was it! If Mom had not been on hospice
through the state insurance, of which we paid over $500 a month for,
they would provide a nurse, but only when needed. They may have
changed now, but then they did not come on a regular basis. The state
would have provided medications, but no supplies. The caregivers were
also not through Medicare. The caregivers were part of the medical
insurance Mom received through the state. I was told if for any reason
Mom went off of the state program, I would lose all the caregivers.
The bottom line is Medicare does not provide caregivers.

The schedule was constantly changing as caregivers changed due to their covering of other patients. Caregivers are somewhat independent in that there is always a need for help and many would change companies with turnover high. Training a new caregiver also took a lot of my time. Just because the caregiver was there didn't mean I could leave the house. I was always extremely visible. When a new caregiver started I wrote down everything for them; Mom's food schedule, her activities, even how to change her after a potty break. Just because they had experience with dementia patients did not hold water for me because each patient is different. I watched them all day. No two are ever alike. They still have their own personalities and level of awareness. On the second day I would be more "hands off" but never left Mom alone with a caregiver. The only exception was unless they were working a steady schedule of at least once a week. Some caregivers found me to be looking over their shoulder too much and expressed a desire to work somewhere else. At times this left me with no caregiver for a couple of days. I told the caregiver company "I really don't care if they do not like how I watch them. It's my Mother, I do not know these ladies at all and they do not know my Mother. So yes, I am going to watch them for a few days."

The first caregiver that came, on that first morning, was a woman named Lois. Lois had cared for her Mom until she passed. Lois was 79 and Mom was 94. Mom took to Lois immediately. I could tell that Lois was a caring person and also very gentle. She spoke very softly to Mom and immediately said to her "Mollie, my name is Lois and I am here to keep you company today." This turned out to be a match made in heaven. Lois became the only caregiver that stayed with my Mother through our journey. That said, when Lois turned 83 and Mom was 98, Lois then became a companion to Mom and would visit. This was not caregiving because she was starting to lose her hearing. We were afraid she would not hear Mom if she needed help. But Lois still came over. While Lois was Mom's caregiver I could always count on her. If we had a doctor appointment and had to leave the house at 9am and the caregiver hours did not start normally until 10:30am when Mom would wake, we could call Lois and she was always available. Always!

Lois really helped me through some difficult times because I had really no idea of Mom's ups and downs or what to expect. Lois was always so patient. It actually calmed me! My Mother always did exactly what she wanted and having dementia was not going to change that. She did not just decide to be a good guest and listen to what I thought was best for her. Oh no, Mom was still in charge! The first day I got her out of bed and took her from the wheelchair to the recliner she had a fit! "I am not going to sit in this chair!" "Oh yes you are," I replied. "Oh no, I am not" she would say as she started scooting down the chair onto the footstool. I would come behind the chair and pick her up and pull her back into the chair. This would go on for three or four times until she realized I wasn't going to give up.

Mom really had no idea she could not walk. She told you she didn't walk, but there were times even she forgot she had said that. Some days it was a constant struggle to keep her in the wheelchair. I began fighting with her and then after the fact realizing "this is my Mother I am yelling at." The first few weeks were very frustrating. Other times my Mother was very understanding and even appreciative of what I was doing for her. She would say "Oh, thank you for that blanket around my shoulders." I had to learn my "new Mother" and her needs and ways of thinking and she had to adjust again to a new home.

Some days were diamonds and some days were stones.

Chapter 49

Caring for Your Loved One

I wanted to write a chapter on this subject because it's very near and dear to me. I wanted to share what I saw, what I learned and to let them know their jobs are very important. Caregivers work for the minimum in some places, actually most places, and their pay goes up by experience. Certified Nursing Assistants (CNA), with CNA's being the highest paid. But for those who are not CNA's don't get caught up in thinking they know more about the little elderly man or lady you are caring for than you. Also, on how you can assist this vulnerable senior citizen or be more attentive or loving. I had a caregiver tell me "You should read a book on dementia." She told me she had taken a class and she felt I did not know enough about how to care for them. Well, let's see what I knew.

I knew my Mom was special. She was different than any other person in the world. We each have our own souls and personalities, our likes and dislikes. There are not two of us alike unless we are identical twins. I knew she liked blueberry muffins and not the banana one, so, I made sure there was blueberry. I did not try to get her to like the other nor did I tell her if she didn't eat that, there was nothing else. I just made sure there was always blueberry. Sometimes we think it's OK to try to have someone eat or sleep on our timeframe. Or as is in most nursing homes, they all get up and go to bed at the same time. I remember about one of the homes Mom stayed in for 5 days. (I was given respite from hospice.) This home was gorgeous. Very expensive. I had to pay the extra $100 since they did not accept the money hospice was allowed. Their routine was still getting everyone up at a specific time and everyone went to bed at the same time. Not Mom! I trusted no one with Mom. So anytime I used respite and Mom went to a home approved by hospice I paid a friend or one of the caregivers that watched Mom to go and be with Mom from the time she woke until 30 minutes after she went to bed.

One specific home I chose since it was suggested by a friend. It was a very nice home and I inspected it first as usual. I remember telling them "Mom does not get up until 10am." They replied that this was fine. No problem. Well, the caregiver, Randa, happened to get there early. She arrived at 9:30am and found Mom up, dressed, in her wheelchair, asleep, with poopy paints. Understand, Mom never wet her pants during the day, even the day she died. Randa was furious and called me. I called the home. They replied "Well, we get them all up at 8am. If you don't like it that is too bad." Yep. Exact words. So of course I called the owner who called back and apologized. I ended up coming home a day early to get her out of there. They were upset saying they did not have her clothes ready. I would have to take her home rather than wait until 6pm for the medical transport. As I was leaving on the day Mom was taken to the home I met a young lady going in. I said "My Mom is only here for 5 days. What loved one of yours is here?" She said "My Aunt and she loves it." I said thanks, went to the car and said a prayer. I was already on alert!! Seems that morning when I was there with Mom this same lady was half asleep at the table and her face was in her cereal. I helped get her head up and called a caregiver. But, the caregiver said "Well, we will clean her up when everyone is done!" When I left her hair and forehead were in the cereal bowl.

What is hard is when the poor elderly don't have the wherewithal to understand what is happening or the communication skills to tell you. This is why the last year Mom was with me I left her once. But, Mom was kept here at home, in her own home. The night caregiver was my wonderful neighbor, Brenda, and the day caregivers were the people she knew and loved her and whom I trusted. Mom was to the point where she could not really remember or communicate to me if there was something that happened that she did not like. As for the caregiver that told me I should read more books on the subject of dementia, I told her I did not beat to the drum of a book, I beat to Mollie's drum. There is no one in any book like Mom. Of course, I had read up on dementia when Mom was first diagnosed. As you read or will read, I even took Mom to the Alzheimer's clinic where they did not just review her, but spent time with me. If Mom didn't want to take a nap, she didn't. Mom never went back to bed. If she was tired she slept in the new recliner we purchased

217

which is suggested for the elderly. It helped us get her up and down. Mom didn't get up until 10 or 10:30am. By the time she was washed and dressed it was 11am. She did not finish breakfast until 12noon. She didn't eat her lunch at the same time each day. Many days she had fruit between meals since it was too late for lunch and we didn't want to spoil her dinner. Again, we beat to Mollie's drum.

I also had a way of getting Mom's attention when she was screaming. Mom never wet her pants. She would tell us "I have to go tinkle." When it was time to transfer her from the wheelchair to the potty she did not understand and would hang on to the wheelchair for dear life, yelling "I need to go tinkle." It was hard to get her attention so that we could explain what we were doing. Mom had no teeth to speak of. She had upper false teeth which no longer fit her mouth and we had the dentist readjust them twice. So Mom would take them out. A trick I learned to get her attention was that I would put my finger across her mouth, not inside as she would try to bite me. She would then look at me and I would be able to talk to her. This worked perfectly! In a minute, she could understand me. But a couple caregivers thought that was harsh. Guess it wasn't in the book, and it was my finger, not hers!

In the six years I was blessed to have the most wonderful caregivers. Lois, Randa, Brenda and Kathy were with me the whole 5 plus years. These were just a few of them. Randa was with me for 4 years. There was only one caregiver company that we had problems with. When a caregiver came for the first time, I did not leave the house. In fact I had written down everything but I was still there. This one caregiver company sent me three different girls in a three day succession which was hard because I had to spend the whole day training them. Any doctor appointments or whatever I had needed had to be cancelled. When I finally called them they said "The caregiver doesn't want to come back because you watch over them all day." I said "Yes, I do. I do not know them. I am not leaving Mom with someone I don't know." If they would have stayed the second or third day they would have seen me gradually release my attention to how they handled Mom.

Caregivers don't realize how important they are. I think it is because they don't get paid a lot. Medicare doesn't pay the caregiving companies much, but I know they could pay the staff more. You, the caregiver, are very important! Without you, many of us who are trying to keep our loved ones at home, would die on the vine!! Keeping a loved one at home takes a village. It takes a good caregiver to fill in those hours. It takes someone with compassion for the elderly and a wanting to see their long hours of sitting in a wheelchair, or being at home all day, make them feel useful. I learned with Mom, who never sat down and loved being in the kitchen, that she never lost her feeling of needing to feel useful. It was Brenda, the caregiver that got Mom interested writing notes. Mom could barely see but she would put a big pen in her hand, get some paper and say "Write a love letter to Rudy." I still have many of those papers. Mom never once said "I can't see." She just wrote!!! When I visited a few nursing homes and even assisted living, I would find some of the dementia patients sitting in what I called "sitting rooms." They had windows, but for how long can you sit and look out the window? What these people need is communication and interaction. If you are working in the kitchen, bring them in. Put them near the table if you don't want them near a stove but put them where you can talk to them. If you're putting other elderly patients to bed, take the person with you (if they are wheelchair bound) and let them hear you talking and helping the others get ready for bed. Even if they don't understand what is going on, they hear talking. They don't feel alone. I don't feel any elderly person in a wheelchair needs to be left alone for any long period of time. As long as they are in hearing distance they don't need to know what you're saying. You don't need to personally converse with them. Yet I would find these people, in very nice homes, sitting alone. They were obviously moved there for the afternoon because, like Mom, they did not watch TV, were not able to play bingo, etc., so they were put in a nice sitting room. Wrong. You could always put them out by the nursing desk.

When Mom was in hospice for 5 days while I went away, they actually moved her over to the nurse's desk. The nurse went about their business but you could tell Mom thought they were talking to her because she talked back. But then Mom talked all the time to those who were there and those who were not! Linda, Susan, Brenda, Lois, Randa, Kathy and Wardine. I want to take this opportunity to thank you, not just from me, but from Mollie, who I know you loved very much. These are just some of the caregivers who not only cared for Mom, but loved her. They treated Mom like she was their Mom. If you do not have the distinction of being a CNA don't sell yourself short. Understand your position is very important. You are the comforter, the friend, the companion at cards and games, the helper with bingo, the person who gave her that great blueberry muffin, her favorite. You are someone who cares and gives! That's why you're called caregivers!!!! Give your name the recognition it deserves. I thank all caregivers everywhere!

Chapter 50

Mom Is Beautiful

March 23 Today Terry Kolence and his wife Karen stopped to visit Mom. It was early so she was still in bed. I am not sure if she remembered them but it was so nice of them to stop while they were visiting friends in Arizona. Of course they still live in Ohio, everyone does! I am the only member of our family that decided they were too old for snow! Today Mom called my name twenty times, over and over. She doesn't settle down so the whole house is in confusion, but I took some videos the last few days and she sure looks great!! I have her playing cards and singing. Lucky for my iPhone.

March 26 What a morning. She started at 7am. Very unusual for her to be awake but she slept all night, no sundowner last night. "Where am I, anybody there, where is my family, Judy it doesn't look like you, help me Judy I need help to get out of here," and on and on. By 8am I quit running in and out of her bedroom. I helped her eat toast and scrambled eggs in bed because the caregiver doesn't come until 10am to get her bathed and dressed. But some of what she says is so funny like "Judy, this cat is sitting on me so I can't get up." She was referring to Loeke, her cat, is sitting on her bed, which Loeke does every day!! If that was not enough Veronica the caregiver decided to try to give her a shower. I wore my bathing suit! She was screaming before even getting in. "They are throwing me down the steps," she says. There are no steps in this house!! We washed her hair and when it was over she looked so nice. They also decided to weigh her. She is down six pounds! I doubt we will shower her much as it's just too traumatic for her. I know I would not like it so why do it to her!

March 29 Mom up, changed, and now eating toast as I write this. I am looking at the picture on the desk of her and her Dad. Mom was beautiful. Mom is beautiful. She is 18 in the picture. She just said "Judy, I just woke up and I am having a nice time." She asks me why I don't become a nurse since I am so good. I guess she has forgotten all the noise she made while we put clean pants on her earlier. The phone just rang to have me substitute teach. Substitute teaching is now out of the question so I need to change that on my school form. I wonder some days where I get my energy and then I say "Thank you, God."

March 30 From 2pm to 5pm Mom never stopped talking. It gives me feelings of helplessness. She was determined she needed a potty. So I put her on and then she says "Why am I here?" She wears herself to a frazzle. I might see about something to calm her but I don't want her to go to sleep or be drugged. I need to find the right medication. I don't care for all the ones they suggest. I have looked them up and maybe if she were a man and was walking and I could not handle her I would need something. But she is little and in a wheelchair. Believe it or not, I am in command! Hahahahahaha!!! I have to remind myself of that!!

March 31 Mom says "I think I would like to go away on a nice trip with Dad!" I took some great movies the last couple weeks and she talks and even knows my name. She asked "Who do you watch this for?" and I say "This is my house." She told me today she watched these two birds all day. That could be when I sat her out on the back porch. The tree is full of birds, but I am surprised she remembered that, if in fact she saw them.

April 4 Easter Sunday Funny, last year I wrote that would be her last Easter, and here she is talking and she says "I am going to eat all these treats and food and I will get tall!" I was thinking today of all my childhood Easter Sundays. We got our good shoes that we would wear all year, our dress that became our Sunday dress all year, Mom's potica which the whole city bought from her. What would Easter be like without potica and ham? My cousin Nancy surprised us and had some mailed to us!!! I have no idea how my family could afford Easter with food, new clothes and church. Thank you God for those days.

April 5 Meanwhile, I need to change the routine. Neither John nor I are getting a break. Mom won't let us get her out of the wheelchair. She hangs on yet she wants out. She is afraid of falling and while this is going on the phone rings. This place is a three ring circus. But the solution would be to give her some medications. I will check with hospice as I trust them. They already know I took her off all the junk they were giving her before she came here. Now she is alert and talking so I am going to be very careful. She is what she is, it is what it is. The circle always meets. I would not want to be medicated all day. Yes, she has these moments, but I took some great videos yesterday. She is so sweet. So in her world. She has a lot of life in that brain. It just takes some patience. If I did not have it I would miss some wonderful moments with her.

Chapter 51

Flapjack Arrives

April 7 I sent Todd a birthday card last week. His birthday was the 21st. Such a cutie. For short we call him "Toddy Mike." Walked to store for ice cream and bananas for Mom. Read Danny's new book *Top Ten Hazards Affecting Your Health.* She had so many questions today. "Why do I not feel like getting up?" "Why can't I iron and help you?" Last week she told me to "Quit ironing and get us some wine!" Yesterday sitting outside she says "Judy, I think I'll go home and see ma and pa." My stomach turned. Why? We know it's near. We want her to be out of this wheelchair, so why would my body say "Oh no." It just did. I know I will never be ready so why try to prepare? But all my life with her was tumultuous, controlling, depressing at times and with her insecurity I never held her up for judgement. She is and always will be, my Mother!

April 8 Mom is eating toast as I am writing in my journal and she says "Judy, I just woke up and am having such a nice day." So glad I am sitting here writing. I am sure I would forget all these cute things she says. I think I will get a book, and keep it in her room and the kitchen, and tell the caregivers to write down anything funny she says. Well, I am taking care of Mom and the angels are taking care of me!

April 9 Beautiful day. Mom again asks whose home this is. I answered that this is my home! Mom says "It's nice to know." So observant considering they told me she was giving up!!! I have begun to create journals for the Phoenix Children's Hospital. I can't write how excited I was when I finished the first, it was really pretty. Can't wait to make another.

April 10 Mom won't let us get her out of the wheelchair. She hangs on, yet wants out. Go figure! She is afraid of falling so she hangs on. And, if that was not crazy, I talked to Jan today about finding a dog for John. He comes home around 5:30pm when Mom is really wound up and it's noisy here! But I need a trained dog. For sure I am not training a dog, so I need to look at the Colorado Women's Correctional where Jan says they have cute dogs and they come with 8 weeks of training. Now that's just what I need, although at this moment I might think about it!!

April 12 Mom is sleeping more and more. Really wants to die. Rightly so. Nathaniel, my grandson, says "I said a prayer for nana to go to God. She can't do anything anymore!" My three grandsons are young. The youngest, Brandon, hesitates when he goes up to my Mother in the wheelchair. Mom says "Give me a kiss," and he just freezes up. So I said "Brandon, someday nana is going to heaven and God will ask her if you were nice to her." So he slowly moved towards her and leaned over, trying not to touch her, and planted a kiss on her cheek and ran! Oh well, one step at a time. *As I am remembering this now in 2017 I recall a friend who wanted to bring her Mother home, but was worried her little grandchildren would not visit. Sometimes little children can be very afraid of the elderly, especially in a wheelchair and not even making sense when they talk. I never gave this a thought with my Mother because I knew I was bringing her home. I knew as they got used to seeing her here they would probably laugh more than be afraid at some of the crazy things she would say. No, she was coming here. Period.*

April 15 Long day today but watching Mom play with her stuffed bunny made it all worthwhile. But, believe me, her independence and stubbornness is still there! Refusing to listen when I say "You have potty pants on" (she has asked me over and over what these pants are), or "No, you can't walk to the store." Today, as she searched in her purse, the one item she never lets go of, she announced "I cannot find the keys to my car." She is a worry wart! I have begun writing down most of her questions because they for sure don't make sense. Reading from my list (and she talked all day) "What are you doing?" "When do we leave?" "Where is everyone?" To which I reply 10 times "Mom, it is just you and me today!"

April 18 Thinking I don't like this med the nurse suggested, Depakote.   Can't read my own writing.   Anyway, I am going to change it. We just started it as a calming during the day and it might be good for some, but I don't like it for Mom. I have watched her every day so I can tell if I don't like what I see or hear! I have left a prayer for my angel because they always come up with the right idea but I am leaning to something natural. And, it would not hurt me to learn more patience. But still, Mom's comments just make my day. Today she says "Judy, you need to get a toilet in this house." Like where has she been sitting for the past four months? But no singing. I notice a difference. Not sure I like it.

April 23   Mom was always so possessive. She always wanted to see me, whatever, whenever. So this has not changed. "Judy, I need you." "Judy, I want to go home." "Judy, can I go outside?" "No Judy, I want to come inside." (she is inside) Today I moved her recliner outside on the porch because the weather is beautiful. Then I hear "fire, fire." I run outside. It's actually the sun shining off the wall. So I call my neighbors to tell them not to worry! They are the best. I could not have introduced Mom to a better neighborhood. They just love her.

April 25   John and I got out! We celebrated my friend Cheryl and husband Jay's anniversary with some other friends, Wanda and Chuck. Cheryl is a gourmet cook, so any time you get invited to go, you go!!! My Mother was a gourmet cook, remember, and there are many times I am not sure I am her daughter. I can't cook and I am a very picky eater. Did I say picky???

April 29   Today is Mom and Dad's anniversary. I put all her pictures out. She was so pretty. He was so handsome. She knew exactly what the picture was, and even said "I never liked my dress, but I was so happy to be married to Dad." Took Mom off those meds. I can see why nurses and doctors are always prescribing meds for dementia patients because they can't have 30 patients talking all day. I have the luxury of seeing my Mother as she is and gently answering all her questions. I get her to sing and forget whatever she was thinking.

April 30   Wow. Did we expect change? We got it! Mom up at 12:30am, still awake at 5am in a state of??? Barely knew me, talking to herself and others, flapping hands, reaching into the air and shouting "We can't get out of here" meaning the bed. Eyes blood shot from no sleep, just no sleep. *This is a long writing, but I wrote 2 pages as so much happened.*

I called the nurse. "I know it's not because she is on a med, I know there is something wrong. I have watched her too much to not realize that. So Mom was exhausted. I left her at 5am and tried to get some sleep but ended up taking a shower. I felt like a drunken sailor. Mom would close her eyes for a short time, then wide open. The hospice nurse came over and said "Some die this way. They literally stay up for four days in the state of anxiety until they go to sleep and fade away." I started to cry and told her "Well Mom sure didn't give me much notice!" I thought she will make it to May, the month of our blessed Mother and I will have some solace in the fact she passed in the most beautiful month of the year. The nurse said she could have a urinary tract infection. I looked this up and it matches Mom's behavior. I cleaned the potty and got a sample of urine for the nurse.

May 1   Mom is still here. She is still not sleeping well, but she is quieter. I gave her toast and juice then put her on the potty at 9am. She was very confused and kept talking. She was dry when I put her on the potty and I thought something was wrong! I understand with urinary infections they can hallucinate. So I put clean clothes on her and she slept for two hours. I called and hospice said yes she did have an infection and they ordered some antibiotics. She had settled down somewhat since we took her off Depakote. We still need one med that she has to take if she goes to a home if we leave for a couple days. I have decided none of these "dementia drugs." I need to look into a calming drug for now in a very low dosage so it is just enough to take the edge off for her! Thank you, God!!!

May 10   We are into May and I don't think Mom is going anywhere!   They gave her some antibiotics for a urinary infection, which does cause tons of anxiety. Now she is back to her pestering and controlling people. She displays more hours of the day being so nice and understanding. I feel so much compassion for her. No life for Mom, no dignity, no real home and no husband. Some of this she knows, some she doesn't. Still asking when Dad is coming to visit.

May 11   She made it! Mother's Day!   She was so alert, so awake, so much talking that you never would have guessed. I told her it was Mother's day and she says "Thank you for telling me," and she repeated that about ten times!! So our new dog Flapjack is coming! Yes, I picked him out and went to check him out. He can come home on the 20th when he finishes his 8 weeks training. He is 8 months old and is a corgi/aussie/shepherd mix. My son Danny brought a food and water dish and a treat can! You would think we were having a baby shower! Johnny and Geri gave me a locket with a picture of Flapjack in it. So exciting, a new member of the family coming! John is still saying "Tell me again why we need a dog."   He is so not into this, but Jan and I know when he meets him he will love him! Oh, and I had to announce to him that we must fly to Denver, but rent a car to come home because they don't allow the dogs to be put on a plane! I would not say this was the best behavior in my marriage of 48 years!

May 20   Well, we got Flapjack and oh, my gosh, John is in love!!!! This little guy is adorable. We drove as far as Albuquerque and stayed with my son Danny and then we drove home! Flapjack is much trained. He does not go into a crate (that's our rule) but he also will not get on the furniture. He slept at the bottom of the bed on a doggie bed from Jan! He is so quiet. He doesn't bark. Not sure why. Not a sound. He also is trained to go potty in the same place. All we do is say "get busy." That is the magic word and he will go to the same place.

May 22   We got him home late last night. So today we went to the hairdresser and took Mom, wheelchair and Flapjack. What happened is too sad to write. Getting back into the SUV, the wheelchair fell out and scared Flapjack who took off. It's now 10pm. John has been crying. We didn't even have him 2 days! We searched, called our kids to search, my hairdresser searched and we could not find him. When I am done here I will put a notice on Craig's list and hope someone picked him up,

May 23   John got up at 5am. I stayed behind to make flyers. On Craig's list I put John's cell phone number. John went canvassing and at 10am he got a call from a woman who said "I have your dog." John was crying so hard he could not even talk to me. Seems her son saw him running down the middle of a busy street, with his leash on, and knew he was someone's dog. He followed him and when Flapjack went down the side street and dipped into the grass, he stopped and picked him up. She said "He is fine. His paws are burned since he was running in the hot pavement and it was 110 degrees." We picked him up and took him to Cheryl since she knows how to care for dogs. She wrapped his paws, and will go to the vet tomorrow. Did we need all this excitement? Oh, God is so good! I also thanked my angels. I would not want to be on this earth without my angels. Going to bed!!!!

Chapter 52

Father's Day

June 1 I would not call my time with Mother at my home stressful. Rather I would say I am on a constant watch. Watch to see if she is comfortable sleeping. Watch to see if she is up too long as a sundowner. Watch to ensure she eats a good breakfast since she sleeps so late and misses lunch. Watch to see if she is scooting to get out of the recliner. Watch how much she drinks, we don't want any more unitary track problems. Watch for new tears on her arms or legs. So it is watch, watch, watch. My motto is "not on my watch" meaning just about everything will not happen!

John and I are going away for 3 days. I have delivered one of my hand made boxes to Travis Murphy's wife. I do this anonymously for police and firemen killed in the line of duty. I know for one of the boxes for a fireman I used a small firetruck for the knob on the top. Creating these boxes has also been a great diversion for me. Mom comes into the studio with me and this is now something we can do together. I probably will write when I get back. Wish me luck.

June 5 I did not make any contact with Mom while I was gone. How did I do that? Well, I knew there was nothing I could do about anything. If I knew she was unhappy it would negate our whole weekend, which I terribly needed. I did not realize, until she was not with me, how much it takes mentally and physically from the moment she awakes. If you asked me if I would change my mind I would say "Not on your life." Remember all the times she watched me? Somehow I feel this is a journey for both of us and I am determined to see it through. Also, I have decided not to trust anyone so I paid the caregiver to be there when she woke up, making sure she eats OK and gets put to bed the way I like it. They told me she was confused from the time she woke up the next morning. I decided to go with the van taking her to the home because I did not want her to go to bed without seeing me. I promised myself I will always do this!! I left instructions but they decided to do things "their way" so this place is off the list for next time. Tonight she went from angry to as sweet as a baby. At 8pm I gave her teddy. Mom burped and then continued to pretend the teddy was burping!

June 8   Mom has been here less than six months so I need to reset where I am. I know where she is! Time to examine my life since I am so busy I have no idea where exactly I am going. Bill Austin passed. He was on *Beth and Bill* on 99.9 radio and I never got to meet him. I really enjoyed him on the radio. For some reason I feel very bad yet I have this feeling his spirit is so happy. The issue here is I am so busy I am forgetting to do something I need to do for me! Certainly I have some caregivers, my husband would never tell me what not to do, so it's all my choice. I have just been so wrapped up in the beginning of caring for Mom that I have to be sure I don't lose sight of my own life. Time for some changes. I will pray. I am guessing John is also praying to God asking him to give me this great idea of getting rid of a lot of my junk!!!! Oh, isn't life interesting.

June 9   I took Mom to the eye doctor today. She has an eye infection. She had 2 corneal transplants years ago and it's a hereditary disease that I also have.   By 6pm she was in full form controlling and anxious. "I am not going to sit in this chair" and then I said "Yes you are." This is my Mother I am talking to, so please forgive me God! I have decided to start her on a regular time schedule for a pill rather than wait until she is out of control. It's amazing that she knows it. She will tell me what she wants and then says "Judy, I am sorry. Please give me a kiss?"   Mom is on this kiss kick, which is all she wants. If we want her to do something we say "If you don't, you don't get a kiss." Works every time. But she does not have severe anger like in Alzheimer's, she just gets so confused. I have decided to just try Tylenol for now. I like this better than the dementia drugs because none of them fit every person. Maybe as time goes on I might have to think of something, but now, this takes the edge off and she is so sweet. Today is also Flapjack's birthday. I watched John play with him this morning. Pure love. And this is the "Why do we need a dog?" duo!!

June 12   Mom was so good this morning. She changes as the day goes on but is it really dementia or is it just old age with her memory and brain just getting old? For sure she is doing more than she did before she came here so she has not gotten worse in 6 months. Today I introduced Mom to emptying the silverware. She continues to ask if she can do something so I am finding things for her to do. I take the insert from the silverware drawer, the dishwasher silverware compartment, put them on the table, put her wheelchair up to the table and ask her to put the silverware away. It's amazing how she can do it and best of all she loves it!!! "Can I do more?" she asks!

June 15   Bad day today. She was great in the am and then around 2:00pm the anxiety strikes. I agreed to give her a new med today, a small amount of Valium. But I want to be very careful.   A caregiver is not allowed to give any meds so I don't need to worry this will happen if I am at the store or elsewhere. Valium is not as harsh as Xanax which is what I know they were giving her at that behavior hospital, the one I have nightmares from. So, no Xanax. Now she is getting so much stimulation from the caregivers. They play solitaire every afternoon. Mom grew up on this game and loves it. Can you believe she still knows a lot about how to play it? She has forgotten somethings but she knows how important the ace is!!! I am amazed lately how much she is doing since I got her started doing small jobs. I have to write this because I will forget. Mom was outside in her chair and she says "Judy, look at these people in the back yard. They are taking our stuff. Shoot um. Shoot um. Why are they all eating here?" She was totally confused. Usually in the evening John takes over. He brings her wheelchair to him in the family room and asks her name, children's names, her birthday etc., just to have a conversation with her. She names them all. But tonight she was confused and didn't want to answer. We have decided when she gets tired, like most of us, she doesn't focus very well. Mom can't say "I am tired." She doesn't recognize that is the problem, but we can. So now we notice it starts around 6:30pm so we are going to move up her bedtime to 7:30pm.

June 16   She was up and down all night to go potty. I get her up because she doesn't understand she has special pants on. At 11:00pm I went to bed and she was still up. I woke up at 5am and found her with no pants! Bed wet through all layers, blankets wet. She was rolled in a ball sleeping, freezing. I wonder how long it had been so I covered her. I did not want to wake her but I tore everything off. She was half asleep and didn't move or acknowledge me. I stripped the bed while she was in it and put clean clothes on her. She was like dressing a rag doll. I even turned her over and washed her bottom with warm water and soap, put on clean pants, a warm blanket and I went back to bed. Some of her being up nights is still the sundowner syndrome, so I am going to focus on this rather than a day med. She needs a med because when we go to San Diego at the end of the month the home demands you give them something for anxiety even though it's only "as needed." So I want to try it first at home. Oh, and Flapjack got his first bath!

June 18 Put Mom on a med, Trazadone, a very small dosage, last night. She slept plus she was not exhausted so early in the day today. I would rather do a night med than a day med. I have purchased this "small portable bike" and I now have her peddling and singing during the day! She still does the silverware and I take any plates or cups from the dishwasher that are still damp, put them on her little table and she dries them. Each day she does better rather than get worse. She still demands she wants to walk, but no anxiety. I think it is because she was sleeping all night. See, that's prayer for you!

Sunday Father's Day I decided tonight to write a tribute to Dad. Happy Father's day Dad! I love you! You chose to come here as a Father, and now you are reflecting on that as you have done many times. This time there is so much happiness and forgiveness. You did everything you should have. You were the best. You have a heart of gold, a soul soft with love and strong with hope and charity. I am so proud of you Dad. Love, Judy.

June 24 No one has yet to figure out the best method for Mom to sleep at night and be up during the day (she refuses naps) yet doesn't have melt downs around 5:30pm like she used to.

June 25 Well, we tried the Trazadone at night but it doesn't matter since different drugs affect people differently. (Just let this show me later that I didn't just settle.) Today she was calm. She helped in the kitchen. She put the chicken on the sticks for the grill and she was in the kitchen with us all evening. Then 6:30pm bang! She wanted to go upstairs. We don't have an upstairs so I took her to the studio to distract her and for about 30 minutes she was fine. Then out of the blue she says

"Why are you so mean to me?" Seroquel is her depression medicine given to her after she went to counseling so this is not the culprit. The nurse says by 6:30pm, as we have noticed, she gets tired. Remember, she is being stimulated all day!!! They go from cards to writing and she does not nap. In 2007 she was diagnosed with "just dementia" but obviously it has gotten worse. The nurse says to give it a couple more days. Remember, we are trying to get her past the sundowner and to sleep at night.

June 27   I was stunned. I went into Mom's room at 5am. Pillows piled on the wheelchair that was moved from the side of the bed to the bottom of the bed. The green afghan is on the chair next to her bed with the rest of her bedding on the floor. I had put the bedding there in case she got out of bed and fell. It was surreal. I will never know how she did all that!! But Mom is very strong!

June 28   I just never know what I will find. I have a baby monitor in my bedroom, and I heard her at 1am. I went in and told her she had to go to sleep to which she replied "Why?" Her standard answer. Now at 6am I go in and it's a mess! Her pants were off, she is all wet, and she is sitting on the side of the bed with her legs between the bars! I cleaned her up, dry clothes, warm blanket and she slept for 2 hours. *The first year was all about finding the right meds. I have always said you can tell the difference between drugged and just being tired. The goal is to get sleep at night and then calm any anxieties that arise around 4pm. But Mom is a sundowner so you have an extra problem. At this point, and as you read further, I feel I have not found the right medication for Mom and I am not settling for just anything.*

July 1   We left for San Diego for 4th of July. The home Mom is at is supposed to be really nice. I always visit a day before and stay with her for dinner the night before we leave. This time I also have Randa going over all morning and Lois coming at 4pm tonight. Taking no chances. I want to feel relaxed this time.

July 2   I am relaxing and realizing I need to get myself organized. Mom's quiet time is the best time plus the 3 hours the caregiver is there during the day. I wonder how I will find her when we return, but so far one day and no bad reports from Randa.

234

July 3 As I continue to review my life with Mom, I realize only I can work this out. Mom is not going to change. Randa says the people in the home don't like her there, but too bad! Randa is not a shrinking violet and loves Mom. She will ensure Mom's needs are met. The only time she is not there is from noon to three, the time Mom should be in a recliner resting, even though she still will not nap.

July 7 Arrived home. Randa told me they had no mat on the floor by her bed and no bedside potty which they had promised! She said they also demanded Mom keep to their schedule. Another promise not kept. Randa refused to allow them to wake her up at 8am! Randa was supposed to come at 10am, since we thought that was when Mom would wake up, but when Randa found her the first day, she then came every day at 8am to ensure they did not wake her up! When the medical van showed up with Mom the first thing I noticed was one of her front teeth (she has upper false teeth) was missing! I called them. They said "She had it when she left here." So are we saying she lost it on the ride home? There is no place we can trust people! I called hospice and told them to take that home off the list!

July 14 Got Mom up today. Brushed her hair and fixed her cereal. Then she fell asleep in her recliner so I am guessing she did not go back to sleep at 2am when I went in to tell her to be quiet to which she replied "Why?" Someday I will miss her "Why?" response!!! She was so sweet all day. Randa put some cream on her back and rubbed her legs. She looked at me and said "You're so beautiful." She is so sweet. Mom has 2 sides to her spirit and her ego. Too bad her ego rules most of her life, but when she is sweet, she is very sweet. I think there is a saying to that!!

July 19 Mom awoke today very confused. "I have to get dressed for the party, Judy. Put out the sausage. When are we leaving?" She says this with a lot of determination. So sure of herself. That's OK, she has dementia. It's expected. It bothers me only a little because she doesn't understand. I feel sorry for her, and no, there is no party! But, wow, do we keep her busy. She now plays "war" with her cards and caregiver. If you have not played, it is easy. The highest card takes the others card!

July 27 My sundowner Mom was up again, this time one half of her clothes off. She must do this very quietly because the monitor is right by my bed. I put her on the potty, put on clean pj's and back to bed. She always tells me she is sorry. She seems to know when I come in that she had done something she should not. I give her "puppy," her small little stuffed dog from hospice, which she cradles in her arms and goes back to sleep. These times I find to be beautiful. I love taking care of her and it shows me she doesn't mean to do what happens. I figure in a nursing home she would be drugged, sleep through all this and maybe, just maybe, be awake during the day. But I see too many still drugged! Later we might discuss increasing the Trazadone which now is a very low dosage. But we have found a medicine that does not find her drugged in the morning.

July 30 I finished two boxes and am finding I can create some art with Mom here. I have scheduled my life to do some when she is sleeping, but more when she is awake because she really likes coming into the studio. She winds ribbon and just looks at all the pretty embellishments. She is still confused when she wakes up but not angry and not demanding. I do not see her getting weaker. Could she live to 100? Probably, but only God knows. We are now giving her very low doses of Trazadone at bedtime. Very low. They say some patients take 600 milligrams, Mom is getting 20!!! I give it to her at 1 or 2am when her sundowner wakes her up. So far so good. *We ended up with Trazadone the rest of her life at night time. Still a very low dosage. It's August. Mom's birthday is August 28th. My brother is coming for her birthday and I am so excited. They have never visited her here. Mom will see Kenny for the first time in almost 10 years. Her cute little blond boy!*

Chapter 53

Oh, You Are My Kenny!

Mom will be 95 and Kenny and his wife, Carolyn are coming to visit! I am so excited. They arrive tomorrow. I have no idea how Mom will react. I hope she is quiet but we never know. Got Mom up and she says "I am ready to go." She says "Go get my books and my sled." Then she says "Oh, I don't know what I want." "How much older than me are you?" she asks. I explained I am her daughter. I tell her that her birthday is coming and I ask her how old she is to which she replies "14, or am I 16?" I say "You are 94 and we are having a party Saturday." She says "Oh, ok, I will be there." She says "I hope my viral clears up so I can enjoy all this." I have no idea what viral means. I think it's just words that seem to come out of her mouth lately.

August 26 All went well. Mom did not know Kenny at first, and Ken was shocked to see how frail and confused she looked. It was a big change from when he saw her 5 years ago when I took her to Cleveland for her 90th birthday. One minute she knew him and 5 minutes later she did not. Ken came very quietly up behind her and said "Hello Mom." The dialogue they had went like this: **Mom** "What is your name?" **Kenny** "Mom, I am Kenny, your son." **Mom** "You don't look like my son Kenny." **Kenny** "Well, did your Kenny like chocolate?" **Mom** "Yes, he did." **Kenny** "Well, so do I." Kenny then asks another question to which Mom responds "Oh, so does my Kenny." Kenny then commented to her about 6 things he liked and she agreed "So does my Kenny." Then that Kodak Moment, which we have a picture of when she looks right at him and says "You are my Kenny! Wonderful moment in time! God is good!

Ken and Carolyn stayed two days and tried to spend as much time with Mom. It was over 100 degrees and I still think how wonderful that they didn't seem to care about the weather. Kenny just wanted to be with his Mom on her birthday!! What is interesting is Mom would many times say "Judy, we have not seen Kenny in a long time." She would say the same about my son Todd. I have no idea how those two names would come up out of the blue but she was right as she had not seen either in a long time. There were many people from her past she had not seen in a while but it was Kenny and Todd whose names she would ask about. Well, thank you Mom for reaching 95. It brought family together. We had great memories. Ken and Carolyn went to our church for mass, a church Mom also went to many times with me. Johnny stood on the kitchen counter to get a good picture of Mom blowing out the candles on her cake. So funny, Mom remembering everything about Kenny. She remembered his eyes, favorite cake, even birthday, and then said to him "You're a nice man but you're not my Kenny!" We laughed. But in the end, Kenny received a beautiful gift which he was hoping for when she acknowledged "You are my Kenny." God is good!!

September 11 Nine eleven! Where was I when it happened? We lived on Viewpoint. The TV was on the wall in the eating area and I heard about the plane crash. They had TV monitors showing the tower and then, before I could even grasp it, there was another plane. You thought you were seeing things, how could this be. I called my son Todd and asked where he was because he was away traveling. He said "I am on the way to the Florida airport, traveling." I said "Don't go. The airport will be shut down and everyone will be trying to get a rental car. Go right to the rental agency and get out of town."

September 20 Mom's confusion isn't going to change. I don't want her drugged. When she seems confused the caregivers talk to her. They're wonderful. Mom has a lot of one-on-one stimulation so we can usually get her back on track. This morning she thinks she is in a hospital and says "Judy, how long do I have to stay?" (Notice she says my name.) I told her, "Mom, this is my home and you stay with me." This lasts all of two minutes. You need to have patience as she says "I want to go home" ten times an hour. Mom loves to eat but she notices little things such as "You dropped something." The kitchen is by the large back window so she can see everyone and the caregiver sits right across from her. Now we get out the dominoes and the tic tac toe. Believe this, Mom can beat you! Yes she can! It's amazing. You think she won't see that last move you make, but she does, and she wins!! I am so proud of her. She continues to do anything you ask and the more we talk to her and find things for her to do, the calmer she is all day. I am beginning to think most of her anxiety was a lack of feeling useful or the need to do something. Remember, my Mother never sat! Never! If she found us kids sitting she would say "I can find something for you to do." To this day, I cannot sit. Even watching TV I have to have something in my hands. I am good for one hour, maybe, if it's a mystery or interesting, otherwise I am up and about.

October 3   Meanwhile, Mom slept her life away for almost 3 days. Then Saturday, Sunday and Monday she was up as early as 5am. Yesterday she stayed up all day. Now at 8:45am she has fallen asleep and we will need to wake her up at 9:3am when hospice comes to give her a bath. It's been hard for her because we have had so many changes in hospice caregivers lately. They come three times a week to bath her. She gets bathed in bed. She hates showers and is too heavy to put into a bathtub. They do these baths so beautifully, they wash everything, even between her toes. They are the ones who, if there are any blisters, will find them. So far Mom has never had a blister on her butt from sitting! She is so funny. She wakes up and I go in there to tell her to go back to sleep and she greets me wide awake, smiling. "Oh hi, Judy. What have you been doing all day?" I say "Mom, it is 5am," to which she replies "Do we have enough potatoes for dinner?" Oh how I will miss her funny responses. I was thinking, as I write this, I never would have seen this side of my Mother. Always so in control, now says things that don't make sense and is so needy! I love you Mom. Lately when I go in in the morning, I find her exactly as we put her to bed. Blankets are on her with puppy next to her. She doesn't seem to move around in bed anymore.

Chapter 54

Oh to God We Give Thee Glory

December 24   Well, our tradition continues as it did at home in Ohio. The kids came over around 8pm. We rented the trolley and took friends and neighbors and their children to see the lights. What they didn't know is we had planted Santa along the route, so when the trolley went past they all screamed "There is Santa." So guess what? Santa boarded the trolley as we had planned. We had gathered some gifts for each child and they were in Santa's sack with their name on it. I remember my grandson Nathaniel was so excited he could hardly talk! It was one of our favorite Christmas's. Mom surprised us all by still being up at midnight! Amazing!!! I wondered if she just knew this is what we did, and she was just following her mind and heart at what was a tradition for over 40 years! Truly, it was a miracle. You had to be there as each person opened a gift and she was so excited for them! Nana was there 100 percent for the family and it was midnight! God is good.

As I write this in 2017 I think back to January 2011 as it was something special for me. I was remembering the day one year ago that I brought Mom home. I looked back on all that had transpired and how far John and I had come with this new journey. I remember reflecting today like it was yesterday. I didn't read my journal. In fact, I never read my journal until I began to write this book. I was surprised at how many times I wondered what the heck we were doing and if we even knew what we were doing. The shock at seeing Mom trying to get out of bed and her funny requests, but most of all my concern to find the right medicine. I don't think I ever want to go through that again. She did get worse and there were some changes but by now I was more confident in my decisions. I think the first 6 months was like having a new baby in the house and being a mother for the first time. You want to do the right thing but the baby has a mind of their own!!! You also know bringing this new addition to your home is a blessing, a journey given to you by God and only unconditional love will ultimately help you make it through. And that I had. I loved my Mother regardless of what she ever did or said. I know she felt the same way about me. After all those screams, not knowing where she was, all her stubbornness, and also all her sweet demeanor just when we needed it, I also knew she was never ever leaving this house. My prayer on Christmas day that year was "God, all I want is for you to allow her to go home while sleeping in her own bed, in my house. Don't ever let anything happen that I will not be here and she will be alone. Amen."

Chapter 55

The Long and Winding Road

2011-2014 Over the next two years we took each day as it came, one day at a time. Mom actually started to calm down even though we did not add any meds. She just had her bedtime med. Or maybe it was because she was now going on 96! I really thought when I brought her home that I would be able to find a nice place near me. On the other street there is a "cottage" type assisted living which they keep very quiet, but I know it's there. I felt as John and I took some time off, I could check out different facilities and for sure find the right one. This idea didn't work at all. I remember one of the places hospice suggested was not far, and it was beautiful. The caregivers were great. I had to pay an extra $100 since this was very expensive and they did not take the total amount offered by hospice. It was so pretty even John said "Wow, do you think we can stay there some day?" The kitchen was a chef's dream and opened to the eating area with huge windows looking outside. I would definitely recommend it. However, most of the residences there were not dementia or Alzheimer's patients but rather just older and not able to be at home. Their rooms were huge with gorgeous bathrooms! As for Mom, it would not have worked because as I sat with her the first night Mom just talked and talked. To that end one of the residents said "I didn't pay all this money to listen to that all night."

I will give credit to the caregivers, they were so great to Mom. Mom was also very aware of everything we did for her. She could not thank us enough and was always asking for a kiss. Her appetite was great. The caregiver came from 10:30am to 3:30pm 4 days a week. Hospice came 3 mornings a week and bathed and dressed her so those three days the caregivers came later from 3:00pm to 8:00pm so they could help me put her to bed. I always went into her room in the morning to say good morning and ask her "What would you like to wear today, Mom?" She would say "Oh Judy, how nice to have you come to see me." I would respond that this was my house. She would say "Oh, can I live here?" and I would tell her yes and show her the closet with her clothes in it! She was so happy. We did this every single morning!! I dressed her so pretty every day with a bow in her hair (She had about 40). My hairdresser Charlyn even bought some ribbon and made her a whole bunch. As for socks, everywhere I went I would pick up a pair of long socks to help protect her fragile skin on her legs. So she had every holiday sock plus pink stripe, purple hearts, you name it. Her bows always coordinated with her socks and her clothes.

In 2011 I quit putting long pants on her because it was too hard to lift her from the wheelchair to the potty and pull down the pants at the same time. The first couple of years Mom was strong enough and she would put her hands on each side of the potty and I would help her stand and she would twist herself around. She was amazing while she still had some strength in her legs. By 2011 her legs were getting weaker. But, I did have two special blankets for her lap. One was a beautiful pink one with pink ribbon my sister Carol made and one was a pretty red one she loved. At no time did I ever want her to see, or know, she had no long pants on and that she could see she was wearing special tinkle pants. I knew she would feel bad. My Mother was always very aware of her female parts and would never wet her pants. She also was very proud of how she dressed, always coordinating her clothes.

The days the caregiver left at 3:30pm gave me a chance to really be with her. Some days I felt they were closer to her than me! It was good because they spent every minute of the time they were here stimulating her with either cards, dominoes, writing letters or even peddling on that little bike. You had to sit across from her and put your feet on each side of it to hold it in place. Some days she didn't want to ride the bike but that meant no kisses! Mom loved those kisses and she loved giving them. At one of the homes she was in, they called her sweet Mollie and even without outbursts, her sweet Mollie shown through. Every day there was a walk outside regardless of the weather. I put them on her, she never tried to take them off or said anything, and she just went with the flow! My next door neighbor taught gymnastics in her garage and I would wheel Mom over there to watch the little girls who were 4 or 5 years old. Mom clapped and clapped for them. She loved it! The girls would say "Hello Mollie."

She went to every celebration be they birthdays, graduations, anniversary, thanksgiving, even Halloween at my son's house! We never left Mom at home. I noticed she really loved the ride in the car. Sometimes she did not take a ride in the car for a month or more because she was such dead weight neither my husband nor I could get her in. When we had help, we would just take her for a ride. Her dementia continued to get worse. One funny episode was when my brother called and we were in the car riding and we handed the phone to Mom. She said "Oh, how nice to hear from you." I am not sure what my brother said but Mom continued on just like she had known him for ever. Then she hung up, handed me the phone, and said "Who was that?"

We had our issues, especially with caregivers from this one company who never showed up. It was OK unless I had a doctor appointment or lunch with friends. I never could understand how a worker, regardless of what their responsibility, just would not show up. I mean, not even a phone call so you could make other arrangements! The only problem I had when I was with Mom alone was lifting her for potty. Other than that I didn't have any trouble caring for her. I took her everywhere in the house, even to my bedroom when I was cleaning it, and I would give her something to dust. I would lay the items on the bed and she could reach them, dust them with her rag and put them back. Mom just loved helping! I don't think there was anything she liked better than when I would tell her "This is your job." Once a month I wheeled her up to the corner hairdresser. They would wash and set her hair. In the beginning she would get upset when they started to wash it, but just like any woman as they massaged her head she loved it! They all began to know Mollie and one of the girls asked to please be the hairdresser to help her. Then we would wheel her home. She always looked so pretty. What was interesting was her constant questions later of "Do I look pretty?" "Judy, is my hair pretty?" Always so insecure!!

The studio I put together to make the journals and later painting and making plaster boxes was a blessing. That is where Mom and I went when we were alone. Just the two of us, her chatting and me painting. For Easter in 2012 I bought her a beautiful navy and white dress and a big white hat!! I still remember picking it out. I thought of all the times we got new Easter clothes, never being able to figure how Mom and Dad could afford it. But on Easter we had new clothes. So I wanted Mom dressed up even though she really didn't realize it. But she did love the white hat, which I still have.

Mom's favorite item to hug and hold all night was "puppy," the pink and white stuffed puppy hospice gave her. She called him "puppy" and he went everywhere with her. I have pictures of Mom in the courtyard and yep, puppy is with her. I bought her a handmade angel doll that was made of cotton and had cotton wings. So pretty. She named her Amelia, which was Mom's real name. She never really clung to her like she did puppy and she was forever forgetting her name. "What is her name Mom?" "I don't know," Mom would reply. I would say "Her name is Amelia," and Mom would say "Oh, that's my name." Not much else changed. She could never remember my name but would say "I don't know your name but I know you're a sweetie pie." I would tell her my name is Judy and I am her daughter and then I would say "So now you know my name," and immediately I would say "So what is it?" She would try every name, but never came up with Judy!

I give all the credit to my caregivers. They were so creative with her and every minute they were there, for 4 hours and later 5 hours a day, they were doing something with her. They took her for a walk every single day. If it was hot, she went out at 7pm before bed. They would wheel her past the flower bushes and let her smell them, sometimes they would pick one off for her. But she never watched TV. If we sat her in front of the TV she would get restless. Some things never change. When she would get loud, John would just turn up the volume. Good John! We would take the glass jar of 40 bows of hers and put them on her little table and tell her to separate them by color or even by which were her favorites. Always another idea with the bows, but she loved them. Mom loved anything you asked her to do, the more the better. What I really noticed, however, was how she emptied the silverware drawer. In the beginning in 2010 when she first came, she did this lickity split! But as the months and years went on it was taking her longer and longer. She would hold the spoon for 4 minutes, deciding where it went. Besides keeping her busy I could see the difference in her ability to remember things she had no trouble earlier.

247

Every 6 months the state came to exam her. To continue on hospice she had to be constantly decreasing in the ability to do even the smallest request. They would also weigh her and check her eating schedule. Weight seemed to be very important in their decision. Then one day, in 2014, the hospice nurse came and said "Your Mother no longer qualifies for hospice since she has not declined according to the weekly visits in the last 30 days." What is interesting about this was, of all times, Mom had quit feeding herself. She was having problems getting the spoon from her dish to her face so we were now starting to feed her. Didn't matter. So what all did that mean for me?

1. I lost the availability of a nurse every week.
2. I lost all the supplies which were very expensive.
3. I lost the table that went with her wheelchair.
4. I also lost the wheelchair.
5. I lost the 3 days a week where they came to bath her.
6. I lost the trust I had in the nurses who prescribed her meds.
7. I lost the 24/7 person on the other end of the line, if something happened to Mom. Now I either took her to the ER or waited for a nurse to come.
8. I lost the immediacy Mom had when she got a bad skin tear. They came out the same day.

I lost a lot. The fact Mom even was put on hospice was a blessing. She was put on when she lived at Copper Village because they said "She is 94 and giving up," and I took her home. They gave me two weeks' notice! So, what to do? They would take the bed and everything but Medicare would replace the bed and the potty. I might have to wait a week for approval on the wheelchair. So what did Mom do? Sit in bed? This was not good news. So I did what I always do, I prayed. I thanked God for the years of help I have had with Mom and realized that I might not have made it unless He was guiding every move. But now there were going to be changes and I just wanted strength. For sure Mom was not going anywhere. I just had to change the schedule a little and I did not lose the caregivers!!! Caregivers came because Mom was still under the state! Medicare doesn't give caregivers. I felt when I went to bed that in the morning God would show me just how to make this journey work.

And He Did!!!

Chapter 56

Those Halloween Handouts

During the next two years, as I went away for any trips, I left Mom at home. Yes, I paid a caregiver, a wonderful lady from the neighborhood, to stay overnight. She came at 8pm when the day caregiver left and stayed until 10am when the day caregiver came. She would feed the cat, take out the garbage and best of all, sit with Mom until she went to sleep. No more taking Mom anyplace. I know everyone told me not to expect the same care Mom got at home with any cottage or nursing home, and that was OK, it just meant she wasn't leaving this house! I had tried probably four different places for Mom when I would leave for no more than 5 days, each time thinking if it worked out maybe this might be good for Mom. Sorry, I am not saying I am "picky," maybe I am, but the issues were not just what they ate, etc., it was that I never felt I could trust them after what happened with Randa finding Mom up, dressed, asleep in her wheelchair with poopy pants. And of course the lady who fell asleep in her soup at dinner and they left here there. "When we clean up at the end we will take care of her."

I had some extra hours each month for what they called respite, and I used them for the time I would be gone. This ended up giving me 8 hours a day, just during that week. I had saved the respite hours each month so I knew how many I had for the year. So the caregiver came at 10am and was off the clock at 6pm. Then she would stay privately for 2 hours until the night lady came at 8pm. It worked perfectly. Mom never ever again had to sleep anywhere but her bed, and would not have to wake up in a strange room. I remember once going to a very nice place in Mesa, where the people seemed very nice and they probably would get her up at 8am, which I hated, but that is not why I decided at the last minute not to take her. It was the bedroom. They showed me her private room and it looked so dark, sparse, not at all like Mom's pretty room. All I could think of was Mom waking up in this dark room. How silly, huh? She would be fine. But it bothered me. I just could not do it. What I did might not be for everyone, you just follow your heart. Hey, it was a private room. What was wrong with me?

But now in 2013, Mom will be 98. She cannot tell me exactly what she ate, what she liked and didn't like and so I could not leave her. I did however put cameras in the house. I put them in over the last couple years for some of the new caregivers that would come. I remember one of them was in the kitchen so I could see Mom in her special place by the window, or even at the table in the kitchen. I turned it on one day and saw Mom but didn't see the caregiver. Then in the background I could see the family room with the TV on. This was unusual because Mom did not watch TV. So I called the house. "How is it going?" I asked. "Oh fine, we are folding some clothes in the kitchen," she replied. I thought "I don't think so." I called a friend and asked her to stop by and innocently say "Oh, did you know there is a camera there?" That did it! But it's sad I had to do that. I also had a camera in her room. I had seen way too many terrible stories. The good thing is, I had 3 caregivers that were with me for 4 of the 5 years. Even though the caregiver company would tell me who was coming, and I knew her from being here before, they could and would change the schedule and a new person would show up! I just could not be sure. John at one point threatened to take my iPhone away because the application to view the cameras was so easy to access and I was constantly checking if there was a new caregiver!

August 24   I enjoyed time with Mom. Today I asked Mom "What are you going to do today?" And she replied "Ask me tonight and I'll tell you." And she has no mind? She tries very hard to remember my name and when she can't she will say "Well, can I still give you a kiss?"

The doctor told me I need a new hip. I told him not while my Mom is here. He tells me it won't last much longer and I tell him what I tell everyone "Nothing will happen to me while Mom is here. God is making sure I complete this journey with Mom." Neither myself, nor Mom ever got the flu or sick. I think Mom got a cough once but so far we are covered. She was very healthy and so was I.

August 27   It's one day before Mom's 98th birthday. I ask her how old she is and she says 55. I tell her she will be 98 to which she gets very excited and in a loud voice says "I am not!" Most of what Mom wants she will either ask or she will just point to it and say "That is mine." She is so loud, probably because she is hard of hearing, but it's actually funny the way she decides "That's mine." She is still a sundowner. No matter what we try, at 1am she wakes up and is quieter then she used to be. I guess she is running out of energy, but she is awake. If she is awake at 2am or later, I will give her a tiny bit of her night med. I do not want her so drugged she sleeps during the day or can't wake up in the morning.

August 28   Happy 98th birthday Mom. I can't tell you how funny she is. I wanted to put her puppy and her angel doll, Amelia on her bed. She is so pretty and I assumed she had dropped them over the edge but I asked anyway. "Mom, where is puppy and Amelia?" to which she responded "I don't know. I think I put them on the employment list." Somethings you never forget. So of course, cake, balloons and visits from neighbors and her grandsons! Oh, and didn't they say "Oh, she is 94 and giving up."

September 9   "Judy, you are the limit, you are a darling Mother, you love everyone," is what Mom said this morning when I went to get her up. She was so quiet and also very negative this morning. I guess we all have our days. But then she came alive. She was talking and talking to the window so I grabbed my iPhone and took a video. I have at least 20 videos of her over the years. Maybe someday I will write a book and put a DVD in it so people will really get to know Mom. You just never know each day how Mom will be.

September 20   The studio I put together in the extra bedroom, because I really needed something to do, a place to go and be alone with Mom, has been a Godsend. Mom loves it in there. I put a table that is low enough for her wheelchair so she can see everything on the table. Then I will gather some embellishments and just lay them out and it keeps her busy!

September 24   Wheeled Mom up to the hairdresser but today she was not as good as usual.   She complained about everything from them "Not rinsing it enough, you need to do it again," to hating getting her hair dried. On the way home I told her "You were a bad girl." She replied that she was scared. I talked to her just like I would to anyone and told her "No Mom, you knew you were at the salon and you just didn't feel like getting your hair done." I came right out and told her "This is not easy, it's tough pushing you up hill just for you to have a fit when you are there." No answer from Mom until supper when she says "I love my hair." I talk to Mom just the way it is. I know she knows what I am saying and I think that kind of dialogue keeps her on her toes and makes her think! I am really trying all the time to stimulate her and help her feel like she is a real person, not someone sitting in a wheelchair at 98.

October 10   Mom was just out of it. Just talking all day to no one. She hardly communicated with us, didn't even want to play cards. Seems when her "friends" come, she can actually leave where she is and join them. I have seen this happen many times, sometimes for a full day.

October 15   I cannot believe how time has gone by. I can't believe how I still walk across the hall almost every night to check on her and see if her sundowner issue has woken her up. Lately with the increase in meds, but same meds for the last 2 years, she is sleeping better or is it she is just more tired. I watch to see if she is drugged still in the morning and that tells me if I need to change and do less as she gets older and more tired.

October 17   I went into the bedroom last night as Mom was awake talking at 2am. I told her again to be quiet, people are sleeping but instead of her regular "Why?" she said very softly "Judy I love you." Even in the dark, she knew my voice. But that reminded me of what happened a few weeks ago. I must write it down now so I remember it although I doubt I will ever forget it. So I had come home from a church sodality meeting and they had talked about something that had made me cry all the way home. I guess something sad. All I wanted to do was get home to my Mother. Amazing how we still want our Mom when we cry. So I went directly into her room. It was 9pm and it was dark. She was sound asleep. I put my head on her chest and cried. Then I felt this hand on my back, and she said "Judy, don't cry." She knew it was me! I was so stunned. First I said a thank you to God, and then I told John that a Mother never forgets the cries of her child! In the dark, not recognizing me for a while, she said my name and knew it was me.

October 23   Mom is really going. Hard time today. Mom ate cereal "Is this ok?" She looks out the window and says "Oh, it's so beautiful outside and I feel crappy." What? Mom says "crappy?" When did that word come into her vocabulary? I say "Why did you say that?" and she replies "She feels sitting is a lot better than standing." For sure that makes sense? The hospice doctor comes about once a month, actually I don't keep track. But this time he says Mom won't be here much longer. Not sure where he got that idea, but she was very quiet and tired when he was here. I feel bad. Why? Ask myself. Don't know. Am I so spiritually connected to Mom my mind spirals out of control as her mind goes down? Nah!

October 31   Halloween and Mom had a great time!! We usually go to my son's and see the grandkids all dressed up but they are getting older and it's getting harder to get Mom over there. Also she doesn't understand when she does get there. Up until this year, we took her every year so this year we set her outside with the table and all the goodies to hand out. She was a hoot! The children would come up and she would love their costumes. She really knew what they were and was amazing until she had to hand them the candy. She had it in her hand but would not put it in their bags. "Mom, put the candy in her bag," as the little girl was getting fidgety, but Mom would reply "It's mine!" "Mom, give the little girl that candy!" "NO, it's mine," she would say and so we would have to either grab it out of her hand or reach in the pail and get another. This is how it went all night! Aren't these memories precious?

November 1   I love the song *We Were Born to Shine*. I decided I want to do a DVD of pictures of Mom, me, the kids and put that music to the background. That would be a nice project. I am always looking for something to keep me busy and still be with Mom. So I will put that on my to-do list!

November 5   Mom woke up at 7am, too early and still tired but had to go potty. I then put her back in bed. She went right to sleep. She goes to bed early, one hour before she used to, and is sleeping later so I told hospice to change the time they come from 9:30am to 10:30am. We have to change as Mom changes.

November 15   Mom slept all night. Both John and I have doctor appointments and makes you realize you're getting older. Mom is 98 and does just fine. She takes no pills except for her depression which she was put on years ago and which hospice says they will probably take her off. They also are taking her off her Namenda which she started when she was about 88. Maybe that's why she didn't show signs of dementia until she was 91, although my doctor says they don't really think that helps. Lois, Mom's caregiver now for 4 years, got a new puppy, a German shepherd. Just what an elderly lady of 84 needs. I told her this dog will get big. But she brings it and we put him, Prince, in the back yard and Mom loves watching him.

December 15 I remember when Mom came to visit for the week of December 5, 1997, before Dad passed. She came for 6 days and we went everywhere shopping and seeing the Christmas lights. She did not bring Dad. She said she could not stay longer because she could not leave Dad alone too long. My brothers would go over every night and the people in the apartment watched over him. But, sadly, she came home on the 10th and Dad passed on the 22nd.

But now, I am sitting with her. She says I am an angel. It was 8pm and I was sitting with her. She is in a beautiful place tonight. No anger. No anxiety. Just sweet. She says "Are you looking for someone?" (I have no idea why she said that.) I replied "Yes, I am looking for my Mother." Oh, she says "Why do you want your Mother? I wish I could help you," she said. I replied, "Because I want to kiss her goodnight." (While writing this I am thinking what made me say that?) So Mom says "Well, come closer and I will give you a kiss and then you can give it to her!" I cry now writing this. But at the time I started to laugh and laugh and she said "Oh, it's so nice to hear someone laugh." Then I said "I found my Mother and her name is Mollie." She says "My name is Mollie" so I hugged and kissed her and said "Oh Mother, I have found you." She says "I am happy I could help you." And I laughed and laughed again!! Then Mom said "I want to find my Mother and her name is Agnes." I say "That's my Grandmother's name." She says "It is? How do you know her?" So I say "Because you're my Mother and that means she is my Grandmother." Mom asks "Well, where is she?" And I replied "That she is in heaven. But that's OK because you have me, Rudy, Louis, Kenny and Carol." Mom then said "Oh, I am so happy, I would love to have a sister like you." *This was taken word for word from my journal. Considering I have not read this journal until writing this book I think tonight I will just cry myself to sleep! Then I will stop crying and thank God for all the beautiful gifts he gave me on this journey.*

MOM IS 98 READING HER CARDS

Chapter 57

You Are My Sunshine

December 30 Happy 73rd birthday to me! I am blessed to have Mom here one more year. I asked her if she and Dad were happy when I was born and the doctor said "It's a girl." Mainly because Dad had 6 brothers and of course their first born was my brother, Louis. But Mom did not comprehend my question. Instead she answers "Oh, is there a girl here? Oh, but you look good, so did you say it was a girl born today?" Mom just woke up and I ask the angels to let Dad know, in case they don't have an idea of time in heaven, that today is my birthday. Later, as if just having Mom here for my birthday was not enough, I asked her the question again and this time she said "Congratulations Mrs. Hoffart, you have a little baby girl, yes, that is what the doctor said." I wish I had written journals all my life because reading this now I realize I probably have forgotten a lot. But I will never forget how wonderful Mom celebrated my birthday. She never gave me presents wrapped like Christmas and my angel food cake was always decorated like New Year's decorations.

January 2 Mom woke up at 9am, early for her, but she had to go potty. I helped her to potty and she says "Thank you miss." She, more and more, calls me everything but Judy. I am not surprised anymore. I think it's sad that she doesn't know it's her daughter. One day she said "Miss, would you take me to my family please." We are putting our presents away today. All my birthday presents were under the tree! I am making a note of them here because some day I will read this journal and we will smile at all the special presents I received "years" ago! I read my book Danny gave me *100 Things You Learn in Art School*. Geri gave me a "Rudolph" cup!!!! Love it. Dad's name. I will put it in the studio to hold some brushes. Add to this an angel picture from Jan and a heart bracelet from Mary! Wow. I am just so blessed to have these friends and family! Wanda gave me a red Christmas tree. If there is anything unusual, Wanda will find it. New years at Sheldon and Susan's. We play a mystery game. So fun. Susan always goes overboard decorating to match the mystery place and time! We called my brother Kenny and wife Carolyn to wish them a happy new year. Boy are we lucky to have Kenny after all his health issues when he was younger. Dan sent everyone his new album. I think I will try to paint the cover of this album on a canvas. Won't that be fun to try? I have to go now. Late. Thank you, God for this day. I try better every day with your help.

January 11   We went to Palm Springs for 3 days. Short trip. Of course Mom was at home with friends and caregivers. She probably didn't even know I was gone. But my initial reaction on seeing Mom after such a short time was a shock because she looked 110!! So old. So small. I bought her two new bows for her hair. I know, all my life when I went somewhere I always brought back something for Mom. I would be in the store and think, "Oh, Mom would love this." We got her up, put the new bow in her hair and while she was sitting with coffee by the window she seemed to come alive. She was smiling and very happy.

January 16   Poor Mom, so confused. I walk in the room and she says "Look who's here, its Judy." Then 5 minutes later it is all "Miss." Last night she was so confused and so tired by 6:30pm. Today is Sunday and the lady came from church, gave her communion and she knew all her prayers. I must thank All Saints' Church. They have been coming ever since Mom came to my house! Today we tried to see where I could sit next to her and hug her! I can't sit with her in the wheelchair, the couch is too low, she is dead weight and I can't pick her back up. So we decided to do this when the caregiver is here. Between the two of us we can get her back in wheelchair. I loved it! Hugged her. Just sat there! Quiet. I think "Why didn't we think of this earlier?" Thank you God for these moments.

January 17   Took Mom to the studio to keep her busy. TV is out. Even cards, which she plays every single day, is out! She is just too tired. But in the studio I can put something in her hands and she loves looking at the glass birds or the metal hearts. I am feeding her more because she takes so long that her food gets cold. After a few bites she wants "My own spoon," she says!

January 21   Scary. Today Mom says "I wish I could jump in the river and drown." She says this while I am putting some grapes in her hand to eat while she is in the recliner. We move her there after no more than two hours in the wheelchair. Last night I had a dream. I scribbled it in my journal when I woke up. So it says that Mom is riding in the car with me and says "You don't have to take me all the way home, it's not that far, I can walk." So in the bathroom I put on the light and wrote down this poem that came to me. *Inside my heart there lives a friend who shares thoughts regardless of how harsh.* I am going back to bed. I have an idea to use Plexiglas for a top on one of my boxes. Wow, cannot wait to try. Maybe in a few days. ***I had no idea until I read this where the idea came from for a Plexiglas top on my plaster boxes, but since I have used it twice and they are just lovely!!***

January 22 Poor Mom. Luckily she has no idea how she has spent the last 4 years. Now today she says she wants to go home to Geneva!! If that's not enough, she says her name is Mollie Skolaris. Yes, Mom grew up in Geneva, Ohio and when single was Mollie Skolaris!!

January 23 New CNA to bathe Mom. Cassia is gone. Nora and Mary now come. Everybody moves on but Mom. She moves downhill not to some new changing style in her life.

January 28 Mom was up at 7am. Way too early! Caregiver comes at 11am. I cannot get her up now because it's a long day and by 6pm she is ready to go to bed. So brought her juice, changed her pants and covered her back up. She isn't focusing much, just wild rambling and wanting kisses. What do we expect? Geez, every day I wonder how much longer for her. She still doesn't nap! She just gets excited. Mom's demeanor all her life was "go go go!" Her body still does not want to stop!

January 29 Well, Mom just keeps amazing us. Today she recognized John. Up until now she calls him "The strange man in the house." She asked him who he was and he told her he was Judy's husband, John. She says "You married Judy?" When he responds with a yes, she reaches for his hand and says "Let me kiss your hand." I would have liked a picture of John's face. Now tell me God, how does this happen??? Only you know!

February 2 Lots happening. Mom was up for 2 hours calling for the Lord and ma and pa. Same thing the night before from 3am to

5am. Meds don't work. Guess I could add more, but I keep thinking she will go to sleep, and for sure at 5am I didn't want to drug her. I get confused and have to make decisions. So afraid to do something wrong. At one point I kissed her head and she said "Don't touch me." She seems to be sleepwalking? I mean she is awake but she is not really with me.

February 5   Danny is going to Flagstaff for a gig and kids go up for the snowboard festival. Sunday he will be at his house in Prescott to paint or update, so we will drive up. It will be a nice drive and a day to get out. John and he will paint, I will go shopping.

February 6   I did not know if I would even go in there and find her alive this morning, but for the last two nights she slept perfectly. She ate breakfast at 11:45 this morning and she looked out the window and said "What a beautiful world, look at the bright light (sun)." In the studio today I thought Mom is getting tired, but as I started to move her wheelchair from the table she found this item, it was gold and round and she said "This looks like a flower." *I have a picture of what I did with this "flower" Mom found. It still hangs on the wall.*

February 09   "Let's all sing our good night song, you sing, you sing," as she points to the air. "Oh, hello Judy, what have you got? A book?" "Yes, I have a writing book," I reply. "Judy, we have to talk to you because I am not sure you're singing the good night song, don't you know it?" I tell her "No." She says "You all go in there (closet) and bless everybody, no, go in the house, oh, you all have to go." (talking to stuffed animals) She says "Judy, what is this?" I say "It's your blanket." She continues "Oh, come and sing the song. Come in the morning and open the door and the good mothers and fathers and everybody sing every Sunday. If you were me I would have you all sit down." *I brought a book I had to write some notes. I did not want to forget so that I had the opportunity to write exactly as she spoke, which of course, made little sense to me! But how cute that she wants to sing a good night song!!!*

February 13   It is bath day. Mom hates it. I get her up a few minutes before hospice comes. There is no hurry and I talk to her and then heat up the towels. When you are sitting on the potty getting your back washed you can feel cold so I always warm up the towels. Sometimes when the girl comes in Mom gets scared. Not sure why because it's the same person every day and they love her. If she really gives them a hard time, I stay, rather than go get her oatmeal. Before they come Mom and I pick out her clothes as she always knows what she wants!! Mom got out for a walk today with Lois because it was 82 and beautiful.

February 14   My favorite day. Dad sent me valentines every single year. He also sent some beautiful ones to Mom when they were married. Very old, beautiful, the kind you don't see anymore. Years old and she kept them in a red box. Mom was in full form so I went again and got this journal. I am not sure how many days I have left but I want to really write down what she says. "Judy, didn't we have the best time? We are so lucky." With that she raises her arms to the sky. "Judy, did you get your communion in the suitcase?" "Yes Mom," I reply. "Judy, we worked so hard but I loved it." "You did?" I asked. "Well, it depends on what it was but Judy didn't we do everything together? I love you so much I could hug you so long." So I gave her a hug and ran for my iPhone to video this. I got some words but for 10 minutes Mom had the best dialog ever! I never saw her laugh so hard in four years and talk about fun times together. It was a treat. ***Reading this I am so lucky I had the journal. I wonder many times how the window opens and God gives us these moments. She mentioned my name so many times and yet over the next months, she never said my name.***

February 24   Sitting here with Mom at 6pm trying to get her to understand how to dry the cups. She understands but does for a second and quits. I know she loves helping me. She used to do this all the time but today I put her hand on the top of the cup for her to feel the wet. Then she understands to dry it. It takes time but it's something for her to do. Tonight I gave her extra Trazadone.

February 25   Amazing. Mom was up until 4am then slept until 10:30am. Had her bath and is very loud today. All she says is she wants to go home. I am amazed she was up all day, no nap and talking all day! Where does she get her strength?

March 1   Mom up again at 3:43am sweet. She sees people but says "Judy" when I come in. When I touch her she screams. I guess someone is there and I am messing up something. Strange! I gave her some meds but this poor old soul needs to sleep. So got back out of bed later to look in on her. Put my hand on her head and asked angels to give her some peaceful dreams. I said "Let her dream of the mountains that talk and the trees that sing!" I can ask for anything from God and so I prayed that I wanted her to go back to sleep. I went back to bed, confident my prayers would be answered, and now it is 8:45am and she is still asleep. You could say it was the meds, but I have given her meds before and they didn't work, so I chose to believe it was my prayer. She slept until 10:30am and woke up hungry!

March 7   Every night almost the same, up and then goes to sleep. Talks and doesn't make sense. Everyone says "It's the sundowner," but now after her bath I can see she is still tired. Not eating unless I feed her. Seems the past 4 nights have been hard. The meds do put her back to sleep but still she is interrupted in sleep for at least an hour or so before she goes back to sleep. This morning she says "Where am I? Did I die? I don't want to die." I tell her she is fine and going to have a blueberry muffin for breakfast.

March 21   Now we are going through no BM's on schedule. So giving her some meds for that. After three days the nurse came with a Fleet enema. My friend Dottie died from a burst bowel so I am very careful. After three days, I want help for Mom. I had given her everything from prune juice to cod liver oil. The nurse has a special recipe of prune juice, butter and milk of magnesia, but I would not make my worst enemy eat that!!!!

March 30   I have 32 kidney stones! Yep. Time to get rid of them! Had surgery scheduled and woke up with pseudo gout. If you have never heard of it, it's like gout, but not from diet. They have no idea what causes it and it never comes in the toe! No, that would be too easy. It hits any joint and comes quickly. If you don't take care of it with doses of prednisone, it travels, and it travels quickly. So I noticed it early in the morning in my ankle. I knew I was going to have surgery so did not want to take a steroid. Wrong. It traveled to the other knee and by 2pm in the afternoon it was in 3 places. Called my surgeon, Dr. Sadeghi, who I am not sure believed this could happen. I went right in for him to see all the swollen joints himself. Once my hand swelled up so bad you could not see the knuckles. So we had to put off the surgery for a week.

April 20 Easter No penny pinching. Another tradition bites the dust! I wonder what happened to Easter when we took the only grandchildren and moved from Ohio to Arizona. How lonely, because my parents loved the boys coming over. Oh, and remember hats!!! We always had to have an Easter hat. Well that was the 60's, when did that stop? Guess we will have to make some new plans for next year, maybe try a sunrise service?

Chapter 58

I Walk With Jesus Every Day

Keep the faith. Every time I pray I always get the same answer "Keep the faith" so this little hiccup up was no different.

May 5 Sure enough, on the 2nd day of the notice, with one week left to figure what to do, I got a phone call. I guess when hospice said they were cancelling Mom, they sent the report to the state. Two days later my state caseworker called to tell me she got the notice. "So what now?" I asked.   Are you ready for her answer? She says "You call another hospice." What? I do not understand. If Medicare says Mom is not eligible because her health has not decreased enough over the last 3 months then how can another hospice sign her up? Well, it seems the government gives hospice the money when they sign up a patient. Those dollars go for the expenses of the patient and we know they always take good care of their patients. When they sign up a patient, if the patient has issues that require the help that hospice provides, the new hospice starts from what level the patient is now. Then they have to report each month, just as the previous hospice did, and the state will come in person every three months, exactly as was done before. She suggested I call three companies. They will come out and evaluate the patient and let me know if they think Mom would qualify. So I set up three appointments. Meanwhile, hospice took the bed but the same day Medicare sent one. Whew! Two of the companies said they needed to take the information back to their head nurse. Now, don't quote me here because with all that was going on I was not really sure just who had to approve this. I just remember neither of them could do it right on the spot. The third came and said "I have the authority to approve or disapprove." So we went to the bedroom to get Mom up. Of course Mom had no idea where she was, she had no idea what you wanted her to do and she said "I don't want to go to school today". Good Mom!

So Hospice of Arizona signed her up. It was the right thing to do. Mom had just made such a downturn, not being able to feed herself.

She was so weak that in the morning she could barely hold her head up on the potty. Every day Mom was with me I thanked God for hospice! Whoever thought up that program deserves a special cloud in heaven so they can look down at the wonderful program they created. I think her age also played a part. She was 97. Again, everyone thought she would be giving up soon! But they thought that when she was 64.

As I write this in 2017 I tried to contact Hospice of Arizona to get some exact dates but seems Hospice of Arizona has closed. For those that worked for them and read this book I want to thank you for every minute of the day ensuring me that someone was there for me and Mom!! And for all those working for hospice now, know your work is very important to us all!!! We love you!

Chapter 59

You Can Not Over Dream God

Now I have to get ready for surgery for my 32 kidney stones.

May 15   Surgery. 32 stones taken out through my back. I had a great Urologist, Dr. Sadeghi . I told him he was the doctor that listened in class! He is the best! I was in the hospital 2 days and carried a bag for 7. They want it to drain but also to ensure they got all the stones. These stones were all stuck together, as big as my fist! I never worried. I had great faith in Dr. Sadeghi!

May 22   In outpatient to close up the hole in my kidney. They did find 3 more. I guess they were hiding. This was really very easy. They keep it open until now because they say they can't go back and open it again, so they want to be sure they get them all. Really wasn't so bad. Meanwhile, we kept Mom at home. I had help from everyone. And Mom was so good. Can you believe it? She slept at night! She ate well. She talked all day, but no emergencies. Now, don't tell me someone isn't looking out for both of us!!! When I came home I went to Mom's bed and hugged her and said, "Mom, I love you so" and asked her if she knew who I was. She said "Judy." With that I cried. I said "Oh Mom, you remembered me." She said "Oh Judy, how could I forget you?" To think I have my Dad to thank for all this, I try to repay him by doing good things like sharing, being nice and like things he did with AA. I know he doesn't like tears. He told me, no crying. "I didn't help you through all this to see you cry." I hear him say this through my heart because he has been gone since 1997. But as God says "Those who believe in Me shall have ever lasting life."

June 6   Danny is moving back to New Mexico from San Diego where he stayed in our condo for a few months. His business, Healthy Living Spaces, is in New Mexico and everyone knows him so I guess he is not ready to retire. In fact he is working on another album. Meanwhile, Mom continues to regress. She now has a swelling problem. So now we are using something special in her drinks. They say soon phlegm will go to her lungs. Then I guess she gets pneumonia and God comes to the rescue??? Oh God, I am living one day at a time. She will be 99. Now I am crying more. I think that if I cry now I won't cry later? Celebrated John's birthday at Johnny's. He says playing in the pool with the grandsons was the best party ever!

June 22 "Be quiet" Mom says to her imaginary friends. Mom is playing cards again by herself. We offer to play with us but she ignores us. She still tries to separate the silverware. She is amazing.

June 24 I remind myself, you do have a life! Kids came to help in restructuring the studio. We put some of the art supplies in the garage, those that could stand the heat, paper and embellishments. A/C is on in the garage. Meanwhile, Debbie is caring for Jim who had a little issue with his leg, but they will do well. He could not have a better nurse!

June 28 Mom's phlegm problem is getting worse. The issue is she talks and talks, gets excited and doesn't swallow which is already a problem. But the phlegm builds up so we are so lucky hospice brought us that breathing machine! The lady who brought the machine said "I can tell you're a good daughter," to which I said, because I am so unsure of myself, "Why?" and she said "I go in many homes and let's just say I can tell." Oh God, at the end of the day today, I sure needed that!!

June 29 Johnny is 49. Actually he is John Anthony Stih the fourth! Accidentally. I really put his middle name as Anthony because in school I always prayed to St. Anthony. John meanwhile signed everything including his marriage license John Joseph. Turned out, John's real name was John Anthony but he took Joseph as his confirmation name. I guess I forgot all about the Anthony. So I was reminded about this after Johnny's christening by my Mother-in-law!   So as he gets older, so do I!! Went to wake Mom and told her "It is Johnny's birthday." Johnny is Mom's first grandson and they were very close. Mom did not understand. I repeated it. Then as clear as day she says "Oh, it is Johnny's birthday." She said it so sweet I know there is a lot of love in that body yet! I returned to give Mom a drink and she was talking to her "babies." She had no problem swelling. Yeah. I put some 40's music on the radio since I know that is what she and Dad listened to and I thought that might calm her today. Actually, today was a beautiful day. *I wrote at the end of my*

267

writing "You cannot over dream God." Not sure what I was thinking but obviously I even felt it was a great day.

July 15   Mom is on baby food because she has a hard time chewing and especially so she can have fruit. I am beginning to make sure I am with her at bedtime, even with a caregiver. She hates getting her back side washed and so I talk to her while she is laying on her side and ask her how her day was. For sure she would not get this in a home! This might not be for everyone, but if you are blessed to have such a journey, you need to thank God.   They say it was a good idea to put her on the baby food but I can't believe she likes it!! My gourmet Mother.

July 17   I was not expecting what happened next. It seemed everything came apart. I came into the room and she was very quiet. She knew me. I asked her for a hug and she gave me one and then said "I have 2 hands. Do it again." She was very good all day and then at 8:30pm, when you would least expect it, she started a rant with whomever she is seeing. She was so loud I could not talk to her. She swatted me and tried to grab a cup of water I had for her. She wanted to "Throw it over the side to him." I got her night meds down her but realized they were not going to be enough. I increased them to the max that the hospice nurse told me to do in an emergency. "They won't kill her" she said. She slept all night. I know everyone will say this would not happen if I had let the experts figure her meds. No thank you! This was OK. I had the right med, working with hospice, and still knew she would be alert in the morning. If she wanted to throw something, go ahead. She is 99 pounds in a bed with sides, no one would get hurt, especially her. What bothers me is I felt she was fighting someone who came to get her and I cannot tell you why I felt that. It was just her words, sometimes not making sense, but she wanted him to "go"!!!

July 20   The next few days were very normal for her. Talking to her imaginary friends and sitting in the recliner with her hands moving as she talked. She ate fine and we did not have any other problems at night.

August 2   I have really begun to meditate a lot, especially in the am before I get up. I don't want to be alone since I have had Mother for 73 years. But I got the feeling whoever was responding to me that it was "So what!" I wonder if other people get messages when they meditate. I received one that said "You have no claims on her soul." For sure that mediation today did relax me!

August 10   Mom ate the Bob Evans muffin with gravy this morning like she was starving. Then I thought maybe baby food is enough protein and carbs for a baby, but not for a full adult! So tomorrow I will make her egg and sausage and cut up the sausage. No more baby cereal. I am thinking we will do what we did when my son Danny was born. He was 9 pounds 12 ounces and 24 inches long and always hungry. I don't remember how old but he was but was still very little. The doctor said to puree whatever we ate and give it to him. If he doesn't handle it, try another food, but he doesn't need baby food. We also started him on beans and he was not even 6 months old!! So tomorrow I am going to do that for Mom.

August 20   The nurse was here to bandage two horrible skin tears on Mom's arms. We now have arm covers.   Tomorrow an MRI on my hip. Doesn't matter as I am not doing anything as long as Mom is here. I have so many videos of Mom. WOW, what would I have done without my iPhone? I need to save them so I am going to a class to save them on a time machine, whatever that is.

August 24   Well, my hip is bad. Don't you just love it!! Ha! Also my art is improving. I just gave a piece to someone who was having a fundraiser for a father who has cancer. No idea who they are. I just drop off stuff. I have decided, even though Danny made me a web site for Mother's Day, I won't sell my art. I would never have realized I could paint on canvas or not just furniture if Mom had not come here and we needed something to do together. It was a gift from God and my art will always be gifts.

August 25   Mom is getting very tired. Twice this week she fell asleep at the table around 6:30pm before I even got her ready for bed. In three days Mom will be 99, if she makes it! She seems to talk then fall asleep in her wheelchair before we can get her to the recliner. I refuse to see her asleep in her wheelchair with her head down. We still will transfer her to the recliner and then she goes back to sleep.

Chapter 60

Through the Years

Through the Years   I love that song by Kenny Rogers and it seems to fit this chapter.

August 28   I have a great picture of Mom and me on her 99th birthday. We had a cake, invited neighbors and took videos. I would ask her how old she was and she said 20! But I realized my Mom has just about left the building. Then I decide to not write that. What I guess I mean is she is no longer my Mom, but more like the little girl I never had. So innocent, sweet, totally needing care but as sweet as ever a little girl could be. When Mom first woke up we told her it was her birthday and she was going to get a bath and put on some new birthday clothes. Her response was "I don't want a bath, I want food." Then she says "Will I have coffee?" Mom loves her coffee so we said yes and she asked "Well, how much will it cost?" Don't you love it! Mom made it. I wrote some cute words from her birthday. I had time sitting in bed tonight and wanted to write them even though I wrote them in the book we kept by the kitchen table to capture all her funny words. J: How old are you? M: 32 J: No you are 99. M: No, I am not. You be 99! J: I'm your daughter, you're my Mother. M: Is there any food here? J: You get a bath first. M: I don't want a bath, I want food. J: Today is your birthday. M: No, my birthday is August 28. J: Today is August 28. M: Oh, is it my birthday? How much is coffee? J: Coffee is free. M: Oh it's free, then I will have a cup! Where is Rudy? J: Rudy is at the radio show. M: Well he isn't supposed to be!

Well, Mom made 99! Who would have guessed? But you have to see her in person. She has a hard time holding her head up so I found an old neck brace we used once and I put it around her. I took a picture. I think by the end of today she knew it was her birthday. But tonight she wanted me to get in bed with her. She says "Come in and see, there is lots of room." So funny as she kept moving over. So to satisfy her I kissed puppy, her favorite. She said "Isn't he adorable?" Many times I have come in between 1am and 3am and she has her babies on her chest, wrapped her arms around them and has said "OK, we are ready to go." I took great pictures and I even took some videos of her playing cards. I don't think I need a video because she has played these cards every day! Is this the last birthday I will celebrate with her? Only God knows. Well, Mom turned 99 this year, Johnny, my eldest son, turned 49, Danny turned 47 and Todd turned 45! Yikes. If I thought Mom was getting older for sure so am I! When your kids are near 50, you know these are your twilight years.

That said, my Mom had two sisters. So there were three girls. Each one of them, Mary, Edith and Mom, had a daughter. Well, now Mary's daughter will be close to 90, Edith's daughter Jeannette has to be close to 85 and I am going to be 74 in December. So we have lots of longevity but I am not sure I want it. My Mother was so healthy, never a new hip or kidney problem, but it was the dementia that got her! Well, Mom still lets us know she is here. Two days ago she woke up at 10:30am and she was letting us know she was here! She was full force all day until 7pm with no nap! "I am going home," she says. "Come to my house and I will love you," and that was at 7pm, still going. However today, her birthday, she had laryngitis! The nurse could not believe it!! Mom with no voice??? My neighbor Brenda brought Mom some flowers. If you're lucky you will have neighbors like we do. I call this the "dream street." They are unbelievable. When John and I wanted to go down the street at 7:30am just for a bagel, we didn't dare leave Mom alone even though she was sleeping. We will call Brenda and let her know we would be gone for an hour and to check the house! Yep.

August 29   Mom was awake at 3am. I think too much excitement yesterday. I came into the room and she had all her babies (puppy, Amelia and bunny) on her chest, wrapped in her arms and says "OK, we are ready to go!"

September 2   Mom was bad today. From the beginning she didn't want to eat. I gave her a blueberry muffin first instead of cereal to entice her to eat and she broke it apart and threw it on the floor! Then she says: "I am going to the meeting," and for the next hour I was #5. We all get numbers! She proceeded to tell everyone what to do and then

271

Angela came and tried to get her to focus, but cards were not to be played. By 2:00pm she was falling asleep. We put her in the recliner and she took a nap, very unusual. Now it's 9pm and she is sound asleep in bed. She must have been very tired, but Mom is getting very tired all the time! So I am going to stop now and listen to Nancy Reyner's DVD. I tried watching it today but way too much confusion. I did get to watch some great techniques. Everyone says I should make some time for myself. Well, 9pm sounds perfect.

September 3 Mom was in full display from the moment she got up. First she let me know she did want to get up and when I said "Well, I will go make you some breakfast," she picked up puppy and put him in her mouth! I explained that was not the food. She didn't want a bath, grabbed the caregivers arm and it takes me and the caregiver to get it off because Mom is so strong! In the kitchen she really didn't want the food and when Angela came she threw her muffin on the floor! First time for everything. She talked and talked and even I was tired just listening. By 3pm in the afternoon she was falling asleep so we put her in her recliner. This was a first. Mom was taking a nap!

September 4 I saw an ant in Mom's room along the molding on the floor. The bedroom is carpeted but it's taken its toll these last few years with having to be cleaned a couple times a year. So I was worried about ants climbing on Mom all night. John was not home. So I called my neighbor Brenda. "Brenda do you know a couple of big guys that can come and pull up this carpet because I don't want Mom sleeping here unless I am sure there are no ants?" She said she would be right over. The doorbell rang in 10 minutes and there appears Brenda and her young daughter and son. I mean they were about 10 and 11 years old!!! I said "You can't do this." She said "Oh yes we can!" Somewhere I have a picture of her, walking out to the rubbish, with the carpet rolled up over her shoulder on the way to the rubbish can!!! Yes, they did it. They moved the dresser to one side, ripped up carpet, moved the bed. Ripped up carpet. I swear in less than 20 minutes they were done. Now that is a neighbor for you! And, in case she forgot when she did this, it's all here in my journal!

September 12   Mom was holding her cards saying "mine," and ordering people around. She was screaming about something and Angela the caregiver tried to get her involved in something to no avail. So I said "No screaming in this house!" She then turns, points to Angela and says "Do you think she heard you?" It was funny, but it was loud. She was like a three year old in a 99 year old body. So I got out one of our emergency pills, which is a very low dose calming pill, and as I put it on her tongue she took it out and said "Give it to her" meaning Angela! She knew she didn't want anything!! So even against her will we got her out of the wheelchair and to the recliner. We have a way of fixing the recliner so she cannot scoot down and try to get out. She is strong. Then tonight as I went in there after she was in bed and all settled down she says very calmly "Come on in my bed, you're so beautiful!" I felt so sorry for her. She has no idea. So cute. So loud. And no, she wants you to join her in her bed! I think "Dear God, if I had not seen my Mother evolve into a childlike little girl I would not believe it and if I did not hear some of the things that come out of her mouth for sure I would not believe it. Thank you for giving me the heart and love that I feel for her rather than be upset with her." I am still amazed at how I react sometimes!

October 4   Mom is alert and she says "It's beautiful" meaning her hair that I fixed today. All the way from her bedroom to the kitchen she remarks "Everything here is beautiful." I give her oatmeal with fresh strawberries and she says "This is the best I ever ate and this is delicious." So I pull out my iPhone and video. I wonder sometimes what I would have done without my iPhone. I would have had to get the movie camera out and for sure that would have taken longer than just picking up the iPhone and pressing video. I think I have almost 100 videos of her, not to mention all the pictures. For 20 minutes all I heard was, "This coffee is so good, I love the muffin, and everything is delicious." Don't we wonder about this wonderful brain we are given?!! Later she said "I wish I was in the corner of the street in Ohio." She is always wanting to go home. I think she says 20 times a day "Please take me home.'" At least 20 times, maybe more!!

October 29   Dan had brought me some twigs from the creek near his house in Santa Fe. I love doing bird paintings and I love painting the twigs. Having them from the creek in Santa Fe is extra special. So I did a canvas with a bird and the twigs painted different colors and wrote "There is a bird that lives in my heart." Then I put a large Plexiglas heart over the bird. Now I have to attach it to the canvas giving it about 3 inches above. I figure I will use screws but then cover the screws with some pretty round embellishments used on bracelets. These moments are really my release from all the noise and confusion, but still I do this with Mom in the studio! I am amazed myself! What is even better is Mom loves the colored birds! She actually focuses when she is in the studio. If Mom had not come to live with me I know for certain I never would have realized I could paint. Yes, I had a shop in Scottsdale where I painted furniture, but painting on canvas was never in my mind. It just sort of evolved. I would get a lot of my ideas from YouTube since I could not leave to take classes. However, once a year, I would sign up for Art Unraveled, an art gathering that came to Arizona once a year. You would sign up in January and there were classes for every art, from painting to jewelry to journaling, you name it. So for 3 days a year I did get out among other artists and take some classes. But Mom loved everything I painted. She did not know my name but she would look at something I created that hung on the wall and say "Judy, I love what you paint." Yes, said my name. Just how can that happen? A gift from God. That is the only answer.

Halloween   Mom was out there, at the table, handing out the goodies. Did I say handing them out? Well this year we decided to put the candy in the bag for the children as they came because last year Mom hung onto the candy saying "This is mine." So Mom got to say hi to the children but we put the candy in the bag, to which she would say "Where is mine? I did not get one," every time. She was the most fun the last three Halloweens she has been here at our house and there is never a dull moment!!! The neighbors walking with their children love seeing her outside and say "Hi Mollie!" By 7:30pm Mom is exhausted so the caregiver puts her to bed. She is so tired she will say "Is that my bed?" Yes Mom, it's your bed. "Can I get in it?"

November 5   Today Mom says "Tell Judy I am her Mother and she needs to come here!" She says this to the caregiver.   So that was where she was today, about 10 times, "Tell Judy I am her Mother and she needs to come here!" The problem was when I would come, maybe not at that exact moment, maybe 5 minutes later, she didn't know me.

November 15   I wanted to have breakfast and write in my journal but could not find it! I panicked. I looked everywhere and then started blaming everyone because every time I start something I get called and so I probably just didn't put it where it belonged! I was very upset. I looked everywhere. So I did what I tell my friends to do "Pray to the angels." So then, guess what? I decided I would sit down, relax, have my coffee, and move on. Wow, next to my chair was my journal! So first I say thanks, have to keep my angels happy! *I just loved reading this now. Yes, it works every time!*

November 18   Today I am watching from the kitchen, and realized there was so much calmness in that room, especially after such a loud and hectic day yesterday. Loeke is such a beautiful cat. When Mom is in the recliner in the family room, Loeke will come off Mom's bed and sit on the arm of the recliner and just purr! I will her miss so much as I know all this is short lived. It's just a matter of time. I will never in my life forget the moment Mom is devouring that cookie, like she never had one, and Loeke is so happy to sit by her! Danny brought her for Mom when he found her under the foundation at his home. She has lived with Mom since Mom moved into her home on McDowell. She is so gentle and I will miss her. Tonight I delivered anonymously a painting to one of the AA meetings. I just go in and hand it to someone. I wrap it and inside I write "You are where you are supposed to be, congratulations." This is why I create, to give. I don't sell my art but I feel I never would have even painted if Mom had not come so I want to give back.

Thanksgiving   Mom was a saint on Thanksgiving. With everyone talking, Mom just seemed to love it all. She sat at the head of the table with myself on one side and Cheryl on the other. We had duck and prime rib. The kids were surprised. Brandon said he missed the turkey. John had gone to a cooking class and had made duck and was so proud of himself he wanted to make it and surprise everyone. Cheryl of course is there for support!!!! Cheryl could cook a duck with her eyes closed!! Friday we went to Herberger Theater as a treat for our anniversary. I love going to live theater.

December 7   In church today my mind wandered. Guess that's not supposed to happen but I am so relaxed in church. I love the singing. For some reason I started thinking about my last 5 years. So much has happened. I have gotten older. Mom has gotten older. Who would have guessed all that has happened? Another Thanksgiving with Mom. I have spent 74 years of Thanksgivings with Mom. I loved every one. I have been given so much. My Dad and Mom were not a president or a CEO, and they didn't get to go to college as I read in some of the obituaries, but I would not have chosen any other two to spend my life with. Yes, I thought of that today. Sorry God, will concentrate on you next Sunday, but actually I am concentrating on you, for it's you, God, that gave all this to me. How can I repay you? R*eading this from my journal I must admit, every time I have ever said "How can I repay you?" all I ever got was the same words of "Keep the faith." Amazing God asks for so little, giving so much.*

December 10   My friend Jan came to visit. She brought me an angel on a stand. Not just an angel on a stand but an antique, a beautiful piece. I love it. I met her friend Craig. John says I was not very nice to him. I guess I am just wanting to be sure the guy who gets Jan treats her exceptionally well! I think it's been three years since I have seen her. For sure I didn't write it in my journal if I had. Everything is here. I even know when Cheryl had her shoulder surgery!!! First, Jan and I went to Merchant Square and also had our nails done, then later we met up with Craig. I guess they came to visit his daughter. Craig's wife Janeanne, who passed, was a good friend of Jan's and she was close with Michele, their daughter. She also came to see me!! I don't care, I am just glad she got here!

December 15   The nurse says Mom needs to ride the bike more. Her legs are getting stiff and we are also adding Tylenol to her list.   But she said something that I knew was coming when she said "The worst is yet to come." I delivered another painting to AA. John says I should not go out at night but most AA meetings are around 7:30pm. It's a nice neighborhood. It is just John is very protective. I keep telling him nothing will happen to me while I am caring for Mom. I just feel that. The nurse also says give Mom more fruit, watermelon and beets. All these things Mom likes but lately she just isn't eating as much. The doctor came with her because it was time to evaluate Mom. Mom is 99 and I am sure they won't take her off. Everyone thinks her days are numbered but they said that when she was 94.

December 22   I sat with Mom tonight at her bedside because she had been so confused all day. All I gave her so far is her sleeping meds at 7pm. It's hard to determine when to give any tiny additional pill. I don't want to but then she will be up talking at 3am. But so far, all these years we have done pretty well. I think the reason we have not had to give her a lot of meds during the day is because the caregiver and I keep her occupied. There is talk, there are things we get her to do. She does get carried off by her "friends" at times and we just let her. I do not try to restrict her natural wanting to talk to whomever. Tonight, as I was sitting with her she says "It's time to get up." I told her everyone is sleeping and its night time and she either did not hear me, or didn't understand because all I got from her was "I want to get up." This is now a 99 year old , who gets up at 11am in the morning, takes no nap, talks all day and is still awake at 8pm. I am tired!!!

December 24   At 9:41pm everyone was gone. No more all-nighters. The tradition finally ends, Rudy Hoffart's families tradition, ours was the last holdout. Mom was so cute. Talking. I went to move her wheelchair to the middle of the room so she could see everyone and she starts waving and saying "goodbye goodbye."

December 25   We got Mom in the car to take her to Johnny's for Christmas day. She slept all the way! So we made it, Christmas with nana, all dressed in red.

December 30   My birthday with Mom. It's so perfect that it rates right up there with my 40th. On my 40th I decided I was going to the mall, alone! I left behind a 15 year old, a 13 year old and an 11 year old and did not care what they did. I wanted to go shopping at the mall, in the ladies department, not children, and I wanted to buy myself a treat. I ended up purchasing 4 turtleneck tops, each a different color and I was a happy camper! What would greet me a home, I didn't even care! I had a wonderful time alone!! But, just walking into the front door, there was a big banner the kids made, "Happy Birthday Mom." Oh, I was so surprised. How cute. Then I walked into the kitchen and was met by a 5 layer cake, almost sliding off its base from all the frosting! If they didn't understand how much I loved what they did, I think they knew in later years because I would tell them my 40th birthday was the best!!! *It was a Kodak Moment because to this day I remember what I wore to the mall, what I purchased, the sign when I came home and every step into the kitchen as I saw the cake on the counter. You just can't beat that birthday. This year, 2014, I went to lunch with my friends and then went home to Mom. Having my Mom still on my birthday was the best present. I sat next to her as we pushed her up to the table and got her to sing happy birthday to???...well Mom would put in "to Mollie" Hahahahah. And I have it on video. Hope I don't lose it. I am so happy. So blessed.*

Chapter 61

Because We Believe

I love this song by Andrea Bocelli.

January 2   Mom made it! But this morning was a sad one for me. Mom slept all night so the morning was a shock to me. When Mom woke up she said "I hurt all over and I want to die. Please let me just lay here." So why am I shocked? She is 99. She is so frail. She can hardly keep her head up and yet she never complains when you ask her to write a love note to Rudy, or put away the silverware. Only thing she does not want to do is ride the bike! So I call hospice. Who else. My angels on the other end of the line. They reminded me they left morphine for emergencies so I should give her just a little since we don't want her to sleep all day but we want to help her with the pain. By 11:30am she was feeling better and asked for coffee! Her legs still hurt so I put a lidocaine patch on them. Then we got her dressed and got her by the big window in the kitchen where she loves to look at the birds. She ate, and then we took her for a walk. It was a beautiful day here. She actually had a good day, playing dominoes, but she took a nap at 3pm. Naps are a new thing for her, but about time! When she woke up she constantly asked me to stay with her. For some reason she seemed to be afraid of something. She sees people. She says "Look at the stuff on the floor. Where is everyone? Let me die." She goes on and on. So just now I gave her the night medicines, because it's 8pm and she needs to settle down! Maybe it was the nap, not sure, but first she wanted to go to bed, now she is there and talking to all her "friends". Is this the beginning of 2015?

January 8   Sunday was scary. Mom not sleeping well even with meds for three nights. We started three years ago with Trazadone 20 milligrams, and now we are at 75. Still the best meds for her and she is alert in the morning. Still up at the sundowner time, but only for a short time. Then she starts saying the "act of contrition." I gave her some morphine for her leg pain but the morphine actually does very little for her anxiety. I am not worried about her anxiety because it's not really bad because I think she is just worn out, period. She is 99!

January 12   Mom slept all night. So, I think she didn't know what to do with all her energy! It was a constant, "No I don't want that, where is everyone, where is my car, I am going home," etc. She was also very cute. Her words are so funny. She says "This house is so noisy, I mean you just have to get out of here!" We went into the studio and I finished an art piece I think I like. They say it's not unusual for an artist to be critical of their work. Well, this one I called "And the rain came." So I will drop it off at an AA meeting, anonymously, but at least Mom and I are doing something together.

January 15   I wanted to see John Edwards. He is in town so I called my friend Judy Falzone and we both decided to go. My sister Carol and I had watched John on TV every week. If I missed a week she would record it for me! Tonight for sure was the most exciting day of my whole life! It has left me with a "Did it really happen to me?" You dream this. You pray for this. You ask God for this, and then it happens, and you're too shocked to do more then go through the motions. They had you fill out a card with your name and information on it. We paid for cheap seats. The line was long and I am guessing there were 400 or more people. When John came on stage he explains what would happen. Of course, Judy and I already know how it works. Then he says that the white cards you filled out, he would start with the first 5 picked and then go through the audience and explain how souls really try so hard to come through. You just never know who will come. Then he picked a card and said "Judy Falzone!" Oh, my gosh. They brought the microphone to Judy and John says "I have a male here whose name starts with the letter "R", do you know who that is?" Judy says "Yes, it is my Father." Then John says "He is telling me he was involved with alcohol." Judy says "No, that would have been my friend's Father." So she hands the microphone to me. I say that is my Father, Rudolph! I am crying as I am writing this and this moment will last my whole life! 400 people and my Dad gets through!! Then John says "He says he has a female with him." And I reply "That would be my sister, Carol," to which he reprimanded me for giving a name. You are not supposed to do that. You just say yes or no. So then again, John says "Well, was your Father involved with alcohol?" I say "Yes, he was in AA for 35 years." John says "He says the month of July is very important." I answer "Yes, that is his birthday." "He also talks about May, do you know what that is?" But I don't. What could May be? I had no idea. Then as fast as he came, he was gone because the next question from John was "He says he has a glass eye." With that, the man behind me stands up and loudly says "that is my Father." Must have been because it for sure wasn't my Dad!!! I sat down. We had been prepared for souls coming and others trying to get through. My Dad was gone. Or was he! I sat down but I was freezing. I felt like I fell into a big freezer and then something said to me "It's because your Dad is here." Judy and I could not quit going over every minute of what happened.

As the night went on, a soul came through that was a boy whose Mom was very involved in caring for gay boys. He talked about all his Mother had done, and she stood up and was crying. "My Dad loves me. My Dad wanted me to know he is with me as I care for Mom. He found a way to reach me. Oh Dad, how wonderful you are. I will hold these moments in my heart of ever. I am so humbled, I love you. God is good." *I have typed this exactly word for word from my journal as I remember it very well!! You had to be there to really feel the love in that room.*

For a while souls came and went and then it seemed the last two stayed for a while. John is not from Arizona, but in the papers just a week earlier they had begun to look at a cold case of where one girl was murdered and then later they found another and were wondering if it was the same killer. It was an unbelievable discussion between the girl and John. It seemed the girl's Uncle was in the audience. He stood up and acknowledged his niece was murdered but he didn't have another relative who was. Then the girl, the soul explained, wasn't a relative. I think her words were "They have yet to know what really happened." The rest of the month of January, Mom seemed to be stable, tired, talking, but still doing the cards.

February sodality meeting For our meeting the priest has a special 6pm mass for us. I love it. Then we go into the large room for our meeting, but tonight I did not stay for the meeting. I have decided I want to be with Mom when she is getting ready for bed. Bedtime is hard for Mom. The caregiver is instructed to really wash her off since during the day we just wipe her. That means she has to turn over and let them wash her back side and Mom hates that. So I have started to talk to her. I go to the other side of the bed, smooth her hair and talk to her so she doesn't pay attention to what they are doing. She still says "Miss, what are they doing to me?" and I say "Mom, they are just washing you, now tell me what did you do today." I love this time and I know she appreciates it. Then we say our prayers. I love to hear her pray because she knows every word of the Our Father and Hail Mary. I believe someday I will look back at these moments with a wonderful feeling.

February 14 Valentine's Day was really made so important years ago when I would receive a valentine from my Dad, every year. Some years he put the date, like 1985! So I put them out along with the gorgeous valentines he sent Mom over the years, some from 1945!!! I dressed Mom in red and bought her and the caregiver some valentine cookies. I tried so hard to let Mom know it was Valentine's Day and for some moments she did, then as usual they were gone. She knew her name was Mollie. She was now into grabbing your arm and kissing it. She, at times, did not want to let go. She was kissing their hands, but with flu season I told them not to, so they would extend their arm which she would grab.

February 17 Tonight I am writing a love letter to Dad. I see the caregivers always asking Mom to write "Rudy" a love letter. So now my love letter to Dad will be in my journal forever. I love you so much. I miss you with all my heart and soul! Yes Dad, I mean you. I realize you are with me, every step, and I feel strength. I am glad Carol is with you. A sweeter person and sister. There never was a better one. She was everything I could want in a sister and I certainly missed out. *My sister Carol was 8 years younger. When I was 16 she was 8. I could have done what most big sisters did, and take her everywhere, but I did not. It seemed I never really paid much attention to whatever she was doing. I cannot remember any great times with her. I was very selfish and very jealous at times as she was so cute. Blond curly hair. My Mom says I was jealous from the start and I guess I never really got to be a big sister until years later as you read. I think I was 40 when we started talking together. I missed a lot. I let her down. In later years I really tried to be with her. For 10 years as I cared for Mom in and out of assisted living we spoke every night at 9pm my time and midnight hers. I was blessed to have 20 years with her before she passed.*

Saturday and Sunday   Saturday and Sunday were scary. I really thought "this is it," yet Sunday Mom ate around 4pm, first food since Friday at 4 and Monday woke up with a smile. I cannot figure it out. Since I was thinking she was going home I would be outside and think "I won't see Mom coming down the street in her wheelchair from the walk." It made me sink inside. But I still could not go into the studio, even with her. I was in a panic mode all day!

Ash Wednesday   I went for ashes. I could not wait. I so much wanted to sit, where there is love, no anger, no anxiety, no frustration. Quiet and peaceful and reflect on where I am and ask God if I am doing this right. I joined the botanical garden four years ago and found it a perfect place to go when caregivers came because I loved sitting by the cafe, reading and watching the squirrels looking for food, and the birds would come right up to my chair! We also went there at Christmas to see the lights and art decorations that lit up the garden and music! I took Mom there one year, but after that she didn't really understand and nighttime she didn't see well. But for sure it was my "special place." Today I brought with me Dad's AA book and his refrigeration bible. Both make me feel close to him. I wish I had talked to him on his first days on the job, giving up his dream at the garage. I wonder if Mom sent him off on his new job with a kiss. Only Mom knows.

It's so quiet here and I can really listen to my thoughts. So God asked me "Judy, what makes your heart light up?" and Dad who was there said "Judy, I did what was needed. I worked but I found time to light my heart and the hearts of others, so no excuses!" Dad acknowledged there were times he was not there for me, as I was not for him which haunts me. But he said I made sure "I still found time to make my heart light up. You need to give up some control of your Mother and give it to God who knows when Mom is leaving you. You can't sit around waiting, as if you can control it. You asked God for some creative ideas yet you never even take one step. No painting lately, no canvas, no brush in hand. You want God to do it all, so you sit and wait and watch your Mother. Listen to your own soul, you ask God to help, so listen to what you shall hear, slow down and listen." *I don't even remember writing this. Obviously, I didn't do much about all this, but maybe I did without remembering because I did start to get out more like lunch with a friend. I did find this very humbling, that I could have such a discussion and not heed what was said actually until after Mom was gone. That said, then I read further down my journal and found this………*

March 12   Coming to terms with Mom and how much both of us can take this. Mentally it's hard for me, and physically it's hard for her. As her anxiety increases we are now giving her some anxiety meds. She talks and talks and doesn't even take a breath. The medicine does help but making her sleep isn't really the answer. I need to get a handle on what would be best. But I am getting out in the evenings. Nothing happening in the studio and that hurts when I see all the paint and stuff I have but I know there will be plenty of time later.

March 14   My brother Kenny's 72nd birthday. My "little" brother. Where did the time go? It's only perfect that Mom would be happy on her little baby boy's birthday because he was so cute. It is bedtime and Mom wants me to sleep with her. Not the first time she has asked. She says she might need me and I tell her I am just in the next room, and I knock on the wall by her bed to show her where I will be. She asked me for a light and I told her I would also bring her a treat. So I went and got her a cookie. They are baby cookies so they melt in her mouth so she won't choke. Then she asked for a cookie "for everyone." "We need one for puppy, bunny and Amelia," so I say I will go and get more. So I left her for 10 minutes, knowing she would start to calm down. When I got back she says "We are having a wedding." So I went along with it and asked "Who is the groom?" She says they had not decided yet. So she takes a bite of cookie, gives one to puppy, takes another bite, takes a drink, kisses puppy, gives a bite to Amelia and this goes on for 30 minutes. Then I say, "It's time for me to go, I will see you in the morning," and she is so calm and says "Yes, I hope we will." She actually was so good today. No extra pills. Nothing. What does she have up her sleeve?!!

March 16   Started out as a horrible day but got it under control with 1/2 of a .25 Xanax. That is very low but seemed to work. Different Mollie, asking for kisses, talking so nice to the caregiver. Had a huge fight with the caregiver company. Their caregivers don't come, then they tell me "they don't want to come." No, she just doesn't have enough to fill in. Then she says "If you don't like a new caregiver every day, then do it yourself." I wonder if her company knew how she talked to customers and how they would accept this. I am told the manager is her friend so she is not going anywhere, so guess we have to move on. Having someone new each day I might as well do it myself to show them everything.

March 20   Comfort Keepers. The manager is Wardine. She came out and visited and saw Mom which no other company had done. She could find the right fit with a caregiver so I can cross one more issue with Mom off my list.

April 1   I listen to family radio every night. I love the pipe organ music and I wonder, why? Then I think I was introduced to it at a very early age by Dad. Going to Euclid Beach and skating because he was going to hear the organ music was very much in our home, thanks to Dad. I wonder if I said that to Mom if she would agree, now at 99 years of age, or if she would remember his record collection took up the whole closet in that small projects home!

April 6 Easter Sunday   I remember when I prayed Mom would make it one more Easter coming out of that so-called behavior hospital, my nightmare, and now here she is again, another Easter with us!! "Happy Easter, Mom," we said. We took lots of pictures with her but she was very low-key today. While eating with her I said "Hi Mom." She says "mum mum, Mommy!" I said "No, it's Judy," to which she responds "You're Judy? I have a Judy, but you don't look like her." Then she says "What will I do, I have no money, where will I live?" It's sad to think here is a lady who is with her family and she doesn't even know it. Looking back at the first two years, she was so much better at understanding but hey, she was 94, now she is 99!

April 19   The doctor told me I am not depressed. I could have told him that. I have just slowed down. I have lost interest in some things like the studio, maybe because Mom has lost interest. Now she doesn't understand why she is in here. "Why are we here?" she asks. I refuse to go to San Diego to the condo. I refuse to go to my friend Mary's in California. Let's face it, I can see Mom's days are numbered. For sure she can't go too much longer. She is very tired. We moved up her bedtime to 6:30pm, at least getting her ready. I feel very alone even though I have friends who understand, and a husband, but for some reason I can't explain it as Mom goes down, I go down. I did a couple small canvases to give to AA places. I titled them "Find the angel in you." I created some angels with encaustic wax and used some lace for their wings and whatever. Now I don't even remember what I did. Mom sleeps better. Little bit of sundowner but she is more tired every day. She does scream when you try to put her on the potty because she doesn't understand, but then she will ask for a kiss and tell you she loves you! Danny's birthday is coming. He will be 48. Wow!

April 22   Mom went for a walk with the caregiver, screaming all the way! Why? No one knows, not even her. "Look what he is doing." Who? "Why is he out here?" Who? "I don't want to go, take me home." Some of this is her regular stubbornness. Tonight she told me to "Turn off the light," which meant she didn't even want to have me sit and talk to her. She is just very tired.

April 24   Mom is like a wilting flower. I was helping the caregiver get her ready for bed and she stretches out her arms and says "Let me hug you." She may have severe dementia and she may not understand things but her soul is a beautiful loving soul. But tonight bedtime was so fun. I gave Mom her night med with peaches which she loves. And then her cat Loeke jumped on the bed and came and sat by her. I picked her up and put her on Mom's tummy so she could see her. "Here is your cat" I said to which Mom responded "Is that my cat?" Mom doesn't always know Loeke, but Loeke knows Mom. She is always with her whether Mom is in the recliner or in bed. I think Loeke is now about 17 and she is a beautiful cat.

April 26   Mom is so funny!!! I sat outside with her for breakfast and we had washed her hair this morning and she had a fit. "I am never coming here again." We laugh. One minute she is mad and the next she is asking for kisses. Danny's birthday is the 30th and Mom and Dad's anniversary is the 29th. They were married in 1939 so that would be 76 years!! I watched Mom try to ride the bike. We do this so she won't get blood clots, and lately she has a fit the whole time. It's sort of funny because Mom always was the person who called the shots and now it's me, who knows what is best for her. She still asks what she can do. She still wants to do something. She sits by the door and tries to open it. She is so strong and then she plays with the belt around her trying to undo it and that can keep her busy for an hour. She has always been very determined on what she wants to do and now it is no different.

May 5   Mom is fading, but then people who have visited her over the past five years will tell you she looked like she was fading then. But, no, she was not at all as frail back then. Tonight she went for her usual walk and was very quiet. I guess we are never satisfied. When she is mad on her walk we are upset, now she is quiet on her walk and we worry. But she knew me at bedtime and called me "Judy." I told her we would have coffee together tomorrow. She asks for everyone, from Dad to her sisters. I told her they are in heaven, but she doesn't understand. Today she said "I wish I were dead." I asked her if she wanted to go to heaven and she asked me what that was and where it was and then replied "I just want to go home."

May 9   Today is the Mother's Day Tea at Hackett house in Tempe, I think. Lately I have forgotten to put the dates on my journal page!! One year Debbie and I took our mothers. How fun. We used to go a few places, the four of us. Debbie's Mother has gone to heaven. It was tough for Debbie. I hope all the crying I do now will help me when the time comes. I should use up all my tears and be happy for Mom. Today was a beautiful day and I thought we would eat our breakfast on the patio but Mom didn't even eat her blueberry muffin. Around 3pm she seemed to be more alert, but I doubt she will make it to her 100th birthday, August 28th.

May 10 Mother's Day   What a special day for me!!! All the mothers came, Geri, Cheryl, Lois, Cathy and Mom!! Mom dressed in a new white top and as alive as ever!!!! At one point we were all talking and Mom raised her hand and said "Hey, I'm Mollie and I am over here!" Absolutely amazing!!! This Sunday at church we honor the Blessed Mother, the Mother who will be there for me long after my Mother is gone. Oh my, did I write that? First time I have acknowledged my Mother being gone. This is good. This should help me when she does leave me. Mom asked where her Mother is, where Rudy is and then calls Judy, Judy, yet when I come she says I am not her Judy. When she didn't want to do something and got stubborn we told her "This is a happy home," and her response, funny as usual, "It is?" Lately she also does some baby talk!

May 26   Today hospice came and still is surprised by Mom's demeanor. Mom was asking for kisses, telling her she looked beautiful, asking her if she would take her home and offering her part of her muffin. Mom put on quite a show. I have to explain to the nurse that for a few days she doesn't eat, doesn't know us, and won't do anything!!!

June 3   John's birthday. Mom gave him the ultimate gift by acknowledging him when I told her that it was his birthday! I pointed to John and she said happy "Happy birthday, John," and just when we thought, wow, this is amazing, she adds "and it's my birthday too." But this has been a tough few days. Mom keeps asking how she can get out of here, where is everyone, can she go home and when you try to answer her she just gets upset and doesn't want to listen. Either that or she just doesn't understand. I got a video of her today, singing! How sweet. But she bobs her head up and down since her muscles are just not strong enough. Just how long can this body handle all this?

June 8   Sunday was not a good day. Sunday was a horrible day. Sunday left behind a lot of sadness and tears. A pill at bedtime might help. I might find some of Mom's, but this had nothing to do with Mom! In fact Mom was the only person who could comfort me. I went to her room. It was dark. I had been gone while they put her to bed. I leaned over the bed and put my head on her chest and cried. All of a sudden I felt this arm patting my back. It was like she (her mind) had never left her. She says "Why are you crying, Judy?" She knew it was me. In the dark room, she knew it was me!! I said "Someone said something that was not very nice to me." She asked me why. I said "long story" and I cried, and she said "Can I help you?" She says "I love you. Can I give you a hug?" I think my tears after that were just realizing my Mom knew me, how wonderful. I was wishing I could lay with her like this all night. At that moment I knew I would always remember that she could not see who it was but she knew it was me! I told John it just tells you that a mother always remembers the cry of her child! It also made me realize she would forever be the person who loves me unconditionally. She has never made fun of me and never will! I also realized tonight that Mom was there for me but she won't always be! It*'s hard to read this and not shed some tears. She had hardly known me for many days yet she knew it was me, crying on her chest. At her funeral I said I had lost the one person who loved me unconditionally, regardless of what I said or what I did. And now looking back at my life with Mom I know it was my unconditional love for her that gave me the strength these last few years.*

July 14   I watch each hour as Mom goes through hell and downhill. Yes, I believe she knows she is unhappy, feels alone, is not home, and is in pain. She calls me constantly yet I am not 100% sure she knows it's me. Today I did not leave the house. I wanted to just stay home with her. Mom has started to get a sore on her back. Something I swore would never happen here! The nurse says it happens to everyone. I said "Not my Mother," so she told me to put this medicine on a cotton swab and put it on the sore twice each day. Instead I dipped the swab in holy water. She had already told me nothing would help this and it happens to all when they sit too long, so I thought why give her the medicine.   I decided I knew God was with me and I would just go with whatever I thought would be the best care.

July 21   The nurse came back today. She checked the sore and says "Well this has all healed but that's impossible because these sores go so deep they never really close." I said that I didn't use the medicine and used holy water and she said "Whatever works." *Maybe sometime the nurse will read this book and she will know that this is exactly what happened to Mollie and she will remember she said "Well, whatever works!"*

July 26   Listening to the sermon today I turned on my iPhone recorder and recorded it because I really liked it. So now I am writing it from my recorder. "God doesn't allow you to get into anything you cannot get yourself out of. He had the solution before you had the problem. Call out to God and he will answer you. God is alpha and omega. The beginning and the end." There is a point where God says "enough is enough." He has already set an end. I have always believed that. It's call faith. What my Mother is dealing with is only temporary. This valley is not her home. God has already purchased her ticket home!

July 27   I went to court for jury duty but was sent home. I got up early and got there early so went to church and home to have breakfast with Mom. The caregiver situation is not good lately and tonight there was no one so John and I put Mom to bed and she was so good. I wonder if she realized we were doing this by ourselves. It's not hard. It just takes time to ensure she sits on the potty long enough to tinkle so there is less wet in the pants in the morning. Then I washed her. She would die if a man, John, washed her! Imagine, 99 and she still knows she does not want a man bathing or changing her. One time a male nurse came to check on Mom and she was so upset when he just listened to her heart under her blouse!!! I hope a caregiver comes tomorrow since I am supposed to get my mammogram.

Chapter 62

We Made it Through the Rain

This is a song by Barry Manilow and I love the words!!

August 28 Mom is 100. No one would have believed it!!! Even I, who have been with her every day since she came at the age of 94, would have thought she would make it. And if that's not enough, today she was amazing. She was talking to neighbors that came in and, of course our biggest surprise of all, my cousins surprised us and came in from Ohio! I remember this day, every minute, so I don't need to read my journal. I had a cake made for her using a copy of one of her playing cards. She had those giant cards and she played every single day, missing maybe 10 days in 6 years!! The store can take the card and make an edible copy and put it on with the frosting!! I took a picture. As soon as she got up we were singing happy birthday. She at first wondered whose birthday it was and we told her she was 100. She kept saying "Not me, not me!" Then we repeated how we were going to celebrate with a cake and some friends and we had balloons outside on the gate. "We are?" she said. I wheeled her out front to see the balloons on the front gate. I said "All for you Mom. You are 100 today." She really didn't sound very excited. She actually was very calm like she understood there was something special going on. Then she saw the balloon tied to her wheelchair.

I had bought her a new cotton and lace top and some new slippers. Her long socks she always wore seemed too tight on her toes, so I picked up some slippers with a pink ribbon. Our neighbor Brenda brought her some flowers. More flowers came from everywhere in Ohio from her niece, Chickie, her sister, Mary's daughter who is now going on 90, and her sons Kenny and Louis. Louis sent her a corsage to wear! I was so caught up in this day that it would take me a few minutes during the day to catch my breath and realize my Mom made it to 100!! We made it to 100!!

I had my camera set on video when these people came in the front door and down to the kitchen. When I saw them, my first thought was "Well, I told all the neighbors this was an open house, but for some reason I don't recognize these neighbors." Then it hit me, they were my cousins Linda and Susan from Ohio, along with Matthew, Linda's son! What? I was in such shock I put down the iPhone and the video. I guess John didn't realize the video was going and no one was taking the picture of all this! Oh, my gosh!!! Linda and Susan were the daughters of Dad's brother John. Linda had cared for her Mom after Uncle John passed. They said they left at 4:30am to catch a flight to Arizona and had just gotten here! I had not seen them since 1997 at Dad's funeral. Linda loved my Mom and Dad. She mentioned many times how Dad had helped her with a boyfriend that would drink and then drive. Dad had told her to call him and he would pick her up, which she did once, and then she stayed at Mom and Dad's overnight. It was Linda and Susan, along with my cousin Janet, who was John's and my flower girl for our wedding and who sent Mom cards every single month. Oh, how Mom loved opening the cards. She would put them in her purse, which of course she had on her lap 99% of the time. Many times when Mom would get very anxious, rather than a pill, we would pull out all the cards she had stuffed in her purse and read them to her, or even let her read them. Mom was sitting in the recliner by the window when they came so we pulled up chairs and they sat and talked to her. They brought her a beautiful soft stuffed kitty, which later Mom added to her "Babies at night." She would say "Let's not forget our new baby," as I would set them up every night at bedtime so she could see them as she laid down.

Yes, everyone remembered Mom's birthday with flowers and cards. My brother Kenny could not fly because he had just had a new pacemaker put in, and I know how bad he felt. He had come for her 95th and I told him he had come at the best time. I know for sure, no matter what he would have said, Mom never would have acknowledged him now, five years later. The kids came over and we took some pictures outside. I have one of Geri, my daughter-in-law that I love. She is kneeling next to Mom. I had that picture sent into this magazine that did an article on Mom and me. Geri loved my Mom from the moment she met her while dating my son Johnny. Johnny always referred to Mom as "nana" even when kids would kid him about that. I remember once hearing one of the kids say "You're supposed to call her your Grandmother." Johnny, who was about 7 at the time replied that she is "my nana!"

So Linda and the gang left Ohio at 4:30am, spent the day and had dinner with us, and then went to the hotel since they were leaving at 5am the next morning for home. They all had to go to work, but they came all that way for such a short time. But when I said it was such a short time, they didn't look at it that way. They felt it was the best thing they ever did and to this day they feel the same way. All I remember is staring at them thinking "I don't remember meeting these neighbors!" They will attest to the fact Mom was so perfect. She sat and talked to them, just loving all the company. There were "no other friends" that appeared to her that day. I hated to see the day end. It was a miracle. I felt like it was a party for everyone!! I wrote in my journal that I had not seen Mom so alive, so aware, so absolutely in the moment, in months. After everyone left, and it was late, I went to her room to kiss her and tell her she was now 100, but she was asleep. I guess her body did realize it was a big day for her and she did not wake up during the night. As you are reading this, did you think she would make it to 100? I have said so many times my Mom was amazing. I know she was tired, her body was tired, her mind was tired and yet, as she did mentally, doing her silverware and writing letters, her body also just didn't give up.

Chapter 63

I Never Saw it Coming

I started to write this chapter, and then after just writing for 5 days I quit. I know what is coming, since I have lived it. So I put this down for the day and went and put together the introduction. So now I am back to reading the journal.

September 4   At 10pm Mom was still awake. This conversation was sweet, but sad. Mom says "Why do you call me Mother?" I told her because she is my Mother and I was born a baby girl to her! She says "You were? You are my family?" Then I told her I was her daughter, Judy. She says "Judy, I am going to the doctor tomorrow, will you drive me?" (total change of issue). So I asked her why she was going to the doctor and I laughed, even though it was not funny! She told me it was because her leg hurt so I went and found a lidocaine patch and put it on her leg. As I write this I think, who would check her at 10pm? If so, who would call her "Mother" so she would feel like she was with her family? I guess sometimes I realize that the care Mother is getting is unavailable when you have 30 patients and three night caregivers. That's why I am so proud of John for letting me care for Mom.

September 8   Mom slept until 1:30am. I had to check to be sure she was alive. When I went in at 11:00pm she was asleep put I figured she had to be soaked in her night pants. So I decided to try to change them. I had tried this once before and I knew I might wake her but I decided to try anyway. She woke up and wondered what I was doing. I was having a hard time getting this soaked diaper from under her, even when she turned over. I almost started crying realizing I might not get this off, and then I said a prayer to "Please give me the strength to just pull this diaper off," and off it came. This was not the first miracle God gave me during the years. I would experience them almost daily. I then put clean pants on and she went back to sleep! Her days are really getting shorter. But again, the caregivers keep her busy all day.

September 25   I can't do it. Again we made arrangements for Mom in a home for the weekend while I go to my shop in California to close it out. After visiting the home, and I will say it was very nice, I just could not do it. I always go the first night and I always have the caregiver stay with Mom. For some reason, I just did not want Mom leaving home. I had made arrangements with Gloria to come Saturday night, the nice lady who has been the night person for the last year. She is wonderful, even feeds the cat!! So I have been calling Gloria and no answer. Where is Gloria??

September 26   No word from Gloria so I called her home one more time and her bishop answered. He told me "Gloria has died!" I told him I had been calling for 3 days. What? Seems Gloria got sick and her husband, who I think has some dementia, didn't realize it so he just left her alone. Then the husband said "Gloria came out of the bedroom last night and said she was cold so he put a pillow down by the heater and she laid down." But Saturday am she did not wake up so he had called their bishop. I had lost my best ever night caregiver. She loved Mom.

October 5   Mom is up and down. Sleeps late, goes to bed early. Went to sodality but did not stay for the meeting. I really wanted to get home to put Mom to bed with the caregiver. I really love that time with her because I know she appreciates it. I would hate to think she was getting washed, which she hated, and laying there alone.

October 17   I had heart palpitations last night. Not the norm for me. Is my body responding to some stress that I cannot identify? Mom is so tired lately yet she sleeps all night with no meds and is very active in the morning. She is so sweet. I gave her silverware to put away today and she tried so hard. I told her "Mom, you are doing your job so perfect," and she looked up at me and with a smile said "I am?" Oh, my gosh I love her so. I know this can't go on forever but I am glad I am here with her now and she is not in Ohio and in a home.

October 24   I feel Mom is less and less able to realize where she is or what she is doing. The older I get the smarter my parents get!! I am thinking of some things Mom would tell me how to handle XYZ. And I would think "Well, that's her, but I am different." No I am not! I was thinking how much Mom and Dad went through but they showed me strength in adversity. *I wrote a whole page on Mom and Dad in my journal that night. Like I was recapping everything they went through and how much I love them. I wrote that "The unconditional love I feel for them will always surpass the pain I feel inside." What I am wondering as I wrote this is why I wrote this. Did I see something that I did not express in my journal up to now?*

October 25   Thank goodness for hospice who came today. They explained how much she is eating and how long she stays awake. It makes no difference. She is going to start shutting down! But she stayed up from 1:00 to 6:00pm and ate some supper. I kept telling her "Mom, I am Judy your daughter," and she did finally say "I love you." But my Mom still plays with her cards! I would have said "I can't see the cards, I am tired, I don't want to do this," but not Mom!!!

October 26   Mom was up for 2 hours from 11:30am to 1:30pm. We put her in her recliner and decided to let her sleep and she will wake up for supper, but she never did! I was up three times hearing her mumbling on the monitor but by 10:30pm she was sound asleep, but me? I am up. I am down. I am beside myself. I am sad just hoping she will wake up for breakfast. I am going to give her a treat with breakfast in bed and I am going to sit with her! I went into the kitchen after checking her at 10:30pm and see her pretty pink cereal dish, her pink tray all ready for tomorrow and my knees get weak. Death is so final and grief so destructive. I want to run, but no place to go. It's like she fell off a cliff, one day doing silverware and now not waking up much. Did I do something wrong? Did she not want to stay here longer?

October 27   11:00am the nurse came. I told him I had blessed Mom with holy water at 4am and she seemed to mumble a little. Nurse was checking her and she woke up so we dressed her and put her in her recliner. She ate the whole baby food jar of fruit. Nurse is amazed. Since it was so nice out we moved her outside, pushing her in the recliner. It was a gorgeous day and she noticed the fountain and the birds drinking from it. I am amazed at how much she can still see. We put her to bed at 5:30pm but she was very vocal!! At 8pm she was still awake and talking, but not as loud. She is upset because she feels she isn't talking right, and that also is amazing. Thank you God for this day!

October 29   We let her eat her muffin in bed because she has a hard time holding up her head. But she was very sweet. At 2:00pm she took a nap. She is very tired because she got a bed bath today and she tried to talk. It was very soft and hard to understand. What I thought I heard was "I wish I could be here when you come home? Or was it come back?" I'm not sure.

October 30   Mom was up today around noon. She fell asleep in the recliner from 3 to 5:30pm. She is more comfortable in bed. I kissed her at 7:30pm because it looked like she was going back to sleep. She kisses my hand when I come to her bed and she knows me! She also still talks although some is garble. Yesterday she said to me "Judy, don't take it so hard." I was shocked! She was so aware.

Halloween 2015   Where is Mollie? That is what everyone asks. Yes, Halloween without Mom! Today Mom was so awake we brought her out to the kitchen. She ate her whole muffin and we took her for a walk outside. It was amazing! It's Halloween and a little girl in a costume asked "Where is Mollie?" I asked her how did she remember Mollie? She said, she would come and watch us next door at the gym practice and she would clap for us! Yes!! Yes! Mom did that!! Mom loved watching the little girls. Mom had fallen asleep at the table at 5:00pm (see picture) so we had put her to bed. I ran into her room after talking to the little girl and put my head on Mom's chest and cried and said "Mom, someone missed you," and then thought this won't be the first time someone asks "Where is Mollie?"

November 1   Amazing. Mom woke up and was hungry! She ate all her cereal and three glasses of water and juice. Then she took a nap at 2:00pm but still sleeping at 8:50 pm!! At 5:30pm when she did not wake, we changed her pants, cleaned her up and put puppy and bunny in her arms and she slept. That was at 5:30pm. Little did we guess four hours later she would still be sleeping. She amazes us. First she sleeps, then she gets up and eats! The nurse told me they get their days and nights mixed up so I wondered if that means she will be up at 3am. Doesn't matter, I will sit up with her. I did not leave the house today. I am not going out of the house until I am sure she wakes up for at least breakfast and talks to us.

November 4   Oh, my gosh, Mom was up and talking at 4am yesterday. Loud and clear!! I went in and told her to talk softly, you will wake up your babies and I put puppy on top of her. And clear as day, after a week of mumbling, she says "I love you!" I was thrilled. Worth waiting for! This morning she seemed tired. I was not surprised at 11:30am she was quiet even while we washed her hair. She did eat a little and fell asleep in the recliner. I knew she might not wake up until 4am or maybe not until tonight at 11:00pm. Seems like we are back to where we were. How will I take this loss! What will I do? I have no idea. She is up, she is down, she eats, and she doesn't eat.

November 5   Bad day. Mom is so unresponsive but she was somehow knowledgeable about what we were doing for her. But she just would not open her eyes. Never opened her eyes. She slept all day. Then at 8pm she is talking away but eyes still closed. Where is she? I was up all last night every time I heard a sound. She would mumble but not acknowledge me. I told her she was a caterpillar and soon will be a butterfly. *Why did I not see this coming??? Why did I not get in bed with her and hold her? Well, you will read why.*

November 7   Last night the kids came over. Geri gave her a hug and the kids understood she is going to heaven. I am remembering the night I came home. In the dark in her room I cried about something and I felt her hand on my back and heard her say "Don't cry, Judy." Oh God, will I ever hear her say my name again? I wanted to hug her hard when she was in the wheelchair or recliner.   I wanted to feel her next to me. I wanted to feel the warmth she always projected. I just wanted to be near her. The nurse came this morning. She said, "Her lungs are clear and her heart is strong, she is not dying. But things will get ugly. Her feet will turn black and you might then want to bring her to hospice." I told him "There is nothing ugly on my Mother and she is not leaving his house." I was crying and he said "Don't worry, she has at least one to two weeks yet." So now, I feel I have more time. But for what? She lays there*. I am not reading from my journal now because I don't need to. I know every single word I said that night as I went to bed. First at 10pm when she did not wake up, I picked her up off the sheet and hugged her. Kissed her on the lips, on her face, everywhere. Remember, at this point she still has 1 week or so. But I just wanted to hold her like she probably held me* *as a baby. She was like a rag doll, my rag doll as I cried. I went to bed and as I laid on my pillow I said to God "Oh God, I am so useless, I cannot buy her favorite muffin, I cannot put another pretty bow in her hair, and there is nothing I can do for her. She belongs to you, you need to decide what to do."*

November 8 6am As soon as I woke up I went to Mom's room because I did not hear anything on the monitor all night. In the dark room her forehead seemed cold so I thought it was the fan I left on and then I realized she had woken up to love and peace and great sunlight. A beautiful garden where the trees talk and the mountains sing. Mom had gone home. Wait, I screamed! Wait. They told me she had a week or more! Why didn't I see it coming?

November 9 10pm I can hardly write this. Oh, how I miss her. Oh Mom, I am so happy for you. No more wheelchair, no more pain, but I am dying inside. My heart is broken. My Mother is gone. My little girl, who was so sweet and loved kisses, is gone. Oh God, help me!!! Her death certificate says she passed from senile dementia. I just say "God brought her home." My Mother's funeral was held two days later. I wanted it over as quickly as I could. I knew I had little time to hold it all together. I had read about people in shock and how they react, like nothing really happened and then the whole body shuts down. Her funeral was handled by the Messinger Mortuary in Scottsdale and they were so nice. Her mass was at our Lady of Perpetual Help Church, the same church I took her to for that Easter I thought she would never see. Yes, Mom was amazing to the end. Even hospice was shocked. The nurse said "Leave it to Mollie to surprise us all." She had been surprising everyone for over 6 years. When my friend Sandy's Mother passed I remember visiting the hospice where she was. Sandy's family was there but I had never met most of them. As I looked at Sandy's Mom I started to cry. I then turned to the family and said "I am not crying because this is sad but because I can see all the angels around here and it's so beautiful." Later Sandy sent me this card, which was so beautiful. I did not want to lose it, so I did an art piece and transferred the words to the canvas.

"She said she usually cried at least once each day not because she was sad   but because the world was so beautiful and life was so short"

I love this piece and now it means even more to me because I know for years there will be tears. I know, for me, it will be because of the beauty of it all. My Mother woke up in glory and found that she was home. But while Mom had earned her place, and she was experiencing it with Rudy, "Her Rudy" as she called him. It was beautiful and her Rudy was there to meet her. Here on earth it was a different setting all together.

I had a visitor..... Grief.

Chapter 64

Love Has No Number

Quoting from the book by Shark, *Glad No Matter What,* "Grief demands to be acknowledged." Well, it did not just come and let me know it was there, it refused to leave!

Now I was not getting any support from my family, other than my husband. My children were very disgruntled with me "After all Mom, nana was 100." Learn from my experience and never say that to someone who has lost an aged parent! They say men show emotions different than women so I guess I could say my sons didn't understand a loss of a loved one and for sure she was loved. Heaven knows she was a great Grandmother, always there if they wanted something, excited to see them. They were her world for many years. When we moved away and took the kids she told me her world stopped. She still wanted me to know I needed to do what was best for my family. And now all they can say is "Geez Mom, she was 100." Well guess what? She was also my Mother! I won't get another one. I don't want another one!

They were still very upset with the fact we did not show up to celebrate Thanksgiving, two weeks after she passed. What exactly did they want me to do, just show up, smile, laugh, totally ignore the fact my Mom was not sitting at the end of the table? That she wasn't in the kitchen washing the dishes? She was always the first to get up when she was well and get started cleaning up. Just because they felt it was time to move on didn't mean I was feeling the same way. I could barely eat. They didn't care that I had a hard time going anywhere where my Mother had been although John felt we needed to leave the house. Oh no, all they thought of was how silly my grief was. It was like they wanted to say "Get over it Mom," but didn't say it out loud.

We did go to California for Thanksgiving to my friend of over 30 years, Mary. With Mary I could cry. We could talk. She understood even though she had not lost her mother. All my friends, Cheryl, Debbie, Sandy, Judy, all of them had lost their mothers. My sons were

302

furious. Actually, I could go as far as to say they thought the whole grief thing was an overkill! Yep. I believe that. So I had grief coming from everywhere. The sadness of the actions of my sons and the death of my Mother. I could not even say her name out loud! I read everything. I went to grieving classes. Here is why the classes did not work for me. I sat there with people who had lost a child or a husband. I was there because my Mom had passed at age 100 plus. I felt bad when I cried and cried when they asked me to talk about my Mother. I could not get the words out. I would look at the faces of the others and realize they could not understand my grief either. I had nowhere to go to express my grief. All the people I loved were gone, except for my husband and my friends. My family totally dismissed me, and my Mom and Dad, who loved me so much, were gone! So, I started to slip into complete depression and guilt over grieving for a Mother who I had the blessing to live with and care for over 6 years. Goodbye to grieving classes. This really was a bad idea. But I knew I was not going back.

People would say to me 'Oh, but how lucky you were to have her for 100 years." Did that mean I could not miss her? Do we ever have enough time? I began to justify my depression and sadness by explaining to myself that "Caring for Mom was my path." Now, I had completed my path and so at any time now I would leave this earth and be with Mom and Dad. I was not unhappy. In fact if I left to go anywhere in the car I would think "Well, maybe I will pass in a car accident." (I never use the word "die" because I don't believe we ever die.) As God said "Those who believe in Me shall have life everlasting." So I waited. I felt I had nothing to lose. Of course, I did not express that to my husband, John, because he had loved my Mother and I knew he also was grieving. I really didn't have to say anything to him. He had been there with me for six years and now the house was so quiet. I also knew it was not my decision when my path was complete. God had made that decision for me long ago.

At Christmas my family was still upset with us for not coming at Thanksgiving. So they decided to change the plans for Christmas. I will never understand that but, at the time, I didn't care. The change in our long traditions meant little to me. I was just existing and they could do whatever they wanted. It did, however, upset my husband. John's family growing up had no traditions and he could actually say he didn't remember any special Christmas. When he married into our family he just loved every way we celebrated. He was so glad when we moved to Arizona that our children wanted us to continue with what they had In Ohio. As far as I was concerned I had lost my sons on November 8, along with my Mother. My depression was so bad even my friends would tell me "Judy, we are worried about you," but nothing worked. To say I was shocked with the level of my grief was putting it mildly.

There was a beautiful scene that happened in California. One of my favorite places and, again a place Mom never went with me, is Seaport Village. There is a coffee shop there called the Upstart Crow Coffeehouse & Bookstore. I love it there. Books, seats by the window and I always just felt so calm sitting there. So for sure I could not wait to get there. This was the Friday after Thanksgiving and the place is extremely busy! The line for coffee was pretty long and so when it was my turn, I ordered my cappuccino, but Mom's picture fell out of my wallet. As I picked it up I began to cry, a silent cry, but a cry. I then went to get the $.69 cents out of my wallet ($5.69) and was having a hard time, so this lady behind me says "I will pay her $.69 cents." (to get the line moving) I turned to her and said "You cannot do a good deed. My Mother just passed and I am doing 100 good deeds because she was 100," and she could see the tears in my eyes. Well, what did she do? She put her arms around me and hugged me. The person behind her, a young girl, gave me a hug also and said "How wonderful that you loved her so much." What did the people in line do? Were they all in a hurry to just get this hugging over? No. None of them were angry, none. They were all so understanding. There were small murmurs from the whole line of people of understanding. Can you believe that? Well, believe it!

Meanwhile, after Mom passed and they took all the hospital beds, etc. out, and before we re-carpeted etc., I would go in there and lay on the bare floor. I felt so close to her. When we returned after Thanksgiving we immediately redid the room. We had taken up the carpet a year before Mom passed so we put down carpet and moved in this headboard I had purchased 3 years earlier at Sweet Salvage. We hung angel pictures on the walls and kept her dresser that Aunt Mary had given her, which by now is about 75 years old or more! I really thought that now I would not have to go past an empty room. But it didn't help. I would go in every

304

morning, just like I had when she was alive, and say "Good Morning Mom." Believe it or not these little things actually helped me! I felt she was still there somehow. Don't ask me how, I really don't know. I had described my Mother's skin as like a caterpillar and then when she passed, being the butterfly. There was a watercolor picture of a butterfly I had purchased in 1986 when we lived in Albuquerque. I had hung it in her room all these years and now it hung in a very special place. Now I felt it really belonged in that room.

So now I had lost my Mother and my kids were so mad at us. Life wasn't looking too good and I didn't see any light at the end of the tunnel. I just existed. Mom passed in November. Her ashes were to be sent to Ohio for burial with my Dad in April. These ashes were in a box in a velvet bag and I took them to bed every night. They were like my security blanket. My husband understood and never said a word. How I could grieve for "nana" when I should be starting to concentrate on traveling and doing things with my husband. Well, at times I thought that also, for about a minute. Actually my sons had never experienced deep grief and so they never understood. I thought about this little girl, because that is what she was like the last year. The little girl I never had. Then I would cry over the loss of my companion. You read where with John working and me retired, Mom went everywhere with me. So people would say, "Well, now go with your husband." John was so understanding. The fact I was so down I did not want to travel and I really felt bad about that, so add that to my depression.

I was sad that I just could not come out of this horrible existence. I wondered if I could ever live my life without thinking or seeing something of my parents. By now you're saying "But Judy, they both caused you a lot of grief during your lifetime." Well, it's natural to remember the good times and God was good that He gave me those wonderful years to realize how much they loved me and how much I loved them. So that thought didn't work. So who came to my aid? My best friend, Jan. She flew from Denver to be with me for a week. It wasn't like my other friends didn't try, but now Jan was actually living with me day by day. She brought along a handmade glass box. She said "If you think you would like to keep some of your Mother's ashes, which is not unusual, you can put a couple teaspoons in this glass box." What? I never thought

305

of that. For sure I could never open this box. But the thought of keeping just a few ashes would certainly be better than sleeping with the whole box every night. She told me when the ashes are gone it was going to be hard for me. She told me I could also order a locket to hold a few ashes. The next day the thought of keeping some of Mom's ashes made me feel so much better! You had to know how I was still in total grief 5 months later with no thoughts of how I could get myself together. So, now back at home I said to Jan "I would like to save some ashes but I cannot open the box. I cannot under any circumstances see the ashes or remove any." So she did! What really got to me was the little metal piece that dropped out. Later I would take it to my orthopedic doctor who asked "Did your Mom ever break her femur?" I said "Yes." He said this is the metal piece we put in during surgery. Thank you God. Now I knew these were Mom's ashes.

Jan stayed for a week. We went to the Mesa Art Museum and just got out. It felt so good, I actually felt like, yes, it's time to put grief to bed! So now I had a few ashes and when it came time to mail the ashes back to Ohio, I felt good about it for two reasons. One, because I felt my brother Kenny deserved to have her ashes in his house for a while, and two, because she would now be with my Dad. I did not go to the burial of the ashes in Ohio. I was still not mentally stable and I knew I was unable to relive the loss of Mom and would just disrupt the whole service. I have the ashes. I am sleeping better, but still crying just saying her name. I prayed so hard. I remember Mom saying to me about a year before she passed, "Judy, don't take it so hard." She didn't preclude that with any other sentence like "I want to be with your Father." Nothing. She just spurted that out. Wow, how did she know!

I have turned to prayer my whole life for everything. In my Catholic grade school religious lessons we were always taught to ask God for help. I used to ask him to help me win the pencil case when Sister Raymond would have a small raffle if we did our homework!!!! I also remember Joel Osteen saying "Remember, you are the daughter of a King and you can ask for anything." Not that my Catholic upbringing didn't tell me the same, but hearing it over and over whenever I needed it. Then, as prayer would have it two things happened. First, I met a stranger at the store. Her elderly Mother was with her. I asked if I could hug her Mom because I had lost mine. She thought that was a beautiful idea. Then after I hugged her I turned away because I was crying. She put her arms around me and talked to me. She told me I really needed to go to grief classes! When I explained how I felt guilty at the classes because people had lost a baby or a son, she said something I will never forget. "LOVE HAS NO NUMBER." Just like that. These people can't say they loved their baby to a #10 and of course my love for my Mom had to be #5 because she was 100. NO NO NO. There is no number on love. We each loved the ones we lost just as much as anyone who lost a loved one. Age or gender has no place in how much we love!! So for some reason I felt a lot better. Just like that. Like one huge piece of my depression over those classes was over. But I still missed Mom. Now I found I was not missing this little girl that at times did not even know me, but instead my Mother! Mom. I missed calling her. I missed just talking to her. And that was natural, except there was something else I could do about that.

And I did.

Chapter 65

Respect and Love

Dad's journey with sobriety brought so many holiday traditions to our home that were just wonderful, especially after all the siblings were married. Those years, with the height of us coming to Mom and Dad's for Easter and Christmas, were my fondest memories. I know my Dad had to think many times during these wonderful family gatherings that all this would never had happened without his sobriety, but Mom is still not to be forgotten. What I found to be such a lesson in strength in adversity is that she went to work each day with such determination to do the best job she could do regardless of what she had left behind. She kept moving up in positions through her work career. She began her career 22 and 1/2 years earlier as just a cook's helper!!!

I am still in awe at all she accomplished. Think about this as you have read about her life on the farm to being a nanny or housekeeper, going through a pregnancy when those were not looked kindly upon, and the issues at home with her and Dad. Then she takes a job and needs to walk to work for probably the first years and here she is being honored at a dinner! You have read the details around the successes of my Mom but here I want to stress that I sometimes think maybe they both, in their own ways, really started to respect each other and maintained that respect through their lives together.

Now, over 50 years later, I can honestly say I saw and better understand the respect and love I did not think I would ever see!!

My Mom and Dad were both worth saving!

Chapter 66

The Tea Reading Experience

I was at an outside event where John worked. We stood in line to have our "tea" read! I did it for the fun. I was talking with a friend while in line so I didn't care about waiting. I have never done this before. Maybe she could tell me something exciting, considering this was after Mom left me with a big lease to try to fix. So she dipped the cup into the tea leaves. I remember this and can see it as it happened. She pulled it out and was silent. Silent. Silent. Finally she said "I have never experienced a reading such as this." "Oh great," I am thinking. She showed me the cup. One half was white. One half was dark. Totally separated, I had to admit it looked amazing, but I didn't realize it was so rare. She said the black means you are going to have some very troubled and dark days. Very dark. I said "Well, I just had a year or so already. Can't get any worse. My Mom has moved on me at least four times, I quit counting." She said, "Yes, it will, your dark days are far from over," but she said "The white means your days will be as wonderful as they were dark. Very wonderful. Beautiful. Beautiful beyond your comprehension."

As time went on I always remembered that reading. I thought about giving up my life, caring for Mom, worrying about caregivers coming, worrying if she did not quality for hospice again, feeling terrible and useless for Mom and her sadness. I was overcome with sadness when she would say "Miss, would you take me to my family?" Were those the dark days she predicted?

It has taken a few years, but now I know I was wrong. I had it backwards. The white was the blessing God gave me in caring for Mom. The black is now the years I have without her.

Amen!

Chapter 67

Love Me, That's All I Ask of You

Well, you have read about Mom through the years with us kids growing up, Dad going from drinking too much to his sobriety and to her 20 years with Euclid School System with the fabulous retirement party they gave her. She is a wonder, but let's talk about Mom and me! We could start with my move from Ohio, where she always followed me, through San Diego, Phoenix, Albuquerque and back to Phoenix. She was always at the end of the line if I needed help. But our lives together went much further over the years and here are some of our most exciting moments together.

Moms 75th birthday. "Mom, I am in New York City for a meeting. Why don't you meet me there and I will take you to see *Phantom of the Opera* for your birthday?" I said on her answering machine! 75 was young for her. She made arrangements, got to the New York airport, found her way to a blue van and arrived at the Marriott Hotel in Times Square. My meetings ended around 3pm and I had left word at the desk to give her a key. Well, she got the key and then proceeded to go out and see New York!! By the time I got through the meetings she was just coming back and had walked everywhere! She had her purse slung around her shoulder and she was ready to go!!

The following morning we walked a little and then went to get ready for the matinee of *Phantom*. We were both so excited. It was 1980. We came home and she decided to take a bath. I hear her holler and went in and she was standing under the shower with blood spurting out of her leg and hitting the back of the tub. I helped her out, put her on the bed and called the desk. In minutes they had paramedics there who determined she just had a small vein that for whatever reason opened. It was not serious, but she could absolutely not walk with it. But that didn't stop Mom, or me!! After they bandaged it up I called down for a wheelchair. I was going to wheel her down Broadway to the show. "Oh, I am sorry we don't allow wheelchairs to leave the hotel" was what they told me, but I wasn't giving up that easy. I explained I had these tickets for a performance. The girl put me on hold, came back and said "Are you with the Motorola group who has been here for 3 days?" "Yes." "Well, the manager says he will allow you to take the wheelchair." So down the street we went, around the corner, down Broadway to the theater. Mom had her leg out in front of her and we were just whizzing down the street. However, when we arrived they explained "We do not have handicap services." Again, we were not giving up. Mom explained the story and how excited we were to get this far. So, the angels realized we needed help and worked their magic. The manager came out and said "We will set the wheelchair along the side of the wall, right up by the front row!" Front row? Yippee!! So I stood behind her to ensure she didn't fall out, as I promised, and we watched the first act. Then, they came up with a little chair so I could sit behind her!!! Don't you wish you could have watched her face as this lady, who grew up on a farm, worked so hard with her children and husband, and now is practically in the front row of a Broadway show? On the way out we bought her a souvenir and I got a t-shirt, which I still wear to this day on special occasions! The following day I wheeled her over to St. Patrick's Cathedral. We did as much as we could before we had to leave. I got her a taxi and even though she said "Hey, I did good coming and can find my way back." I still got the taxi. That was far from the end of our adventures.

A year later I was in New Orleans on business and called her. I would be finished on Friday at noon so we would only have that afternoon and Saturday so I wondered if she was in for a couple days in New Orleans. She had never been there, nor had I. It's always more fun when you take the adventure with someone. Mom who by now was 77, never held me back, she was always ready to go. Same thing, I got out of the meeting and she was in the hotel having already walked around town. We went to all the special places in New Orleans, loving the inside of the cathedral, walking down Royal Street, the historic neighborhood and at night the French Quarter. The next day she said she wanted to go down the river on the paddle boat!! So we did. We ordered drinks and sat at a table outside right by the edge of the boat security fence. She ordered us both pina coladas!!! Believe it or not we were also there while they were doing some filming. We just mixed in with the crowd which was told to follow this horse drawn carriage. After 5 takes we left!!! And let's not forget the trolley ride through the area of vintage homes. We both loved that! We both went to the airport together. She caught the Ohio flight and I returned to Arizona!

What was special was some of the little things we did together. She was always available!! John and I had to move from our home in Scottsdale, which we sold in one day, something we just decided to try since all the kids had left and were shocked when it sold so quickly. John was working out of town, so I moved into a condo we had purchased when we moved to Albuquerque so we would have a place to stay when we would take trips back to Arizona. It was only 700 sq. feet. We had to use the outside storage for my clothes closet! John had to drag me into that home and then had to try to drag me out!! We found we loved it. He was traveling and with a small place we would take a Southwest flight every other weekend to California. We had no home to maintain. It was like a vacation. Then we had to reinvest the money from the big house. The law has changed since then but we had 18 months. So as John was leaving to go out of town for two weeks he told me "You need to go buy a house and you have 20 days for it to transfer or we are going to pay a big fine." Well, long story short, I found one. Moving day was two days before I had to leave for a business trip and would be gone a week so I called Mom. She came down on Saturday. All the boxes were in the kitchen and garage. So she said "What if I just unpack the kitchen while you're gone?" Great idea. When I came back everything was unpacked. For the three years I lived in that house I never knew where anything was, but I didn't care. Mom said she had so much fun, moving into a brand new kitchen. That was Mom!

When she moved to her home on McDowell, I left for Palm Springs for John and my regular week to golf. Something happened and John could not join me but I still had 4 days so I called Mom. "Mom," I said. "I will buy you a ticket. You need to go to the bus station and tell them you are going to Palm Springs and there is a paid ticket for you." I knew when the bus was supposed to arrive and I waited, right where it would stop. Meanwhile, Mom got on the bus. It was a 5.5 hour ride, not 3 hours which it is by car. Mom says she loved talking to everyone and for a few times she wondered if I would be there or get the time wrong. I have a picture of her exiting the bus, her pink hat on, her purse around her shoulders. As she exited everyone on the bus stopped to tell her to have a good time. When she spotted me she says "Oh Judy, I was so happy to see you. It was a long ride." I remember the author that helped me during my "author in residence" program for 3 months. Three authors, 3 months. It was the second author that said to me "Judy, details!" I had written, "Mom and I went to Palm Springs and had a good time," to which he said, "Judy details, details."

So, here are the details of that fun trip when we went to the Marriott hotel where the window goes up and the boats go out into the water. I had been there dozens of times but never took the ride. Well, I did this time!! As we were driving, we saw these million dollar homes and there was one with an open house. Actually, it was Mom who noticed it and said "Hey Judy, let's go through that house." "Great idea Mom." I did not give her any instructions. She was on her own. So the real estate lady asks us what we are looking for, to which Mom responds, "Well, my husband and I had a grand home in Ohio, but he has passed and I am considering making Palm Springs my home." My Mom went on to say "I definitely want a shower with multiple shower heads!" What???? Where did Mom ever see those, for sure never in one of her homes! She laid it on the whole time. Then the agent says "I think this house would really fit your needs," to which Mom responded, "Well, I definitely don't like the color it's painted on the outside and this red carpet is horrible." How funny. I still remember this. The red carpet being horrible??? Anyway, I took some pictures of her out by the flowers at the hotel but many nights I wondered what she would decide to do next. Obviously going to Palm Springs with your Mother, who is 87 years old, was not boring.

My Mother took many trips to San Diego with me since I was retired and John was still working. John came down every other week and stayed 4 days so I would put Mom on a plane and pick up John. Mom loved being there. I would go golfing and she would keep busy. I have a picture of her sweeping the sidewalk which she did every morning. I also have a picture of the two of us on the beach. It was Mother's day weekend. I decided that week I was taking Mom to San Diego for a week. Little did I know it would be the last time she went there. She had her walker and I would roller skate on the beach and she would zip along on her walker. Then, since we both were known "home house hunters," we found one right there on the beach. So yes, we went in. Mom said it was too small. But as we came out I wanted to take her picture and someone came by and took us together. One of my favorite pictures and a wonderful Mother's day trip.

After Mom left her home and went to assisted living homes, I was there to pick her up for ice cream or whatever. It would be so hot there were not too many places we could go so we went to the ice cream shop or the mall. Both we decided were either too expensive or bad for the hips!! I saw my Mother almost every day when she lived in her own home on McDowell. If I had to go anywhere, even just to the grocery store for a couple items, I would stop and pick her up. She was not just my Mother, she was my friend, my constant companion, and the person who I knew would love me, no matter what I said or what I did. I will forever miss her, but so happy for the fun we had together

CAMERON MACKINTOSH and
THE REALLY USEFUL THEATRE COMPANY INC.
present

The
PHANTOM
of the
OPERA

starring
MARCUS LOVETT
MARY D'ARCY
KEITH BUTERBAUGH

JEFF KELLER   **GEORGE LEE ANDREWS**   **ELENA JEANNE BATMAN**
LEILA MARTIN   **GARY RIDEOUT**   **TENER BROWN**

At certain performances
LUANN ARONSON
plays the role of 'Christine'

Music by
ANDREW LLOYD WEBBER
Lyrics by **CHARLES HART**

Additional lyrics by **RICHARD STILGOE**
Book by **RICHARD STILGOE & ANDREW LLOYD WEBBER**
Based on the novel 'Le Fantôme de l'Opéra' by **GASTON LEROUX**
Production design by **MARIA BJÖRNSON**   Lighting by **ANDREW BRIDGE**
Sound by **MARTIN LEVAN**   Musical Director **JACK GAUGHAN**
Musical Supervision & Direction **DAVID CADDICK**
Orchestrations by **DAVID CULLEN & ANDREW LLOYD WEBBER**
Casting by **JOHNSON-LIFF & ZERMAN**   General Management **ALAN WASSER**
Musical Staging & Choreography by **GILLIAN LYNNE**

Directed by **HAROLD PRINCE**

MAJESTIC THEATRE
247 W. 44th STREET
Broadway Premiere 26th January 1988

315

Chapter 68

The Medium

March 16   One of the most important days of my life. My Mom and Dad came to visit today. I knew they would. I swept the porch, went to church and thanked God for letting them come and talk to me. I talked all day about "Mom and Dad are coming today and it will be the most important day of my life," and it was. Jeff McKeehan had been featured in the newspaper two years earlier. My friend Judy Falzone had told me about him. This was before Mom passed. I thought how interesting it would be for me to see if Dad would come through. But for whatever reason I never got that far. When Mom passed and my grief was so overwhelming I had been to grief counseling as I wrote about. I began to make some progress, but now I found myself missing Mom! Mom had not been around for a few years, as a Mom, and now I missed her! Her! So, I got the idea of calling Jeff. But I could not find him. I tried the old newspapers, called Judy, and did whatever I could to locate him. So I figured it was not meant to be. Then one night I woke up with an idea and at 2am in the morning I went to my computer and opened my bookmarks!!! There he was! I called him the next day, Sunday, and he arrived the next day.

Jeff came at 1:00pm and did not leave until 2:30pm. He walked in the door and all of a sudden said "Wow, my ears are ringing. Sometimes they do that but now both are ringing so much I can barely hear you. Can we go outside to calm down?" I said "Sure," but before we even got to the kitchen he said "Wow, there is a female who says hey! You walked by my picture and didn't say how beautiful I am. She says her name is Mollie!" Well, I almost cried. I was like "Oh, my gosh." I walked him back to where we have a long table near the entry and yes, there was Mom at age 18 in a mixed media art frame I had done for her. I said, "Here is Mollie and, yes, you walked past her picture." So we then went outside to calm him down.

He immediately said "There is a lot going on here," and I was like "Oh, thank you God"! He saw our dog Flapjack, barking though the door window in the bedroom. We put Flapjack in there because he always, even though he is a service dog, barks at new people in the house. Jeff turned to me and said "Where is the puppy?" "Puppy," I asked? "We do not have a puppy. We have a cat but no puppy." "No, your Mother says you have a puppy." So now I am getting nervous. For sure we do not have, nor have we had, a puppy! But then Jeff cupped his hands together and said "Your Mother says you have a puppy!" Oh, my gosh, puppy! I screamed and ran to the bedroom. I am sure Jeff wondered what the heck was going on. I ran into the bedroom and there on my bed was puppy! Puppy was a small pink stuffed dog (see picture) that hospice had given my Mom about three years ago. As you read about Mom you remember how many times I explained how Mom loved puppy who went everywhere with her. We did not dare, for any reason, forget to put puppy in Mom's arms when putting her to bed or Mom would call and call for puppy! Puppy went everywhere with Mom. She loved him. She talked to him at night. We would give puppy to Mom when she would have some anxiety moments. Mom never really gave him a name, just called him "puppy." Mom remembered puppy! After that emotional experience, I held puppy and we went back into the house.

From then on, the whole time was amazing. If you have watched John Edwards when he had his own show, or any medium, you just are not sure what is going to happen. Whether true or not true you do not want to remove yourself from the screen. But there was something totally different about Jeff. Jeff did not talk to Mom or ask me questions like other mediums did. Like he did not say "Judy your Mother says xxxx. Is that true?" No no no . When we got to Mom's room where I decided to sit, I said "Please tell Mom now much I miss her," and he said "You tell her. She is right here." My Father came but he was only there for a minute. Jeff said, your Dad says "I am leaving so she can spend time with her Mother." Just like Dad. From then on, Jeff never asked one single question. Anything I wanted to know I would try to face where he said my Mother was, and talk to her. Jeff then would repeat what Mom said. You have probably watched some mediums and I am betting they ask you a lot of questions. Well next time just say "Excuse me, I would like to ask my loved one the question and would be very happy if you would just repeat for me what she or he says." I said "I have wanted her to come and I felt she forgot me." He said "She says she has been here and the dog sees her. But for some reason she isn't that good enough yet of letting you know she is here like your Father does, coming in dreams, etc." Yes!!! My Dad had come in my dreams!!! So Mom knew that!!! Then Jeff said that my Dad has had 15 years' experience and Mom has only been gone 5 months. He said that is very early for her to be able to do what she is doing and that my Dad had probably helped her.

Writing this I remembered when I laid my head on Mom's chest and said one night "Mom, when you go to heaven will you promise not to forget me?" and she said "Judy, I will never forget you." She even said my name, something I had not heard from her lips in months. Jeff and I were sitting in her room, of course it is beautiful now with white carpet and angels on the walls. He said "She said she was not always in this room. She was in another home but her health started to fail and so you brought her here. She says you did everything you could for her and she felt bad that she did not understand everything you wanted her to do. Nor could she do it, but she tried. She tried for you because she knew you were so worried about her. She mentioned when we sat down she was with Rudy." Jeff called them all by name. I asked her if she were happy. She answered saying they were very happy, she and Dad. They have no regrets and they are not angry with each other. They have lived their lives and there is no anger where they are. I asked her if her sisters were nice to her. I felt Aunt Mary always bullied her. She said "I feel none of that. There is nothing like that here. We are all fine." Again, I am asking the questions of my Mother. My Mother said "Judy felt a few times when I was failing that I was coming back and she would do everything and then say "See, she is coming back!" That is true. I would do that because I thought that is what she was working so hard for, but after a while I could not keep it up." These are Mom's exact words! How true. See, hospice told me not to give food, just water, but I really thought she was waking up so I said, "I think she is coming back so I will try some of her favorite baby peaches on the sponge. But it drooled out of her mouth onto puppy." No one knew I had tried that but you can see Mom knew! Jeff says "Your Mom's soul left her body 2 days before she

318

died." You would believe that because she was a rag doll. I would dress her but she never opened her eyes. The pictures I showed of her in her recliner with her "hug me" sweater, a picture of her the day before she died and then the following day sitting with me, she really was not there. He was right. She was gone. I just didn't know it because she was breathing. I said. "Could you tell her how much I miss her?" He said "You tell her, she can hear you!" He said "She is around more then you know." Jeff told me "Take a bath with lavender salts. That is the best way to get the body to relax so someone can come through. Xanax or other meds where you relax prohibit the spirits from coming through!"

Dad had left but he had explained to me years earlier that when you surrendered all your bad habits to God he takes care of everything, but when you do that you cannot take them back!! Obviously Dad didn't. Through Jeff my Mom said "Your Mom says you have a son Danny and he wears his hair like Jesus." This was first time Mom mentioned the name Jesus! How funny, Mom never cared for Danny's long hair and always wanted me to ask him to cut it. Again, I notice how Jeff mentions the people by name! He says "Your Mom says he has a business where he does something that is dangerous, some kind of smell. He has become lax in what he does which if he does not change will affect him terribly." She says "He is OK now. He needs to write down every single step he takes so he can find what it is he is forgetting to do." So I passed it on to Danny and I hope he listened, but I doubt it.

Some people do not believe in mediums. I told my Mother I was having a hard time and not sure how to move on. She said "Do not chain yourself to my bed. You have a life. Your art was supposed to be your path. I am sorry, but better late than never. I wanted to be a sculptor or play a harp or piano or be an artist." I said "Yes, but you were a great cook." She said "Because I felt very insecure and felt if I did not do something good you would all cast me off as being nothing important. I was very insecure." She is right. I always felt she was insecure, always. The counselor even mentioned it.

Then, I let her know I knew about how horrible her life was when she married my Dad and had to move into Grandma's house and people where nasty to her. I said I was so mad when I heard that, I cried. I would

319

have told them off when I was there years ago if I knew that. She said "It was not that bad! Yes, it was small quarters with everyone and it had its days, but I was so in love with your Father, I was so happy just to be married to him. I was just giddy over him and so I didn't mind it all that much!" My Mother used that word giddy a few times when we would do something crazy like go through million dollar homes. She would say "I feel giddy today, let's do something different." Anyway, here I was upset thinking my Mom was pregnant and had to move into Grandma's house where people were not nice to her. Now Mom was letting me know it wasn't so bad.

Now Jeff is here and it's been 40 minutes. He is exhausted. He says your Mom wants you to now go and live your life as you were supposed to. Follow your path, she is just fine and she is with you. She cannot see your face all the time but she knows where you are and she knows where she is. For example, when she comes to your house the dog sees her! She says the dog barks at her! Oh, my gosh, Flapjack is a service dog for John. He is trained not to bark unless someone actually comes into the house. But lately he had been barking and John would have to get up and see if someone was at the door. Many times he didn't even look toward the door. So John had discussed the fact he needed to take him back to training as this barking was driving him crazy. Jeff also told me I could tell when Mom or Dad was here because I would get very cold and sometimes a chill for about 3 seconds when they would appear. Yes, I remembered how cold I felt after Dad came at the John Edwards night. Yes. I had felt that since Dad died. I can always tell when Dad is around. I get chills. I shake. I know, Dad, you are here!

My Mother did mention something else, which I was not sure I would repeat in the book but have decided to do so. She said "I go and visit Geri. I want to help her, but I think I scared her or made her nervous so I backed off." Only Geri knows what this means, or now knows how she felt at times. But Geri really loved my Mom. So I wanted to tell her Mom was trying to be with her at times. I cried and asked Mom if I was always so emotional. She answered that in fact I was very strong. I would bite my nails until my fingers bled and when she would ask me if it hurt I would say "Oh no." Now, a believer or not, no one knew that! Only I remember my nails bleeding. She told me "I am sorry I screamed so much but there were times I did not know what I was supposed to do." I told her I loved watching her. She replied that she knew it was hard. But I said "I would do it again Mom." Mom said "I know you would but don't sugarcoat it," then I laughed. Mom would tell me plenty of times "Don't sugarcoat this, Judy." The one I remember best was when she said "I know I have caused you to worry about me so don't sugarcoat it." Those were her words just before she quit running back and forth from Arizona to Ohio, and when she finally agreed to purchase a house here and settle down! I also had 2 pieces of clothing my Mother had saved in a box and I asked her what they were. She explained one was a christening gown and the other was an apron her Mom made before she got married. She instructed me to pull down the hem and I would see the letters "am", for Agnes Markovich, Grandma's maiden name!!

When Jeff left I could not wait to do this. There was "am" inside the hem! Mom was insistent I give it all away. Her words were "get rid of it" along with Dad's hairbrush and all the stuff I had laid out on the bed for her to see. I was so excited to show her how I kept and loved the things she had saved, but she was not impressed. Actually, I was hurt for days after. I thought they would be so proud of me. She even told me to do the same with her tapestry purse I bought her when I was 18 and which she carried with her every day stuffed with her cards. "Tear them apart and use them in your art." But, I have not done that!

So you can imagine how my life has changed. I was wearing her clothes, pj's and slippers and now I realize she doesn't care. She doesn't care about anything she had here. She loved puppy. That was about the most of what was here that she mentioned. She for sure has moved to another world which she deserves after 100 years here. She doesn't feel any of the neglect she had as a child. She feels nothing. She says "We are happy here. There is only peace and love." I admitted to her that I had kept some of her ashes to which she replied "I don't care where my ashes are." Yep. Her exact words. People say she has to be buried with Dad. Well, she was with Dad. Dad was there with her. She even said "I am so happy to be with Rudy." Jeff mentioned that with all his reading he has never heard one person say "Jesus met me at the gate." Never a mention. Why? Maybe because these souls have not reached the end of

321

their journey. They have not grown to where they are supposed to. We can only speculate.

So that day was such a total change for me. I feel like, wow! I hardly know this lady. For sure it's not the lady or Mother I took care of for 18 years since Dad passed. The lady who was in my house, a sweet old lady. This lady is smart, beautiful, happy, even young speaking. Very much in control! She is like my Mother when she was 40? 30?? Thank you, God. Now I have to decide what to do. Jeff tells me to get out and meet people. Do something more with your art. Your Mother said your art was supposed to be your original path. She said she wanted to do art and she wants you to know. Unchain yourself from her bed as she said! Sounds awfully cold to me. I have cried for her every day. "I miss you Mom," I said, but for Mom it was like her replying "Judy, hang it up, move on." What she said was "I love you, I want you to someday be here. But not now and be at peace." I realize many do not believe in mediums. That's OK. We all have our thoughts and we all have different beliefs just like we believe Arizona is a horribly hot place to live, but many like it!

Jeff is not like any medium I ever watched or met. If you live outside Arizona and would really like to see if your loved ones' spirit can come to you, write to Jeff at jeff@jeffthemedium.com and ask him for a referral. I am sure he can direct you to qualified mediums. Oh, and don't let them charge you an arm and a leg. Jeff charges $150. If the spirt does not come though, there is no charge. There is not an instruction sheet for this. There are not 5 steps to hearing a spirit. It doesn't work that way. You need to believe, have a good aura about you, and yes, feel love. Love is the answer!! I know my sister Carol was watching and smiling. After all the shows of John Edwards we watched, and the book she sent me written by John Edwards I am betting she says "go girl!!"

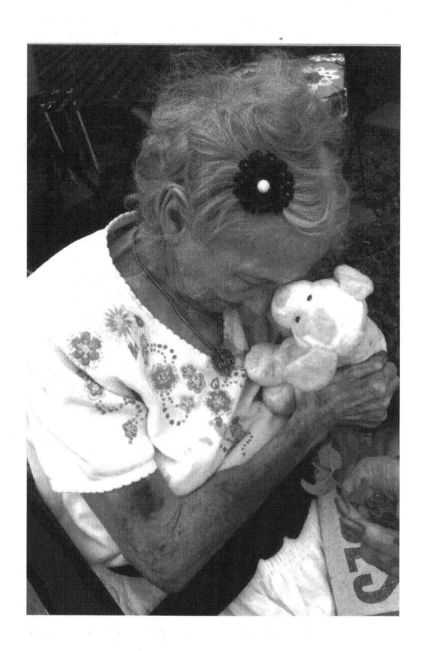

324

Amen!

It has taken me a year to write this story of strength in adversity by both my Mother and my Father, and let's not forget my siblings! I put it down at one point because it was very hard to relive some of the moments, yet necessary. As it was once said you can't understand what it's like to be happy and secure in what you're doing, unless you have spent some time being unhappy and insecure. So I needed the readers to see just where Mom and Dad's life began and to understand where life took them. I didn't plan on writing a book. I wanted to just get Dad's story of his strength though sobriety to hopefully help someone in AA, or someone wondering just where to start, or who thought it was impossible. To see it was possible. Along the way, I could not leave out Mom's unbelievable ability to keep the family together, go to work and twenty years later have a retirement party with newspaper exposure.

Many times I felt I was useless, even as Mom was dying. Only with prayer could I get up every day and try again to do my best, to understand how every little bit I did, was better than doing nothing. Growing up, there were many times I could not help either one of them, but when Dad asked to come back home, I was there for him. When Mom needed help I was there for her! I knew it was time for me to give Mom the security that she had given to our family all those years. Visiting her in the cottage, or taking her with me on trips, I loved every minute. I realized how deeply I loved them both. Never once did I find them to be a burden. It was prayer, and it was answered prayers. I had as much an idea of how to care for her as you probably would if you brought a loved one home today. But I hope this book inspires you to try. It is not for everyone. There are different circumstances, but the most important points I want to make are:

- Research what drugs are best for your loved one based on their specific circumstance.
- If they go to a home, put together a village, to ensure they are really taken care of and don't be afraid to speak up!

- If you bring them home, there is help through state programs and if you don't qualify, again look to friends and family.

One of the issues I feel best about is how I found drugs to calm my Mother and help her sundowner issue without creating a "rag doll' during the day. Remember, my Mother was severely drugged on two occasions by others, so I was determined not to let that happen. By using what worked for Mom and not just what was written in books, most days Mom was able to communicate, even if it didn't make sense. She was alert and alive and never drugged to the point she could not get out of bed.   When I was alone with her and she would get very anxious and then scream, because she did not know how to express what she wanted to say, I would come behind her wheelchair, put my head on her shoulder and whisper in her ear how pretty she was and how I loved the dress she was wearing. Again, pray for patience. None of us can do all this alone. We must remember we are never alone!

So now, it's time to find my own path, as my Mom encouraged me to do. Neither her or my Dad wished those years to happen for any of us, but I know they would be very happy if they saw me smiling and not crying. I hope they are proud of themselves. I know my siblings, Louis, Kenny and Carol are very proud of them!

I have no idea how many books will sell but I do know my plan is to benefit a non-profit. I would like to set up a scholarship program for those in AA who cannot go to a vocational school like Dad did. Some hardly can make ends meet. I realize I cannot do all of this, but maybe with some funds we can put together a "village" and provide some help to all those who are "worth saving" because everyone is!!! I hope this book helps them take the first step.

And never forget...everyone should have a place to go for help.

AMEN!

Made in the USA
San Bernardino, CA
17 November 2017